MAHLER

MAHLER

A Biography

Jonathan Carr

THE OVERLOOK PRESS

NEW YORK

This edition first published in paperback in the United States in 2011 by
The Overlook Press, Peter Mayer Publishers, Inc.
141 Wooster Street
New York, NY 10012
www.overlookpress.com

For bulk and special sales, please contact sales@overlookny.com

Library of Congress Cataloging-in-Publication Data

Carr, Jonathan.
Mahler / Jonathan Carr.
p.   cm.
1. Mahler, Gustav, 1860-1911.
2. Composers—Austria—Biography.
I. Title

Manufactured in the United States of America
1 3 5 7 9 8 6 4 2
ISBN 978-1-59020-514-3

In memory of my mother

MABEL CARR

Contents

Acknowledgements

Many people gave me unstinting help as I prepared and wrote this book. Above all I am indebted to four great Mahlerians whom I am proud to count as friends: Kurt and Herta Blaukopf in Vienna, Gilbert Kaplan in New York and Knud Martner in Copenhagen. Their suggestions and corrections were invaluable. Responsibility for any remaining errors is, of course, mine.

Sincere thanks for aid and advice also to, in particular, Norman Lebrecht in London; Robert Becqué, Frans Bouwman and Willem Smith in Holland; Susan Filler, Gail Ross and Stan Ruttenberg in the United States. A special word of acknowledgement goes to Dr Nicholas Christy (Florida and Rhode Island), who extracted from Dr George Baehr, one of Mahler's last physicians, the key diagnostic information cited in the last chapter. Thanks also to libraries and research institutes on two continents; especially to Emmy Hauswirth and the dedicated staff of the vital, sadly under-funded Internationale Gustav Mahler Gesellschaft in Vienna.

While drawing on published sources listed in the Bibliography, I have in many cases amended the translations from the German; in cases where there is no published text in English, the translations are my own.

Caroline Dawnay, my agent, and Carol O'Brien, of Constable, have been patient and determined far beyond the call of duty.

Last – and most – love and thanks, as ever, to my wife Dorothea who makes it all worthwhile.

List of Illustrations

Abbreviations

BMGM – Bibliothèque Musicale Gustav Mahler, Paris
IGMG – Internationale Gustav Mahler Gesellschaft, Vienna
KF – The Kaplan Foundation, New York
MR – The Mahler Rosé Collection, The Music Library, University of Western Ontario, London, Ontario
ÖNB-BA – Bild-Archiv der Österreichischen Nationalbibliothek, Vienna

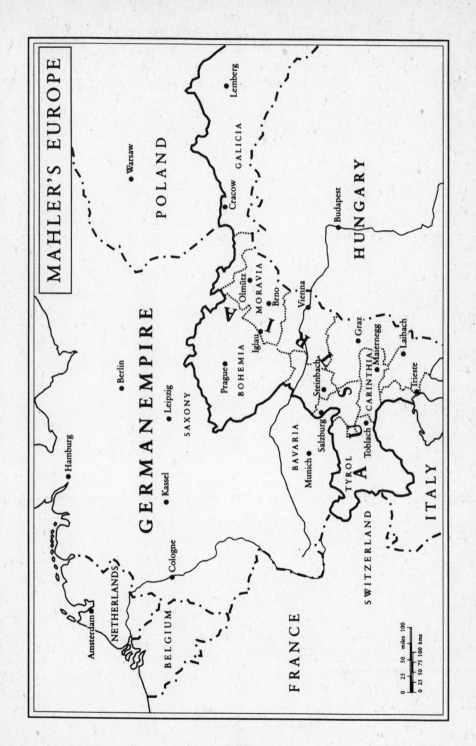

MAHLER'S EUROPE

Introduction

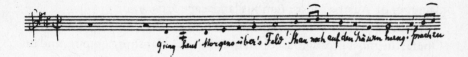

DURING ITS 700-year history the village of Grinzing has grown used to invasion. Set among vineyards in the hills north-west of Vienna, a strategic point for armies advancing on the capital, it was sacked by the Turks in the sixteenth and seventeenth centuries and by the French at the start of the nineteenth. A decade or two after the French marched away the Viennese finally adopted the place, flocking out to drink sour new Heuriger wine and dream to sentimental music in the taverns and gardens. Franz Schubert was one of the Grinzing regulars.

Today, in the summer at least, the locals are far outnumbered by the busloads of tourists shuttled up from town to see 'a typical old wine village'. Schedules are usually tight and few trippers get around to leaving the din of the main street for a stroll through the side roads. Those who do find themselves rewarded, unexpectedly, with one of the finest of the many panoramas of Vienna. The bird's-eye view from the towering Kahlenberg heights further north is much more famous but the quiet vantage point above Grinzing has an appeal all its own. It is high enough above the city to reveal most of the distant landmarks – the bulk of the opera house squatting on the Ringstrasse, the spires of St Stephen's cathedral and, hard by the Danube, the giant wheel revolving in the Prater park. But it is also set in a district unusually rich, even for Vienna, in musical history and drama.

Ludwig van Beethoven worked close by on his 'Eroica' and 'Pastoral' Symphonies and, as deafness claimed him, penned his despairing Testament in the neighbouring village of Heiligenstadt. Just down the hill Johann Strauss the younger, flouting his father's orders to stay out of the music business, won early fame in a dance hall his father had inaugurated years before. Round the corner at a neat little Biedermeier house lent him by friends, Hugo Wolf composed dozens of his *Goethe Lieder* in happier times before be began to go insane. And just a few streets away from there, on a winter's evening in 1901, Wolf's erstwhile friend Gustav Mahler proposed marriage (rather clumsily) to Alma Maria Schindler, daughter of Austria's most famous landscape artist.

Mahler was then at the height of his power as director of the Vienna Opera, the most prestigious job in music in the Habsburg empire, and he was close to something of a breakthrough as a composer. Alma was young, talented, alluring. On the face of it a brilliant match – yet within a decade it was all over. In 1907 Mahler resigned his post, many claimed was driven from it, and went with Alma to America. Four years later, his health in ruins and his marriage crumbling, he returned to Vienna and died there on 18th May 1911, a few weeks before his fifty-first birthday. He was buried four days later in Grinzing cemetery next to his little daughter Maria, who had succumbed to scarlet fever and diphtheria in that same fateful year of 1907.

Mahler had asked for a simple funeral and on the whole he got one. There were no big speeches and no music. But despite the teeming rain on that blustery Monday afternoon, hundreds of ordinary Viennese crowded outside the little church where the service was held and the coffin blessed. Only a minority had come to pay tribute to Mahler the composer. His gigantic symphonies had rarely gone down well in Vienna and not a single one had been premièred there. But Mahler the opera director – that was another matter. In a few stormy years he had lashed the institution at the heart of the city's cultural life to a peak of excellence it might never reach again. Many Viennese had acknowledged as much while Mahler was still at the helm. Now some of his erstwhile critics were starting to do so too. As one contemptuous Mahler fan put it, 'the same sneering somebodies' who had attacked every Mahler production were now 'keen to belong to the exclusive circle of Mahlerites'.

For his friends and – the word is unavoidable – disciples, Mahler was not just a conductor/director of genius but a great creative artist, for some even a saint. To the 'holy Gustav Mahler' and the 'immortal example of his work and deeds' ran the dedication on one of the hundreds of wreaths laid beside the route between church and graveside. It came from Arnold Schönberg, often helped by Mahler with cash and counsel, and other pioneers of the atonal school including Alban Berg and Anton Webern.

Schönberg was one of those who, huddled under umbrellas, trudged slowly behind the coffin as it was borne away from the church. So was the conductor Bruno Walter, destined to fight for wider recognition of Mahler's music on two continents over the next half-century. So was Anna Bahr-Mildenburg, Mahler's greatest love before his marriage and transformed by him from a promising young singer into a dramatic soprano without peer. There too were Mahler's revolutionary stage designer Alfred Roller, the poet and dramatist Hugo von Hofmannsthal and the painter Gustav Klimt, one of Alma's old flames. Alma herself did not attend – on doctor's orders, it was said.

The mourners were not only from Vienna. As the cortège wound its way through the cemetery the many stations of Mahler's restless life seemed to pass in review. There were representatives from the opera houses of Leipzig, Prague and Budapest, where Mahler had begun to win fame as a conductor; from Amsterdam, where his music had been valued highly from the first; from Berlin, where it was regularly pulverised by the critics; and from Munich, where the public had jeered the première of the Fourth Symphony and cheered that of the Eighth.

It took a good fifteen minutes for the throng to reach the graveside. Sceptics may discount what is said to have happened next but several of those present later gave matching accounts. As the coffin was lowered the sun suddenly broke through at last and a bird began to sing. One eye-witness called it a scene staged by heaven. The drama would certainly have appealed to Mahler, nothing if not a man of the theatre as composer as well as conductor. He had realised just such a moment in his Second Symphony, when after an orchestral storm a lonely flute ushers in a choral finale promising resurrection.

At Mahler's express wish his gravestone bears only his name. 'Those who seek me know who I was,' he explained. 'The others do not need to know.' The second part of that statement is clearly true, the first is doubtful even now. Schönberg called Mahler a saint, orchestral players who suffered under his fury and sarcasm thought him devilish. Some of them even plotted to mug him. To many of his contemporaries Mahler was a naïve idealist, to others a string-pulling careerist who neatly switched from Judaism to Catholicism to help win the Vienna post. According to

[3]

many accounts Mahler was athletic, full of fun, a 'ladies' man', even a roué. Other versions, including much of his wife's, draw him as sickly, complexed and introverted, a view given wider currency in modern times by Visconti's film *Death in Venice* and Ken Russell's *Mahler*. As for Mahler's work, it has been called almost everything over the years. Praise for it nowadays is about as extreme as the abuse often heaped on it nearly a century ago.

A detective trying to untangle all this evidence might conclude in exasperation that several different people called Gustav Mahler lie buried in Grinzing cemetery. Which of them is the real Mahler?

Chapter One

From Province
to Promised Land

THE SCENE: a forest in early morning. The mist is starting to lift and sun-light to flicker through the trees, but still every shape is indistinct. Only sounds seem half-way real; a cuckoo's call, a distant flourish of trumpets, a burst of laughter and what could be a folk tune. It might be just a dream – of Arcadia perhaps. Then the locals give the game away with a rumbus-tious, thigh-slapping dance. We are surely in Austria, or thereabouts.

With this nature tone poem Mahler begins his First Symphony. Parts of it so far might have been composed by contemporaries like Antonín Dvořák or Bedřich Smetana, but Mahler goes on to shatter the idyll in his own unique way. Groans and squawks from instruments playing at their limits parody a funeral march on the theme 'Bruder Martin' ('Frère Jacques'). Snatches of Jewish melody slide in, then fade into a resigned lullaby which brings no real rest. The last movement storms in without a pause, sweeping away idyll and parody with a triumphant, at least implacable, march. *Dall' Inferno al Paradiso* Mahler called it; then, as he often did, withdrew the title. If people could not grasp what he meant from the music itself then words would not help.

Many people could not. 'One of us must be crazy and it isn't me,' wrote Vienna's most influential critic Eduard Hanslick, baffled by the symphony's apparent lack of form and mish-mash of styles. Others were still less charitable, snarling about a 'cacophony', a 'monstrosity', even 'Jewish gibberish'.

It is easy to tut-tut such lack of insight now that the work is firmly entrenched in the repertoire. Perhaps too firmly. Frequent repetition can dull the shock-effect of this revolutionary symphonic début; and Mahler certainly did mean to shock. He took it as a small triumph when, at the Budapest première, a lady listener jumped with alarm at the finale's first *fortissimo* crash and scattered her belongings on the floor. Searing pain and wry humour, dreamy introspection and animal high spirits, a will to emerge on top come what may; there are already plenty of clues in this First Symphony to its creator, especially to his complex and often mis-construed early life.

The complexities start with a definition problem. Leonard Bernstein underlined it when he called Mahler 'a little German-Czech-Moravian-Jewish-Polish boy'. He was wrong about the Polish part and he might have said Austrian rather than German but the rest is quite correct. Mahler came from the very centre of volatile central Europe. He was born to Jewish parents on 7th July 1860, in a poor Bohemian village called Kalischt (Kaliště) roughly midway between Prague and Vienna. As a child he got to know dozens of Czech folk melodies, some of which strayed into his music, and as a man he still seems to have understood the Czech language passably well. But when he was only a few months old the family moved to the nearest town of Iglau (Jihlava) in neighbouring Moravia.

A move to the next province as such was not an enormous upheaval. Bohemia and Moravia shared much common history. They had once been linked as the so-called 'lands of St Wenceslas' crown' and the border between them was never sharply defined. But Iglau itself was a largely German-speaking enclave, thanks to an inflow of Austrian and Bavarian workers which had begun centuries before. There Mahler began to devour the classics of German literature and first heard German music. Iglau was not, strictly speaking, German all the same. Like the rest of Moravia and Bohemia, Hungary and Galicia, Croatia and Transylvania, even Lombardy in north Italy, it was part of the polyglot Austrian empire, ruled for centuries from Vienna by the Habsburg dynasty and, in Mahler's time, on the decay. In 1866, a few days before Mahler's sixth birthday, Bismarck's Prussian army smashed the imperial

Austrian forces near Königgrätz in Bohemia, less than 100 miles north of Iglau. Indeed, for a few months Iglau became a Prussian-occupied town. A year later the Habsburg empire split into two unequal halves, a Hungarian and an Austrian one, though with the same painstaking, well-intentioned Franz Joseph I as their common sovereign. Four years after that a united German empire, excluding Austria-Hungary, emerged under Prussian leadership as the dominant power in Europe.

Paradoxically the kind of Europe into which Mahler was born seems closer these days than it did in the Iron Curtain era, when East and West were brutally divided and the so-called 'People's Democracies' were held under Moscow's thumb. Now Germany (albeit a very different one from Bismarck's) has reunited and the two halves of the continent are trying to come together, despite signs of resurgent nationalism, in a rather fuzzy European Union. Franz Joseph's empire was hardly less fuzzy than the present European club centred on Brussels. What had mainly held its millions of Germans and Magyars, Czechs and Slovaks, Poles and Serbs and Slovenes together was loyalty to a single ruling house. That loyalty began to crumble as the empire's peoples sought to realise a growing sense of cultural and national identity. The Germans, the biggest and most powerful group, felt torn two ways – to Franz Joseph in Vienna and to Bismarck's Reich.

Mahler can have known little in detail about this when he was a child and later he showed only a very fleeting interest in politics. But he surely sensed the strains of a world in upheaval, of growing national feeling all around, of battles fought almost on his doorstep. Much more directly he felt the tension of being born a Jew.

In later life Mahler claimed to be 'thrice homeless, as a native of Bohemia in Austria, as an Austrian among Germans and as a Jew throughout the world. Everywhere an intruder, never welcomed.' That oft-quoted statement is somewhat disingenuous. Mahler was not a refugee shunted willy-nilly from one spot to another. Most of the time he chose to move because he received offers of better jobs. But it is true that from early on he was aware of being part of a minority which did not fit in, and into which, moreover, he did not fit. In Bohemia and Moravia, easily the most advanced part of the empire with good communications and fast-developing industry, Jews made up less than two per cent of the population. Hard-working and relatively well-educated, most of them prized German as the language of a great culture and of the empire's élite, as something you had to master to get ahead. They saw towns like Iglau and, above all, Vienna as a promised land, but one which long stayed a mirage because Jews were not allowed to move about the empire and settle at will. That was changing when Mahler was born, thanks to liberalisation steps decreed by Franz Joseph. The Jews, among them the Mahlers, began a long march into the towns. However hard many of them tried, they did not become truly German in the eyes of the native Germans. But they tended to be seen as a kind of Germanic fifth column by, among others, the increasingly assertive Czechs.

It was against this background that Mahler grew up although Iglau itself, where he spent his first fifteen years and many holidays afterwards, was a tolerant spot. Some accounts suggest it was not so much tolerant as stultifyingly dull (a 'hick town' the composer Ernst Krenek called it) but they are too harsh by half. Back in the Middle Ages Iglau was one of Europe's main silver-mining centres and for a time housed the royal mint. Later it became a leather and textiles centre important enough to have the main imperial post route from Vienna to Prague rerouted through it. In Mahler's time it was a thriving community of more than 20,000 people, famed for good schools, a strong choral tradition and, not least, for its huge square, more than 1000 feet long, surrounded by brightly decorated houses and dotted with fountains.

Most of the spots Mahler knew best were either on the square or within a minute or two's walk of it. One was the German *Gymnasium* (high school) where Mahler later claimed to have 'learned nothing'. That remark was made tongue-in-cheek although it is a fact that Mahler tended to dream over his books and picked up more outside the class-room than inside it. Also nearby was the municipal theatre, accomplished (or at least ambitious) enough to put on operas like Mozart's *Don Giovanni* and Bellini's *Norma*. The ten-year-old 'Maler', as a local paper called him, gave his first reported piano recital there and won an ovation despite the ropy instrument on which he had to play. By that time he was already something of a veteran. He had first begun thumping on a dusty old piano he found as an adventurous little boy in his maternal grandparents' attic. The next day the instrument was trundled round to Gustav's home by ox-cart and from then on he never looked back. More musical input came from the local Roman Catholic church of St James (Jakobskirche).

Although Jewish, Mahler was allowed to sing in the choir there and had some private lessons in harmony from the choirmaster, Heinrich Fischer.

Around the corner from the theatre was a barracks from which Mahler must first have heard the sound of trumpet calls and marches. Perhaps he even saw troops setting off for the slaughter at Königgrätz or the wounded returning with the Prussians at their heels. At any rate from very early on martial music filled him with mingled fascination and fright. When he was about three he trotted out of the house, dressed only in his shirt, and clutching an accordion, and was drawn away Pied Piper-like by a passing military band. He got lost and bystanders agreed to take him home only when he played them the tune he had heard from the soldiers. Around the same time his fine ear won Mahler a less admiring audience at the newly built synagogue (razed by the Nazis in 1939). Vexed by what struck him as the ugly noise made by the congregation, he bawled for silence and, to his mother's horror, broke into his favourite street song – a ditty partly in polka rhythm about a wayfarer dancing wildly at an inn. Meanwhile he was beginning to compose. His first known piece was a polka preceded by a funeral march.

Just off the lower end of the square are the two houses where the Mahlers lived, the first rented on arrival in Iglau, the second bought twelve years later. They are solid, spacious, buildings with two upper storeys – far more prepossessing than the long, low dwelling lacking glass in the windows from which the family had moved in Kalischt. Upstairs Mahler's father, Bernard, built up quite a library and later proudly displayed in a glass frame a certificate showing he had been made a freeman of Iglau. A servant, a nurse and a cook were employed to help out with the huge family – fourteen children in all, although around half died young, including Gustav's favourite brother Ernst. Downstairs Bernard established his business, mainly making and selling liquor with a bakery on the side. As trade grew he set up branches elsewhere in town.

Bernard has sometimes been called 'an assimilated Jew' but clearly he did not turn his back on Judaism altogether. He was elected a committee member of the local Jewish community and his wife and children, at least, attended the synagogue. How often Bernard went along too is unclear. Probably he was far more dedicated to his business than to religious observance, or indeed anything else. The Mahlers never became rich and as a student in Vienna Gustav was always strapped for cash, but the evidence does not show he was brought up in squalor. He was possibly a little ashamed of the way his father earned a living, although that does not mean he was ashamed of his father. In 1904 he asked a biographer, Richard Specht, to call Bernard simply 'a tradesman'. That may look like a cover-up but then Specht had proposed writing that Bernard ran 'a pothouse'. Arguably Mahler was more accurate.

Does it matter much whether he was or not? The issue may seem dangerously close to the world of *How many children had Lady Macbeth?*, that fine satire on fanatics for detail whose labours add not a jot to our understanding of Shakespeare. But 'the impressions of Mahler's youth', as one close friend put it, 'run like a scarlet thread through his whole life.' And, one should add, through his whole work. Mahler once compared composing to playing with building blocks gathered in childhood. Identify those early impressions wrongly and the 'scarlet thread' will lead to an absorbing caricature of a composer, but not to Mahler.

Mahler's home life is often said to have been sheer hell. His widow, Alma, set the pattern in her hugely readable but error-ridden memoirs. According to her, Mahler 'dreamed his way through family life and childhood. He saw nothing of the unending tortures his mother had to endure from the brutality of his father, who ran after every servant, domineered over his delicate wife and flogged the children.'

If Mahler had really seen nothing of the tortures it is unclear how Alma knew about them. But she has naturally been treated as a prime source and the few early photos available seem on the face of it to confirm her dire picture. Here is Bernard, fist clenched on a table and glaring out over his walrus moustache as though warning, 'Just wait till I catch you.' And there is Gustav aged about six, wide-eyed and lip-biting, evidently poised for flight. How easy to put two and two together – and make five. In a passing remark years later Mahler recalled the photo session. He had been scared to death because he thought that he was about to be scooped up, stuffed inside the camera and then stuck on a piece of cardboard.

Bernard was certainly no saint but the evidence does not show he was a devil either. He was blunt and ambitious, energetic and overweeningly persistent. Much of that he inherited from his mother, a stubborn old bird who was still peddling drapery from door to door in a heavy box at the age of eighty. One tale has it that when given what she felt was an unjust fine, she tramped off to Vienna, won an audience with Franz Joseph himself and the fine was dropped. No doubt the story is apochryphal but because it fitted her so well it was often retold.

Bernard had a travelling sales job too but he went one better than his mother and got hold of a horse and cart. Reckoning that knowledge was power he read books voraciously, even studied French, in spare moments on trips. It was no love match on either side when in 1857 he married Maria Hermann (usually called Marie), daughter of a soap-boiler and, at nineteen, ten years his junior. She limped and had a weak heart but arguably it was a step up socially for Bernard and he would have got a dowry. The first child, Isidor, died soon after birth in 1858. The second was Gustav.

An authoritarian father, a suffering, constantly pregnant mother, brothers and sisters borne off regularly in coffins; that, alas, was still an all too familiar picture in the nineteenth century. It did not necessarily mean that children grew up psychologically maimed, still less that the pressures turned them into great creative artists. All the same, Mahler's family background makes it sorely (for many irresistibly) tempting to try to fathom him and his music via the psychiatrist's couch. None other than Sigmund Freud did just that; at least, he made a stab at analysing Mahler during a few hours' stroll round the Dutch town of Leiden in 1910. The outcome was predictable. Freud concluded that Mahler had a Holy Mary complex (mother fixation) and unearthed an early incident which seemed to explain much about the character of Mahler's work. Mahler is said to have remembered that after a 'specially painful scene' between his parents, he ran out of the house and heard a passing barrel organ grinding out a popular tune, '*Ach, du lieber Augustin*'. Hence, we are told, the stark contrast between the tragic and the banal became fixed in his mind for life. According to Freud's biographer, Ernest Jones, Mahler even 'suddenly said that now he understood why his music had always been prevented from achieving the highest rank through the noblest passages ... being spoilt by the intrusion of some commonplace melody.'

This is absorbing but dangerous stuff. The barrel organ tale comes from a summary by Jones of an unpublished letter which Freud wrote to a confidante in 1925 and which may not fairly reflect what was said at the Leiden meeting fifteen years earlier. True enough, the tragic or noble and the banal are often juxtaposed in Mahler's work. That is one important reason why it is so intense and, for Mahler's fans and foes alike, memorable. But it is hard indeed to believe Mahler really identified this as something involuntary which kept his music 'from achieving the highest rank'. He was certainly a self-critical composer, constantly revamping his orchestration and even urging conductors to do the same after his death if they felt something sounded wrong. But there is no sign either before or after the alleged revelation in Leiden that he tried to revise out of his work intrusive 'banalities'. On the contrary there is a great deal of evidence that he knew just what he was doing when he put them in.

Freud's comment about a 'Holy Mary complex' has helped sustain a distorted view of Mahler's relations with his parents. Despite the 'dreaming' which Alma reports, Mahler was under no illusions about how things really were between Bernard and Marie. 'They were as ill-suited as fire and water,' he told a lady-friend when he was in his mid-thirties. 'He was all obstinacy, she was gentleness itself.' Blunt words but not enough to justify the frequent claim that Mahler hated his father and so identified with his mother that throughout his life he unconsciously imitated her limp. Demonstrably there was much of both his parents in Mahler, of Bernard certainly no less than of Marie. He needed no barrel organ incident to fix the pain of stark contrast in his mind. It was already there. The battle between fire and water, as it were, was implanted in Mahler at birth and it never ceased to rage.

Mahler always referred to his mother with love and claimed that in his Fourth Symphony's bitter-sweet Adagio, perhaps his loveliest, he pictured her smiling through tears. Still, when told in 1889 that she was at death's door he neither pulled out of the performance he was down to conduct that evening nor, it seems, did he get to her funeral a few days later (though he had attended his father's earlier the same year). He was surely grief-stricken but he bottled up his feelings because his duties came first. That does not prove he was callous but nor does it suggest a 'mother fixation'.

As for imitating his mother's limp, that too belongs in the bulky file of 'great Mahler myths'. Mahler did have a very odd, jerky walk which no one who saw him could fail to notice. Some called it a nervous tic but this was denied by his daughter Anna, who as a little girl often went strolling with him. She said Mahler simply changed his rhythm every few steps.

Why he did so is unclear. Perhaps his mind was full of those passages with abruptly shifting pace and beat so characteristic of his work. At any rate this oddity of rhythm was not confined to his gait. One exasperated rowing partner reported that Mahler constantly changed his stroke without warning, then blamed others for the resulting confusion.

Mahler's feelings for his father were surely quite different, but it is debatable whether they amounted to hatred. During his spell as a conductor in Hamburg, after Bernard's death, Mahler showed a visitor round his flat and told him, 'On that chair my good father used to work.' Perhaps 'good father' was just a form of words. The Mahler children often referred to 'dear father' in their letters, even when they were seething over some real or imagined paternal misdeed. But if Mahler had despised his father, would he have been carting that battered armchair about? It must have been a sign, if not of love, at least of a certain gratitude and respect. After all, it was Bernard who had encouraged Gustav to pursue the piano, no doubt hoping his son would become a money-spinning virtuoso, and who later let him study at the Vienna conservatory, though evidently not helping him much to pay the fees. When young Gustav was mistreated by a family with whom he had been sent to stay in Prague, a wrathful Bernard descended, packed his son's things and took him straight home. He had unwittingly got Gustav into the jam in the first place, but he acted with typical dispatch once he heard what was going on.

From his father Mahler inherited, among other things, voracious ambition and unshakeable will. If he had not he would probably have got little further in life than conductor of the Iglau choral society. Like his father too he was not squeamish in his methods. At six or seven he was already giving piano lessons for about 5 crowns an hour and boxing his pupils sharply on the ears whenever they played a wrong note. Later as a piano accompanist he gave warning kicks to the victim employed to turn the pages of his score. The page-turner decided to kick back. 'You *Schweinehund*,' shouted Mahler when the piece was over.

Mahler also had traits Bernard lacked – a sense of diplomacy, an ability to pull strings behind the scenes and a readiness to flatter obsequiously when he felt this would serve his cause. He would have gone far in politics, had he wished. He might also have made his mark as a writer. Early on he began poking into his father's Iglau library and later became a real

[13]

bookworm, weeping with laughter over Cervantes' *Don Quixote*, devouring Dostoyevsky, especially *The Brothers Karamazov*, and ploughing through the German classics. Throughout his life he shot off thousands of letters. Hundreds survive, often thoughtful, vivid, funny. When in his twenties, he was advised by a scholarly friend to drop composing for writing because he had 'such a sovereign command of words and so penetrating an insight into human psychology'. 'I can't help it,' Mahler replied. 'I just have to compose.'

It was not all an indoor life of books and music. Although he was small and rather pale, young Gustav had plenty of friends and spent a lot of time out of doors. When his comrades came round to his house to play in the courtyard and cellars, as like as not it was Gustav who led the pack and suggested new games. In summer he spent long hours with them splashing around in the municipal baths and hiking through the surrounding Bohemian-Moravian highlands – full of beauty and mystery with their thick forests, streams, castles and ancient burial mounds.

They were full of music too. It is hard to fathom just why an area within a radius of only about 150 miles from Mahler's birthplace should have produced so rich a harvest of composers; Smetana, Dvořák, Janáček and Suk in the nineteenth century, Krommer, Dušek and the Wranitzky brothers in the eighteenth and dozens of others, often hugely productive. The reasons are many, from the backing of music-loving aristocrats to the special skills of teachers and instrument-makers. But part of the answer must lie in the mystery and beauty of the landscape itself and of the sounds which belonged to it. In Mahler's case there is no doubt about it. 'Nothing but the sounds of nature' is how he once (oversimply) defined his work. He should at least have added 'and the sounds of man in nature', like the distant call of the post-coachman's horn which he heard so often as a child. Sometimes two coaches would pass and each virtuoso aboard would try to outdo the other, sending one brilliant fanfare after another resounding across the countryside. Mahler recalls such episodes above all in the Scherzando movement of his Third Symphony. He does so with a deep nostalgia. The world was soon to have no more need of post-coaches and their ebullient musicians.

More input for a budding composer came from the little country bands, usually just a few strings with clarinet, trumpet or bagpipes. Mahler often trekked off to hear them. Friedrich (Fritz) Löhr, a close friend who went with him on one such outing, recalled that 'there was dancing, there was rhythm, causing heart and senses to vibrate as though intoxicated. There was the zest for life and sorrow too' as girls dressed in bright petticoats and with heads bowed to their partners' chests circled as though in a solemn ritual. Zest and sorrow together: Löhr might have been describing so many ambivalent passages in Mahler's work.

The picture of Mahler the solitary dreamer is not wrong, but merely incomplete. Alma tells how Bernard once took Gustav on a walk in the woods, then had to pop home for something. He got involved in other matters and temporarily forgot he had left his son behind. Hours later, after nightfall, he found Gustav sitting unafraid in the same spot, lost in contemplation. There is no reason to doubt Alma here since so many other witnesses over the years tell similar tales; of the absent-minded Mahler who stirred his tea with his cigarette; of the self-absorbed Mahler who sat studying a score for ages in a motionless train, unaware the engine had been uncoupled; of the moody Mahler who would switch from eloquence to silence in a trice for no apparent reason; of the creative Mahler who shut himself away in isolated country huts and who wrote '*Ich bin der Welt abhanden gekommen*' ('I am lost to the world'), one of his – or anyone's – finest songs.

Even if we knew none of these tales, Mahler handily supplies quite a rounded self-portrait in just three early letters. One of them, very long and histrionic, was written to a student friend when Mahler was not quite nineteen and giving piano lessons to a family in a village in Hungary. It was a lonely spot. At sunset Mahler would climb a linden tree on the heath, gaze out over the Danube and listen to the melancholy croaking of a frog in the reeds. In his letter he sadly recalls his dead brother Ernst (Mahler had been sketching, but then abandoned, an opera called *Herzog Ernst von Schwaben*) and rails against 'modern hypocrisy and mendacity' in art and life, asking, 'What way out is there but self-annihilation?' He ends: 'Oh my beloved earth, when, oh when, wilt thou take the abandoned one unto thy breast? Behold! Mankind has banished him from itself, and he flees from its cold and heartless bosom to thee! Oh, care for the friend-less one, for the restless one, Universal Mother!'

Few of Mahler's letters are quoted as often as that one. It is held to reveal even at that early stage so many features of the mature composer – uprooted, solitary, introspective, nature-intoxicated, near-suicidal. Some commentators find in it uncanny links with *Das Lied von der Erde (The Song of the Earth)*, one of Mahler's farewell works written three decades later. None of that is wholly off target. But a few months later Mahler, in the throes of an unhappy love affair with Josephine Poisl, daughter of Iglau's chief telegraphist, writes to another student friend. This letter is less well known.

'My dear friend, I have got myself quite badly entangled in the silken chains of the darling of the gods. The hero "now sighs, now wrings his hands, now groans, now entreats", etc., etc. I have really spent most of the time, indulging in every kind of bitter-sweet daydream; I have said "Ah" when I got up and "Oh" when I went to bed . . . My eyes are like a couple of squeezed-out lemons, and there is not a single tear left in them.' Having unburdened himself of that Mahler adds a PS, 'If you can, lend me a fiver, but only if this is absolutely convenient,' and then a PPS, 'I have now been carrying this letter around in my pocket for two weeks already. Reply *immediately!*'

How different the tone; more to the point, how intentionally different. In the second letter Mahler writes that 'I have forced myself into a facetious pastoral style so as not to fall into the old, trite lamentations.' However intense the pain, and no doubt unrequited love in Iglau hurt him just as much as his *Weltschmerz* in Hungary, Mahler compels himself with a strong dose of irony to snap out of it. Evidently his self-discipline did not extend to posting the letter promptly but maybe in the mere writing of it he achieved his main, cathartic purpose. Perhaps, too, three songs he dedicated to Josephine at around that time had a similar effect.

When he wrote those letters Mahler had already passed out of the Vienna conservatory. Four years earlier, in 1875, he was still pining to go there and looking for allies who would help persuade a doubtful Bernard. He struck gold with Gustav Schwarz, manager of an estate in Morawan north of Iglau, who heard Gustav play the piano and said he should study music. Knowing that an estate manager was just the kind of person his father would listen to, Mahler wrote Schwarz a letter which, for a fifteen-year-old, was a masterpiece of diplomacy. Couched in the politest terms, Mahler said his 'dear father' was hesitating to agree to 'our plan' because he feared Gustav would neglect his academic work and get into bad company if he went to Vienna.

'Even when he seems to be inclining to our side,' Mahler wrote, 'you must remember that I . . . have only myself to rely on in my struggle against the superior power of so many "reasonable and mature people". That is why I beg you to be kind enough to call on us on Saturday, 4 September, for you are the only person who can really win my father over.' Schwarz called and Bernard gave in, though he insisted that Mahler pursue his schoolwork as an external student in Iglau as well as music in Vienna.

There are two versions of what happened next. One is that Bernard took Mahler to Vienna to seek expert advice from Julius Epstein, professor of piano at the conservatory. Epstein is said to have come out of lectures, heard Mahler play for five minutes at most and announced, 'Mr Mahler, your son is a born musician . . . I could not be wrong.' It is an engaging tale told by Epstein himself, albeit nearly four decades later when he was nearly eighty. The other version comes from Schwarz who says he took Mahler to see Epstein at Baden, near Vienna. According to Schwarz, the professor was not at all impressed by Mahler's pianistic skill but recognised his talent when the boy finally played some pieces of his own.

Whichever account is right (perhaps there were really two visits, one by a still sceptical Bernard following up one by Schwarz), the result was the same. Mahler enrolled at the conservatory on 10th September, two months after his fifteenth birthday.

In principle Vienna should have dazzled anyone from the provinces, especially an impressionable youngster. Magnificently defying the gloomy signs of the times, the capital in 1875 was in the throes of a huge construction programme as though the empire were set to last for ever. By order of Franz Joseph, the fortifications encircling the old city had been torn down to make way for a wide, tree-lined Ring boulevard flanked by grand new buildings. No expense was spared. Twenty types of marble alone were going into the erection of a new (albeit largely powerless) parliament. Semiprecious stones were being used to decorate the new Burgtheater, not so much a playhouse as a temple of German drama. Inside the 'K.K. Hofoperntheater', the Imperial and Royal Court Opera opened six years before, gold and cream filigree work glowed in the light of 4000 gas lamps. Outside, fountains spouted fresh water carried direct to Vienna from the mountains by a new irrigation scheme.

The Ring's construction naturally gave the Viennese great scope for their favourite sport – grumbling. The coffee houses hummed with complaints about soaring costs, filthy road works and, worst of all in a city where culture counted above convenience, repellent design. Malicious criticism drove one of the opera house's two architects to suicide. The other died soon afterwards of heart failure. But all that aside, the new boulevard was as fine as any being planned for Paris in the same era by the much-acclaimed Baron Haussmann. Even the teenage Adolf Hitler, on a trip to Vienna three decades later, reported with a rare flash of poetry that the Ring was 'like an enchantment out of the Thousand-and-One Nights'.

If Mahler was similarly impressed there is no record of it. That may just be because this time of his life is not well documented anyway. On the other hand, at least until his marriage in 1902 Mahler showed little interest in the visual arts, even disdained them as far inferior to music. A letter written in 1890 on his first visit to Florence gives no hint that he saw a single picture there. Rome he remembered chiefly for its dreadful orchestra. So perhaps Mahler really did not not think much of the architectural splendours of Vienna, not even of the fine neo-classical Musikverein building close to the Ring where the conservatory had just been rehoused and where he had to spend so much time.

Surely, one would think, the student Mahler must have haunted the Court Opera which he was to take over in triumph two decades later. But what evidence there is, including accounts that when he took up conducting he had to learn many operas from scratch, suggests that his attendance in those early years was infrequent. This is sometimes put down to his chronic lack of cash and it is true that he rarely had the price of a square meal. He was constantly on the move from one dingy lodging to another, absent-mindedly leaving behind items of clothing in each – much to the despair of his mother who warned that he would soon have nothing left to wear. Trying to help out, Bernard sent a green coat so comically oversized that it trailed along the ground when Mahler put it on. Still, most of Mahler's conservatory friends were just as poor but they somehow got to the opera all the same. Hugo Wolf, for instance, spent much of his student life queuing for entry to the Vierte Galerie (the gods) and writing ecstatic letters home, especially about his idol Richard Wagner.

'The Master of Bayreuth' had visited Vienna sporadically since 1832, running up huge debts which helps explain why he did not come more often. His revolutionary music, abrasive personality and trenchant writings about art and life divided the city into warring factions. Symptomatically, Wagner had scored a hit in Vienna in 1861 with *Lohengrin* but his later and – to his critics – abominably discordant *Tristan und Isolde* had been abandoned there as unplayable after more than seventy rehearsals. In 1875, when he was back again to conduct concerts and supervise the production of *Tannhäuser*, the battle over him was, if anything, fiercer than ever. The contras, grouped around the venerable Johannes Brahms, included the critic Hanslick, lampooned by Wagner as the pedantic Beckmesser in *Die Meistersinger von Nürnberg*, and much of the old guard at the conservatory. The pros included Anton Bruckner, somewhat oddly as he was a humbly devout composer and teacher ill-suited to any kind of earthly conflict, and several music students – especially Wolf. When Wagner was in town, Wolf hung around for hours so that he could open the carriage door for the great man as he left his hotel for the opera. Wolf then raced along the Ring to be on the spot to open the door again when Wagner arrived.

Mahler did not waste his time on gestures like that although he too fell under Wagner's spell, sometimes with painful results. When he, Wolf and another music student, Rudolf Krzyzanowski, began to bawl part of *Götterdämmerung* at the digs they shared, a furious landlady pushed them out into the street and locked the door behind them. Still, that show of enthusiasm for Wagner's music does not prove that Mahler was keen to see Wagner's works, or anyone else's, in the opera house, especially not in static, unimaginative productions at least as common then as now. Even when Mahler attended or conducted symphony concerts, there was generally a yawning gulf between what he heard and what his inner ear told him was in the score. In the opera house the gap was wider still – between what he believed the music expressed and what he witnessed on stage. That helps explain his lifelong exasperation with the opera business in general and why, after a couple of early efforts, he wrote no more works in the genre. Wagner felt much the same as Mahler about conventional opera houses but he drew a different conclusion, creating the

Bayreuth Festival Theatre to give at least his own works the staging and acoustic he felt they deserved.

There is a triple irony here. Mahler despised much about opera but conducted it, not least Wagner, supremely well. Bayreuth was one theatre he really did admire but, because of the anti-Semitism of Wagner's widow Cosima, he never conducted there. Moreover, whatever skills Mahler may have learned in his three years at the Vienna conservatory, conducting was not among them. There was still no course for it in those days although orchestras had grown much larger and scores more complicated. Conductors simply emerged thanks to their wide musical knowledge, leadership qualities and, when they could get it, practice. There was a conservatory orchestra in which Mahler played the percussion but there is no record that he took up the baton. If he did, evidently the result was not thought worth a mention.

So what did Mahler learn? Not as much as he should have done, according to Guido Adler, five years older than Mahler and a close but critical friend for more than three decades. Curiously, although Adler was highly musical and came from a Jewish family in Iglau, he and Mahler did not meet until both were in Vienna. Adler had already passed through the conservatory when Mahler entered it, but he stayed on in town studying music history at the university. Sometime in the second half of the 1870s, the paths of the two fellow Iglauites crossed. Adler writes that although Mahler 'had good teachers in piano playing and harmony, his introduction to the higher theoretical subjects (counterpoint and composition) was anything but profound and purposeful. His talent had to overcome this defective education and only years later . . . could Mahler remedy these deficiencies.'

Harsh though that view sounds, Adler was never a man to overstate his case. Certainly Mahler thought little of most of the conservatory staff and made that plain. His harmony teacher, Robert Fuchs, was a composer of pleasant orchestral serenades who later remarked with some perplexity that Mahler played truant and yet knew everything. Counterpoint Mahler learned (or, according to Adler, did not learn) from Franz Krenn, a dry disciplinarian whose deadly dull tuition helped persuade Wolf to abandon his conservatory studies prematurely. Mahler announced he was dropping out too but, more purposeful than the explosive Wolf, he soon wrote a grovelling letter to the director, Joseph

Hellmesberger, begging for reinstatement. Hellmesberger agreed but Mahler can hardly have recalled him with affection. Although leader of a fine string quartet which Mahler surely heard and admired, the director was a choleric anti-Semite. When Mahler made copy errors in the score of a symphony he had written for performance by the conservatory orchestra, Hellmesberger hurled the manuscript to the ground and refused to conduct it even when the mistakes had been corrected. Mahler promptly composed a piano suite instead. 'Since it was a much weaker and more superficial work,' he noted later, 'it won a prize while my good things were all rejected by the worthy judges.'

Only two of Mahler's teachers really impressed him. One was that same Professor Epstein, elegant pianist and publisher of Schubert's piano works, who had recommended him for the conservatory and who soon became his mentor and friend. When Mahler had to write to the conservatory's governors asking to be let off all tuition fees, Epstein added a postscript offering to guarantee half the sums due. He also helped out by finding piano pupils, including his own son, for his impoverished student. Mahler was duly grateful. Long after he had left the conservatory he still wrote back to his old master telling him his career was going well and, wryly, that he was just as arrogant as ever.

Under Epstein's watchful eye Mahler became a fine player, carrying off the top piano prize in his first year with a performance of part of a Schubert sonata. Could he have made his career as a concert pianist? Four piano rolls he recorded in 1905 of excerpts from his songs and symphonies, the only aural evidence we have of Mahler the interpreter, raise doubts. Indispensable though the recordings are, above all as a guide to the tempi he wanted, they are rather sloppily played. No doubt Mahler by then was out of practice. In any case it is a boon that he took the conducting road instead. Without that long experience wrestling with often recalcitrant players in many different halls, his orchestration would surely have been less expert.

The other teacher to impress Mahler was Anton Bruckner, albeit through example not instruction. So much folklore has grown up about the ties between the two that it is not easy to get at the truth. For instance, Mahler and Bruckner were absurdly bracketed together for decades mainly because they both wrote nine big symphonies (even that is not quite true) widely thought not worth playing. Alma claims in her memoirs that Mahler gave a complete Bruckner cycle in the United States, but he only conducted three of the symphonies anywhere (plus, once, a single movement of a fourth). One biographer writes that Mahler religiously attended all Bruckner's lectures, another that his attendance was sporadic, yet another that Bruckner thought so much of his young pupil that he always walked with him down several flights of stairs when saying goodbye.

Mahler said flatly in a letter written in 1902 that 'I was never a pupil of Bruckner's; this rumour must have arisen from the fact that I was continually seen about with him in my earlier days in Vienna, and that I was certainly one of his most enthusiastic admirers and publicists. Indeed, I believe at that time I was the only one there was, apart from my friend [Rudolf] Krzyzanowski.' Here Mahler's recollection is partly at fault. Bruckner had many keen followers, at least among the students. For them he was both an eminent master and, although he was already in his fifties, a naïve but agreeable companion. On the one hand he was instructor in harmony and counterpoint at both the conservatory and Vienna university, as well as a genius in improvising at the organ. On the other he liked little better than to stump off in his baggy old trousers for a chat over a few beers, or to stand at concerts with young people rather than sit with his prim and proper peers.

Bruckner showed Mahler that even a composer who venerated Wagner could still find fulfilment writing symphonies, which Wagner had soon abandoned. Perhaps the near-Wagnerian scale on which Bruckner built his works influenced Mahler too. Apart from that the two had little in common. Mahler's orchestral palette is far more varied than Bruckner's, or indeed almost anyone else's. With Bruckner melody generally dominates, with Mahler development. Although Mahler, like Bruckner, uses folk-dance (especially ländler) and chorale themes, he tends to set them in a context which casts doubt on the simple joy they express. For Mahler peace of mind is never attainable for long; for Bruckner it usually seems secure – though not quite always. The massive discord which climaxes the Adagio of Bruckner's unfinished Ninth Symphony, his last, matches almost anything in Mahler for desolation.

No wonder even Bruckner's faith wavered at times. On 16th December 1877 he conducted the Vienna Philharmonic in the first performance of his Third Symphony. It was a fiasco for him and a bitter but salutary lesson for Mahler. The orchestra, which had rejected Bruckner's First Symphony as 'wild' and his second as 'nonsense', hardly put its heart into the première of the Third. Whistling and jeering soon erupted, especially from the anti-Wagnerites. Gradually the hall emptied. At the end only a few dozen students were left, among them Mahler who had seen Hellmesberger joining in the jeers. Soon afterwards Mahler presented a grateful Bruckner with a piano-duet version which he had made of the ill-fated Third, possibly with Krzyzanowski's help. According to Alma, he later used part of his own royalties to help promote Bruckner's work, though proof of this is lacking. At any rate, from that December night at the latest, he can have had no illusions about what the world, especially the 'music capital' Vienna, could throw at a composer determined to go his own way.

That lesson alone surely did not decide Mahler's future course but it must have weighed heavily. He wanted to compose but vividly saw the danger of trying to subsist on that alone. A career at the piano seemed too restrictive. He was not a born teacher although much later he was offered, and refused, the directorship of the conservatory. That left the supremely taxing compromise solution he finally adopted until his death – conducting to earn his keep and 'part-time' composing, usually in his summer holidays. Later Mahler claimed that had he won the coveted Beethoven prize with his cantata *Das klagende Lied (The Song of Lament)* when he was just twenty-one, he would never have got caught on the conducting treadmill. Perhaps he really believed that. More likely the Bernard in him meant he was too practical and ambitious to risk working for reward only in heaven. Bruckner could do that, but then he generally seemed certain that heaven really existed. In any case a jury which included Brahms and Hellmesberger awarded the Beethoven prize to Mahler's harmony teacher Robert Fuchs. *Das klagende Lied* did not even take second or third place.

It was not least that steel in Mahler which marked him out from his student friends. Wolf, with Schubert perhaps the greatest of all songwriters, felt Mahler had stolen his idea for an opera called *Rübezahl* and broke with him for many years. He finally died insane. So did Hans Rott, said by Mahler to be as gifted as himself, soon after being advised by the grumpy Brahms to give up composing. So did Anton Krisper, who wrote music and wrote about it but was not really happy doing either. Of those conservatory comrades who did make their way, Krzyzanowski became conductor in Weimar (after an uneasy spell sharing duties with Mahler in Hamburg), Adler developed into Austria's most distinguished musicologist and Arnold Rosé became leader of the Vienna Philharmonic, subsequently marrying Mahler's eldest sister Justine. But none of them showed Mahler's drive, even ruthlessness.

It would be easy to end this account of the first Vienna years there. Apart from a fragment of a piano quartet and a few songs, none of Mahler's music before *Das klagende Lied* has survived; indeed Mahler claims he never finished the works he began in those days because he so quickly became dissatisfied with them. After passing out of the conservatory in 1878 with a diploma (but without one of the coveted silver medals for exceptional achievement won by nine of his fellow graduates), he went on to study at the university. Evidently he did not learn much there, later admitting he only attended the 'Vienna woods' with any regularity. Finally in 1880 an agent called Gustav Lewy signed him up and found him his first job. It was a summer one conducting bits and scraps, as well as setting up music stands and stacking chairs, before dozy guests in an Austrian provincial spa called Bad Hall. Mahler had grave doubts whether to take Lewy's offer, desperate though he was for cash, but wise old Epstein advised him to do so at once because 'you'll very soon work your way up'. That forecast proved more accurate than even Epstein can have expected.

Well before leaving Vienna, however, Mahler became involved with a strange character called Siegfried Lipiner who had a big, probably decisive, influence on him. This part of Mahler's story is often skirted, partly because it seems to have little directly to do with music, partly because even in German-speaking countries Lipiner's name is not widely known nowadays. But back in the late 1870s Lipiner, a Jew from Galicia in the far east of the Habsburg empire and only four years older than Mahler, was already being spoken of as a prodigiously gifted poet and dramatist. Friedrich Nietzsche and Wagner, no less, were among his early admirers. His eloquence was legendary. Although stunted like a gnome, he at once caught the attention of any gathering with his hypnotic eyes and intense rhetoric. Mahler was not easily impressed by his contemporaries and, when he was around, the spotlight rarely fell on others. Lipiner was an exception. In his letters, Mahler usually referred to him as 'dearest Siegfried' and expressed boundless enthusiasm for his work. Apart from a break of several years after Mahler's marriage, the two remained in close contact for the rest of their lives and died within months of one another. Significantly Alma, who resented most of her husband's old friends, particularly the closest ones, reserved special venom for Lipiner.

It is not clear when the two first met but it was probably around 1878 at a meeting of one or other of those hodgepodge bands of German nationalists and socialists, Wagnerians and literary buffs, vegetarians and bon vivants typical of Vienna in that era. One such group, hundreds strong, was the Leseverein der deutschen Studenten (Reading Society of German Students) which aimed to 'preserve the German character' of Vienna university. Another, more select, was the Pernerstorfer Circle (named after its socialist founder Engelbert Pernerstorfer), which exalted German culture and sought the unity of all German-speaking peoples. In such circles talented Jews like Lipiner and Mahler, drawn both by the finest products of the German mind and by a simple desire to belong, seemed more German than the Germans. At one gathering when those present sang '*Deutschland, Deutschland über alles*' reportedly to a particularly fiery march tune, it was Mahler who pounded out the piano accompaniment. One of those singing along on that occasion was another Jewish friend of Mahler's called Victor Adler (no relation to Guido). Adler later even made common cause with Georg von Schönerer, one of Hitler's early heroes, before breaking with extreme nationalism and founding the Austrian Social Democratic Party.

For Mahler, the political element in all this ran only skin-deep. Decades later when he was in principle an 'establishment figure' as director of the Vienna Opera he did vote for Victor Adler and even briefly joined in a workers' May Day demonstration; but that is all that is known (and probably all there is to know) about his post-student involvement with politics. Nor did he stick very long to the modish vegetarianism prescribed (though not adopted) by Wagner in his *Religion und Kunst (Religion and Art)* to achieve 'a thorough-going regeneration of the human race'. Although Mahler often joined Adler, Lipiner and others at a gloomy cellar-restaurant in Vienna to dine on spinach and the like, we find him some years later in Budapest tucking into knucklebone and horseradish sauce.

If that had been the sum of Mahler's non-musical activity in those days it would be worth no more than a wry smile. But it was very probably at that stage in Vienna, not more than a decade later in Hamburg as is often assumed, that Mahler first came to grips with German philosophy. His later letters and the accounts of those close to him show how intensely he studied not just works by famous thinkers like Arthur Schopenhauer and Nietzsche, but also those by relatively obscure ones like Gustav Theodor Fechner (1801–87) and Rudolf Hermann Lotze (1817–81), who both sought a synthesis between science and metaphysics. In all likelihood it was Lipiner who back in the late 1870s either first fired Mahler's interest in these writers or at least acted as a major catalyst. After all, by the time he met Mahler, Lipiner had already written a major work on Schopenhauer, he had studied under Fechner in Leipzig and he personally knew Nietzsche who called him 'a veritable genius'. That background and Lipiner's fervour must have made a deep impression on the young musician, with his hitherto largely undirected fascination for literature and ideas.

To point to Mahler's interest in philosophy is one thing, to show it had an influence on his approach to music quite another. He did not need Schopenhauer to tell him that music was the highest of the arts, though no doubt he was happy to have his own view confirmed from so renowned a source. Superficially, Nietzsche's impact is easier to show, though Mahler eventually rejected Nietzsche who had the effrontery to turn bitterly against Wagner. Mahler used a Nietzsche text from *Also Sprach Zarathustra (Thus Spake Zarathustra)* in his Third Symphony and even briefly dubbed the whole work, after Nietzsche, *Die fröhliche Wissenschaft (The Joyful Science)*. The symphony's brutal contrasts, from a percussive free-for-all at the start to a concluding rapt Adagio, he explained in part as frenzied nature under the god Pan finally being refined into the world of the spirit. Here too Nietzsche is close – the Nietzsche of *Die Geburt der Tragödie (The Birth of Tragedy)* who sought to show that great art emerges only through a fusion of the ecstatic, 'Dionysiac' world and the calm 'Apollonian' one.

True though that is, it does not get to the heart of the matter. What really absorbed Mahler was not this or that theory about art, let alone finding a handy text for his song-symphonies. Something much more vital was involved. As he later wrote in a bid to explain what was at stake in his 'Resurrection' Symphony, 'What did you live for? Why did you suffer? Is it only a vast terrifying joke? We have to answer those questions somehow if we are to go on living – indeed, even if we are only to go on dying!'

Nietzsche gave an answer of a kind with his doctrine of 'eternal recurrence'; namely that everything in history comes round again in vast cycles and hence that we should only live in a way we are willing to see repeated for ever. Fechner, for whom stones and plants as well as animals had souls, took another view of immortality. For him mankind passed through three stages; the lowest an unbroken sleep until birth, the next – earthly life – an uneasy alternation of sleeping and waking, and the highest an eternal awakening through death, which was really a second birth. Schopenhauer, a keen student of oriental religion, saw salvation from the world he detested in an ascetic self-denial much like the Buddhist ideal of Nirvana. A similar notion mightily impressed Wagner too. In a letter to Liszt in 1855, Wagner extolled the Buddhist view that living creatures went on being reborn, and their souls refined, until they caused no more pain to others. 'How sublime and uniquely satisfying is this teaching,' wrote Wagner, 'in contrast to the Christian-Judaic dogma according to which each human being . . . merely has to behave himself in the eyes of the church through the short space of his life on earth, in order to lead an extremely easy life for the rest of eternity.' Time after time Wagner toyed with the idea of an opera on the Buddha, but he never got round to it.

That Mahler imbibed much of this is clear, not least from comments he made to Specht, his biographer. 'We will all return,' Mahler said. 'Our life only has sense if it is shot through with this certainty and it is wholly unimportant whether in a later reincarnation we recall an earlier one. What counts is not the individual and his memory . . . but only that great movement towards perfection, that purification which progresses with each reincarnation. That is why I have to live ethically, to spare my Self a part of the road when it returns.'

Did Mahler believe those remarks and similar ones he made at other times? He desperately wanted to. But he never stopped looking for further evidence, whether in the latest discoveries in the natural sciences (he kept in close contact for years with the distinguished physicist Arnold Berliner), in the dialogue between Ivan and Alyosha on the existence of

God in *The Brothers Karamazov* or in Goethe's speculation about redemption and rebirth. Most of all he sought for proof through his own work. 'Goethe said immortal things on this subject,' Mahler noted once during a talk about man's role in the cosmos. 'What I want to say I am naturally only able to express fully in music. . . . That is what has been given to me and for that I will be called to account.'

That does not mean Mahler's works are simply potted Schopenhauer, Nietzsche and Co. set to music; that we can identify this or that philosophical proposition as we can, say, the baby's howl or the mother's tantrum in Richard Strauss's tone poem *Sinfonia Domestica*. But all Mahler's symphonies, including *Das Lied von der Erde*, are attacks from different angles on the biggest issues man faces, the meaning of life and the paradox of death. Sometimes the assault is explicit, as in the 'Resurrection' Symphony or in the Eighth with its setting of the last scene of Goethe's *Faust*. Sometimes it is implicit, as in the non-vocal Fifth Symphony which begins with a funeral march and struggles through to a joyful chorale even Bruckner would have been proud of. It is even implicit in Mahler's decision, after early flirtation with opera and chamber music, to express himself almost entirely in symphonic form. Only the symphony offered him the scale and structure to seek in music what his favourite thinkers expressed in words. That he then enlarged the scale and almost burst the structure is testimony, not to love of gigantism for its own sake, but to the intensity of the search.

This is not the place to delve deeper into the symphonies. It is enough to note here that when Mahler, aged not quite twenty, left Vienna for that dismal little job in Bad Hall, his head was not only full of the sound of folk-song and Bohemian bands, trumpet calls and marches, Bruckner chorales and Schubert sonatas. It was also throbbing with the problems of philosophy and metaphysics he had thrashed out, above all, with Lipiner. That too helped form Mahler the composer.

Chapter Two

On the Road

'I SEE GATHERED around me a throng of artists whom any general might be proud to lead to victory. It must fill each one of us with pride to belong to an establishment . . . that forms the focal point of Hungary's artistic endeavours and at the same time is the pride of the nation.'

It is October 1888, and the new artistic director and chief conductor of the Royal Hungarian Court Opera is introducing himself with a few flattering words to the assembled company. In principle he is taking on an enviable job which gives him virtually supreme power over one of the most modern theatres in Europe. Completed only four years earlier, the imposing building on Andrassy Street in the heart of Budapest has 1200 seats and the very latest in hydraulic stage machinery. What's more, the new man has a ten-year contract in his pocket and is to be paid an unusually handsome 10,000 florins annually.

There are, however, a few drawbacks. The previous director proved a flop despite his pedigree as a son of the composer Ferenc Erkel, the founder of Hungarian national opera. The house is in dire financial straits, its artists demoralised and undisciplined. Thanks to frequent visits by 'stars', local singers get too little chance to shine and the orchestral playing is often mediocre. This is shaming and intolerable for the second capital of the Habsburg empire, determined to show that anything Vienna can do it can do better.

A rescuer is badly needed, ideally one who combines brilliance as a conductor and producer with proven administrative skill and a burning desire to stage Hungarian works. The already legendary Arthur Nikisch, Hungarian-born chief conductor in Leipzig, is approached but he takes one look at the shambles and says no. So does Felix Mottl, conductor in Karlsruhe and a protégé of Liszt, the outstanding Hungarian composer and pianist of the age. Small wonder that many jaws drop when the choice finally falls on an abrasive twenty-eight-year-old Bohemian-born Jew called Mahler, who is expert above all in the German repertoire and who speaks hardly a word of Hungarian (though he promises to learn). His career so far has taken him on a zigzag course in and out of the empire, never staying anywhere very long and sometimes leaving amid more than a whiff of scandal.

Mahler's takeover as director of the Vienna Court Opera at the age of only thirty-seven has often been called an extraordinary coup. So it was. But in some ways his appointment to the challenging and well-paid Budapest post, only eight years after his début as a penniless novice in Bad Hall, was more remarkable still. Neither the longing to compose, nor bouts of near-suicidal depression, nor philosophical speculation, nor a string of love affairs, checked the upwardly mobile career conductor for long. He squeezed all he could from each job and turned temporary setbacks into springboards to the next rung of the ladder.

The first rung after Bad Hall was Laibach, now Ljubljana in Slovenia (ex-Yugoslavia) but then capital of the duchy of Krain and still well within Habsburg borders. The orchestra of the Landestheater there had only eighteen members and the chorus only fourteen, which may be why some commentators rank Mahler's Laibach period as hardly less amateurish and demeaning than the one in Bad Hall. There are also several comic but suspect tales that the young conductor found himself having to sing or whistle the parts of performers there who unexpectedly failed to appear on-stage.

In fact the Laibach company, though small, had a good reputation and Mahler was lucky to win the job. He mainly had Lewy, his agent, to thank for it, but there is evidence that he also drummed up support via another ex-conservatory student, Anton Krisper, whose father was an influential

Laibach merchant. If indeed he did so it was wholly in character. Mahler was a generous but demanding friend who knew how to work the 'old boys' (and girls') network' for all it was worth. He could also be a canny business negotiator, not averse to the odd white lie if he felt this would, for example, help him to obtain a better post or tempt a reluctant diva to appear as a guest artist. The strange thing is that despite his hard-headedness and comparatively spartan way of life he was perennially short of cash. Later that may have been partly because he financed his younger brothers and sisters after his parents died, but by then he was earning very well. The truth is that he simply could not handle his own money, or at least could not be bothered to. Lewy, for one, seems to have realised that. After a while he insisted on a change of contract to ensure that he got his commission paid through direct debit at source by Mahler's employers.

Mahler held the Laibach post for only one short season, from September 1881 to March 1882, but local press reports suggest that he made a success of it. He certainly learned a lot, making his operatic début with Giuseppe Verdi's *Il Trovatore* and going on to conduct a string of works including Otto Nicolai's *Die lustigen Weiber von Windsor*, Carl Maria von Weber's *Der Freischütz*, Gioacchino Rossini's *Il Barbiere di Siviglia* and, to his greatest joy, Mozart's *Die Zauberflöte*. The critics were generally favourable and at a benefit performance in his honour (meaning he received the takings) Mahler was presented with a laurel wreath: not bad for a starter just turned twenty-one.

After Laibach, Mahler's next post in Olmütz (Olomouc) really did mark a plunge into the murkiest depths of provincial music-making. In principle it should not have been as bad as all that. As the second largest town in Moravia, only about 60 miles from Mahler's Iglau home, Olmütz had the wherewithal to support a passable theatre. Instead the house there was in need of almost everything – cash, repairs and, in January 1883, a new conductor to replace the previous incumbent, who had been dismissed after performing an 'unmentionable act' during Giacomo Meyerbeer's *L'Africaine*. Mahler got the job but he began to regret it even before he lifted his baton. 'I am crippled like a man who has fallen from heaven,' he wrote to his friend Fritz Löhr, who for years received some of Mahler's frankest letters. 'From the moment I crossed the threshold of the Olmütz theatre, I felt like one awaiting the wrath of God. When you harness a noble steed to a cart drawn by oxen, all it can do is sweat and drag along with them.'

The 'oxen', as Mahler termed his fellow musicians, had been warned by the theatre director that the new conductor was something of a genius but distinctly odd. They soon found out just how odd – as a baritone called Jacques Manheit, then a soloist with the Olmütz company, vividly recalled in an article years later. At the very first rehearsal the members of the chorus retreated after an hour saying they were completely hoarse and unable to sing another note. The soloists then filed into the rehearsal room to find Mahler sitting at the piano warming his hands in his coat tails. He had long, dishevelled hair and a shadow of black beard, and wore a large horn-rimmed pince-nez which tended to slip off his nose as soon as he began his wildly energetic conducting. Mahler tried to secure the glasses with ribbon wound around his head but the result looked so absurd that the singers doubled up with laughter. Otherwise they had nothing to laugh about. Mahler did not bother to introduce himself. He curtly demanded complete obedience and ignored the obvious hostility shown him by almost everyone but Manheit.

Even at the local tavern Mahler managed to put people's backs up. Still in his vegetarian phase and to the disgust of the waiter, he ordered only water, spinach and apples, then got into a fierce argument with another guest who finally retreated, snarling that the new Kapellmeister had best leave town double-quick. Manheit, seeking to avoid further scandal, hastily took Mahler off to a nearby café for a game of billiards. Even that did not go smoothly. Mahler began dancing about and brandishing his cue so wildly that officers from the local garrison came over to see what was going on. The cue-waver explained that he had been practising conducting the first act of Meyerbeer's *Les Huguenots* for the benefit of Manheit's 'esteemed colleagues' who were wholly unable to follow his beat.

Mahler stuck it out in Olmütz until the end of the season in mid-March. It was his shortest and, with Bad Hall, least glorious spell in any theatre. Yet it is astonishing how much of the later maestro, fêted and feared in the grandest opera houses, was discernible even then. Mahler had shown in Laibach that he was a workaholic who could master a new score as quickly as most people could skim a book, but his feats in Olmütz were still more striking. In just over two months he lashed the benighted company into learning five new operas, including Georges Bizet's *Carmen* and Etienne Méhul's *Joseph*. The latter needs fourteen solo singers and the theatre could muster only twelve but Mahler liked the piece and insisted it be performed all the same. He even had a spot of praise for the singers who despite 'unspeakable insensitivity' went about their task 'rather more seriously' than usual. Still, that modest success did not tempt him into putting on Mozart or Wagner operas. Sure that works by two of the composers he loved most would only be sullied if taken up by the Olmütz company, he successfully intrigued to have them struck from the repertoire.

Just how intensely Mahler felt about Wagner even then can be judged from another Manheit report. The singer found Mahler in a café looking glum because he had heard from home that his father was ill. The next day Manheit bumped into Mahler again, this time running down the street, sobbing and pressing a handkerchief to his eyes. 'In heaven's name, has something happened to your father?' Manheit asked. 'Worse, worse, much worse,' Mahler wailed. 'The Master is dead.' Clearly news could travel fast even then. It was 13th February 1883, the day Wagner expired in Venice. Five months later Mahler made his first pilgrimage to Bayreuth for *Parsifal* and left the Festival Theatre claiming he had 'come to understand all that is greatest and most painful and that I would bear it within me, inviolate, for the rest of my life'.

Even without Mozart and Wagner on the programme in Olmütz, Mahler still felt that he was suffering, as he put it, 'for the sake of my Masters and . . . to set a spark of their fire alight in the souls of these poor people'. It is a tellingly evangelical remark. For Mahler a conductor who was a 'mere musician' was not good enough, however great his technical mastery. 'What is needed,' he insisted, 'is a complete and superior human being – one capable of thinking and feeling as the composer thought and felt when he wrote the work.' No doubt most conductors believe much the same even if they tend not to say so with quite Mahler's blithe self-assurance. But then Mahler was a composer himself, albeit a fledgeling one in the Olmütz era. He identified himself utterly with the work in hand as though it were his own and treated as a personal insult performances which fell below his standards. Not surprisingly, most of them did. In Mahler's view it was not enough for a player to give his all. 'He must go a step beyond his own capacity. And I force them to do it;

for each one feels that I'll immediately pounce on him and tear him to pieces if he doesn't give me what I want.'

Mahler did not exaggerate about the fear he inspired throughout his career. His rages were legendary. The odd wrong note he could just about tolerate if the spirit of the performance was right; routine, indifferent playing – never. 'Where music is, the demon must be,' he would say. When his players fell short he became demonic himself. His whole body trembled, his face turned pale and two veins on his temples began to throb like lines of blue lightning. Counter-productively, some of the errant musicians on whom he turned his hypnotic glare became so petrified that they could hardly lift their instruments.

Those describing Mahler's approach to conducting often resorted to zoological comparisons. One said Mahler treated his musicians like a lion-tamer his animals. Another, that Mahler on the podium looked like a cat with convulsions. Max Graf, a critic in Vienna, said that Mahler 'let his baton shoot forward suddenly, like the tongue of a poisonous snake. With his right hand he seemed to pull the music out of the orchestra as if out of the bottom of a chest of drawers.' The *Deutsche Zeitung*, an anti-Semitic newspaper in Vienna, was even more explicit. 'Mahler's left hand often jerks convulsively,' it wrote, 'marking the Bohemian magic circle, digging for treasure, fluttering, snatching, strangling, thrashing the waves, throttling babes-in-arms, kneading, performing sleights of hand – in short, it is often lost in delirium tremens, but it does not conduct.' Hostile though that report was meant to be, no doubt the acrobatics it described fired the curiosity even of the unmusical. Later in his career Mahler became calmer, relying on darting glances and flicks of the wrists. The result seems to have been, if anything, still more riveting. Eyewitnesses described the contrast between the uproar of the orchestra and Mahler's near-immobility as positively eerie.

Manheit's account shows that in Olmütz Mahler was already firmly into the 'lion-tamer/convulsive cat' phase. Loathed though he was, his approach paid off. Shortly before his departure, the initially hostile local press began to praise the orchestra for its 'magnificent playing'. Mahler not only conducted. He coached the singers, produced and stage-managed, often leaping across the orchestra from the podium to position the choir or correct a soloist's stance. Two decades later in Vienna he was still doing much the same. His agility earned him, behind his back, the title of 'the Jewish monkey' and drew from a court official the dry remark that Mahler did 'not have to move the scenery too'.

Mahler not only won over the press. As luck would have it Karl Ueberhorst, senior stage manager of the Dresden Court Opera, passed through Olmütz talent-scouting – in principle for singers. Not surprisingly it was the conductor who literally took his breath away. 'You can only gasp at a man who manages to bring off a performance like that,' he conceded after hearing Mahler conduct *Joseph*. Unfortunately artistic merit alone was not enough to win a job at the Dresden Opera. Ueberhorst felt the young maestro's 'figure and appearance' made him unsuitable for so dignified a house, but he was more than ready to give him a testimonial for somewhere else. It was with the help of this document, praising him not least for energy and 'tact' (!), that Mahler soon got a post in Kassel, capital of the Prussian province of Hessen-Nassau. It turned out to be no less stormy than the one in Olmütz although the resources on offer were far better.

In moving to Kassel, Mahler for the first time left relatively easy-going Habsburg lands and promptly collided with Prussian discipline. In principle that should not have bothered a person so keen on discipline himself, at least when he was the one to impose it. But Kassel's Royal (Prussian) Theatre, ultimately responsible to Berlin, was an extreme case. The place was run like a military academy by its general manager Adolph Freiherr (Baron) von und zu Gilsa, a veteran of the Franco-Prussian War and holder of the Iron Cross. Those who broke ranks even over minor matters had their names entered in a black book. Mahler was soon caught out, among other things for stamping his foot on stage and podium. As though that were not demeaning enough, he was forbidden to make cuts without prior approval or (an irksome but not wholly superfluous rule) to rehearse with any lady member of the company unless a third party were present.

Worse still, although Mahler was called 'royal musical and choral director' he was only second-in-command after an uninspiring Kapellmeister from Graz called Wilhelm Treiber, who usually kept the weightiest works for himself. After deliberately keeping clear of Mozart and Wagner in Olmütz, Mahler often found himself in Kassel doomed to conduct potboilers like Viktor Nessler's *Der Rattenfänger von Hameln (The Pied Piper of Hamelin)*. As in Olmütz, he won over the public and critics but quickly antagonised singers and orchestra. Mahler later claimed that on one occasion he faced down musicians who turned up for rehearsal armed with cudgels to beat him up. Perhaps he embellished a little but the tale is not impossible. On a similar occasion in Hamburg Mahler had to call the police. In Budapest he received a challenge to a duel (which he ignored) and in Leipzig orchestral players appealed to the town council for protection against his 'unworthy' treatment of them and his 'impossible demands'.

Mahler may have hoped a similar fate might befall Hofkapellmeister Treiber, unlikely though that seemed. In a letter to Lewy full of self-praise at Treiber's expense, Mahler hinted that 'it is not entirely impossible that something unpleasant might happen to the above-mentioned gentleman. I don't want to speak more plainly.' In fact nothing happened to Treiber and Mahler soon began looking for another job. His first – known – attempt rebounded badly.

In January 1884 the Meiningen Court Orchestra under its founder and director Hans von Bülow gave two concerts in Kassel. They were cardinal musical events comparable, at least in advance ballyhoo and soaring ticket prices, to tour appearances by the Berlin Philharmonic under Herbert von Karajan in more recent times. Von Bülow, the most famous conductor and one of the finest pianists of his age, was not only a former right-hand man of Wagner (who seduced and later married von Bülow's wife Cosima) but also, remarkably, a backer of Brahms whom so many Wagnerites despised. Splenetic and sarcastic, he turned the provincial Meiningen band into about the best-drilled orchestra in Europe and forced its members to play from memory standing up.

It was from this martinet that Mahler sought help. Bowled over by one of the concerts, he tried to see von Bülow at his hotel but was turned away by the hall porter. Undeterred, Mahler wrote a letter to the 'most honoured master' praising his 'incomparable art' and begging to become his pupil even if he had to pay the tuition fees with his blood. Mahler explained that 'after the most wretched wanderings' he had become assistant conductor at the local theatre. 'You will know only too well whether this hollow activity can satisfy one who believes in art with all his heart and soul and sees it travestied everywhere in every conceivable way.' Mahler frankly admitted that 'what I can do – or what I might do – I do not know; but you will soon find out.'

[36]

Von Bülow thought not. It is often claimed that he did not even bother to answer. In fact he sent Mahler a few contorted lines telling him, in essence, to buzz off. Still less kindly, he sent Mahler's letter to Treiber who in turn, no doubt with glee, gave the incriminating document to von Gilsa. The latter, to his credit, took no disciplinary action. But by then, at the latest, Mahler's masters knew just what he thought about their theatre and his job.

The paths of von Bülow and Mahler were to cross years later in much happier circumstances. But for the time being the young assistant could only struggle on with his 'hollow activity' and spray job applications in all directions. He had no luck for a year and then, as such things happen, he struck gold twice over. He was contracted to take over as a conductor at the prestigious Leipzig Municipal Theatre from mid-1886 and, to bridge the gap until then, he won a post at the Royal German Theatre in Prague. With these engagements in his pocket, he left Kassel after an event which brought him his greatest glory there and caused the biggest uproar. It was also the first known occasion on which he was subjected to anti-Semitic attack in public.

Apart from his activities in the theatre, Mahler had been building up a strong reputation on the side as a choral conductor. It therefore seemed natural that, when a music festival was scheduled in Kassel in summer 1885, the organisers should ask Mahler to take on the performance of Felix Mendelssohn-Bartholdy's oratorio *St Paul*. Natural – but not diplomatic. Evidently furious that he was being passed over, Treiber intrigued to get the job himself. Von Gilsa too tried to get Mahler to stand down, appealing to his 'sense of nobility'. It was all to no avail. Mahler too much relished the prospect of leading the theatre orchestra, choirs 400-strong and fine soloists, including a mezzo-soprano from Vienna called Rosa Papier who years later would play a vital role in his career. The best Treiber could hope for, it seemed, was to rehearse the orchestra for Mahler's performance. This was too much for a local news-paper which whined that 'the Germans do the work and the Jew gets the honour'. Kassel, it claimed, had better and far more beloved conductors than 'the Jew Mahler'. In the midst of the mud-slinging the orchestra decided, at least partly under pressure from Treiber, to pull out of the performance.

That seemed to be that. No orchestra, no oratorio. Mahler did not see it that way. He scoured towns far and wide for musicians, commandeered a band from a Kassel infantry regiment and the performance went ahead in a local drill hall. It was a huge success. Mahler was showered with valuable gifts which was just as well because he was once more so bereft of cash that he had pawned his watch.

Amid all these professional battles Mahler found time to fall in love with a shapely, blue-eyed soprano at the Kassel theatre called Johanna Richter. Mahler claimed that 'she is everything lovable in this world' and that he would shed every drop of his blood for her. The affair surely had more substance than Mahler's crush a few years earlier on Josephine Poisl but it ended no more happily. Mahler wrote to Fritz Löhr that on the last night of 1884 he sat alone with Johanna awaiting the New Year. Both were weeping. 'Nameless grief had risen up between us like an everlasting partition-wall, and there was nothing I could do but press her hand and go. As I came out of the door, the bells were ringing and the solemn chorale sounded from the tower.' Tears and jubilation – and bitter irony too. By chance, Johanna lived in the same house as Mahler's despised superior Wilhelm Treiber. It was, Mahler wrote, 'as though the great director of the universe had meant to stage-manage it perfectly'.

Did the poignancy of that very scene flow into Mahler's work? We only know that even before that mournful New Year's Eve Mahler had written six poems dedicated to Johanna and that he set four of them to music in a cycle called *Lieder eines fahrenden Gesellen (Songs of a Wayfarer)*. To be strictly accurate the words of the first song, sometimes attributed to Mahler, were in fact copied by him almost word for word from *Des Knaben Wunderhorn (The Child's Magic Horn)*, a collection of old German folk poems he loved and often quarried for material. Still, it would be hard for the uninitiated to guess which passages have been 'borrowed', so well does Mahler latch on to the *Wunderhorn* style. More to the point, the music piercingly conveys the spurned lover's despair, his torment at the memory of his sweetheart's blue eyes and silvery laughter, his exhaustion as he plods off alone into the night.

In its first version, for voice and piano, Mahler's cycle expresses much of the numbed hopelessness of the wanderer in Franz Schubert's *Winterreise*. But his later arrangement for voice and orchestra hits harder, with tortured brass, feverishly shuddering strings and woodwind cackling like hobgoblins. More subtly, the songs drift from one key to another like the restless anti-hero they bring to life. Here it is not so much Schubert who springs to mind as Hector Berlioz. It is as though Berlioz had injected the nightmarish spirit of his *Symphonie Fantastique* into his richly romantic orchestral song-settings *Les Nuits d'Été (Summer Nights)*.

That link is unexpected, but it is not the only one between the central European Jew steeped in the German tradition and his great French predecessor. Both were revolutionaries as orchestrators and symphonists (though admittedly Berlioz concentrated far less than Mahler on the latter), both were masterful conductors, neither did things by half. 'The ordinary orchestra, the ordinary chorus, the ordinary concert-room would never do for him,' wrote the English critic Ernest Newman. 'Everything must be magnified beyond life-size. . . . A thing is never beautiful or ugly for him, it is all either divine or horrible.' The remark was about Berlioz but it applies just as well to Mahler.

Lieder eines fahrenden Gesellen is often called Mahler's first masterpiece. That is rather hard on *Das klagende Lied* which predates it, a cantata about fratricide which, with its off-stage band, already explores the kind of dramatic spatial effects Mahler perfected later. Still, the later work is even more original and certainly more subtle. One wonders whether Johanna Richter ever heard the cycle – perhaps she even sang it herself although strictly speaking it is composed for a lower voice than hers. She had a long but not particularly distinguished career as performer and then as teacher right up to the Second World War. Some suggest she was the real reason why Mahler left Kassel, but that is just as unlikely as the claim that another affair a decade later caused him to abandon Hamburg. In these and other cases he moved on to better himself and always, it seems, with the highest post of all firmly in mind. That, at least, emerges from a letter he wrote only three weeks after his painful parting from Johanna. He asks a friend to spread the news that he has gained a new job in Leipzig and adds, 'I no longer have many more rungs to climb. But my ultimate goal is and must remain Vienna.'

For a second conductor aged twenty-four about to leave Kassel under a cloud, that seems a somewhat unrealistic boast. But Mahler knew what he wanted and he was ready to make almost any sacrifice to achieve it. That included swallowing his pride. One might have thought that after the frustrations he suffered at the Kassel theatre, he would never have wanted to hear the name of von Gilsa again. But at the end of 1885 Mahler wrote to his former boss to wish him, no doubt to von Gilsa's astonishment, a happy New Year.

'I cannot avoid taking this opportunity,' Mahler bubbles, 'to express my thanks for all the goodness and friendliness you showed me during the time when I had the good fortune to be allowed to pursue my artistic aims under your direction. In your school I learned what is hardest of all, namely to obey so that one is able to command, faithfully to fulfil one's duty so that one is able to demand this from others. . . . I hope to be able to show you from now on that I will not put my master to shame.'

There are three possible explanations for this gushing epistle. One is that Mahler meant what he said. Most of what we know about his struggles in Kassel suggests that is unlikely. Another is that Mahler was simply being ironic; but why should he have suddenly decided to give himself that pleasure nearly half a year after moving on? The most plausible explanation is that Mahler realised ex-bosses, whatever his personal feelings about them, could help or hinder his career. Why not, therefore, try to ensure their goodwill with a few flattering words which cost nothing? Politic though such a strategy may be, in this case it did not work. Less than a year later Mahler wrote again asking if von Gilsa would help him find a new job. The director would not but, as was his wont, he carefully filed the letter away.

Although Mahler had Vienna as his firm aim, for the time being he had to 'make do' with Prague. Beautiful though the Bohemian capital was, with its majestic cathedral and castle on the Hradcany hill and its wooded pastures sloping down to the River Vltava, Mahler had only bitter memories of it from his brief stay there as a schoolboy. Moreover he was only to be a junior conductor at the German Theatre there which had suffered a fall in status, like much else German in the Habsburg provinces in those restless times. The increasingly self-confident Czechs had recently set up a fine National Theatre of their own in Prague and the German house, under a lack-lustre manager who had only just been replaced, was being badly squeezed by the competition. Mahler initially saw his job there as a mere stop-gap until Leipzig. In fact he came to love it so much that he tried vainly to stay on.

Mahler turned out to be unexpectedly lucky in his timing. Angelo Neumann, the new manager who signed him up, was a go-ahead former operatic tenor with business sense and a fine eye for talent. Thanks to him the German Theatre soon began to make up lost ground, not least with performances of Wagner which Neumann loved. He had his rows with his young and uppity appointee whom he judged 'too fidgety' on the rostrum, but for Mahler the Prague job spelled joyful release from the Kassel strait-jacket. All the more so since Anton Seidl, the chief conductor and an experienced Wagner-hand, took a job at the Metropolitan Opera in New York soon after Mahler arrived. The other conductor, Ludwig Slansky, was a popular local man but not inclined to overexertion. Hence virtually by default, Mahler suddenly found himself in charge of several of the works he loved most and with which he was later particularly identified like Wagner's *Die Meistersinger* and *Die Walküre* and Beethoven's *Fidelio*. He even took on delightedly Mozart's *Don Giovanni*, premièred in Prague under its composer a century earlier, because Slansky was not keen to conduct that either. To cap it all Mahler at last had the chance to do more non-operatic conducting and gave his first performance of Beethoven's Ninth Symphony. It turned out so well that leaders of the local German community, among them Mahler's old friend Guido Adler who was then teaching at Prague's German university, sent him a special letter of congratulation.

Despite all this German-ness, Mahler did not turn his back on what the Czech competition was doing. He was, after all, Bohemia-born. On his nights off, he would stroll round to the Czech National Theatre a few streets away to hear works by Dvořák and, to his special delight, Smetana. 'I must confess that Smetana in particular strikes me as very remarkable,' he wrote to Max Staegemann, director of the Leipzig Municipal Theatre. 'Even if his operas will never form part of the repertoire in Germany, it would be worth while presenting such an entirely original and individual composer to audiences as cultivated as those in Leipzig.'

By the time he wrote that letter in summer 1886, with its diplomatic praise for the Leipzigers, Mahler had finally resigned himself to leaving Prague. He had tried hard to get out of his contract with Leipzig but Staegemann, no doubt impressed by reports of the y[ ] growing success, insisted on holding him to it. So Ma[ ] once more, again leaving behind a tearful soprano. Th[ ] Betty Frank. She sang at the German Theatre, took [ ] triumphant performance of the Beethoven Ninth and, in a concert at a Prague hotel which put her in the music history books, gave the première of three early Mahler songs with the composer at the piano. The affair between the two brought so much tongue-wagging that word of it even reached Mahler's acquaintances, and perhaps his family, in Iglau. But it did not last long. Once Mahler got to Leipzig he found his hands more than full – with a new flame and with his most dangerous rival so far.

Hitherto Mahler had played (perhaps sometimes even secretly enjoyed) the role of hothead young genius, wringing fine performances from vile material, as in Olmütz, or showing up conductors nominally his superiors, as in Kassel and Prague. Leipzig offered a challenge of quite a different order. The city where J.S. Bach had spent much of his working life, and where Wagner was born, enjoyed fine choirs and the famed Gewandhaus Orchestra, a body raised to excellence by Felix Mendelssohn nearly half a century before. When Mahler came on the scene Leipzig's grand music tradition was personified above all in Arthur Nikisch, chief conductor at the Municipal Theatre and at least as phenomenal a master of the orchestra as his new underling from Prague.

Had Nikisch belonged to an older generation like von Bülow (born in 1830), Mahler might have found it easier to settle for second place – at least for a time. But Nikisch was only five years Mahler's senior and seemed to have achieved fame with an irritating ease. Born in Hungary in 1855, he entered the Vienna conservatory as a piano prodigy at the age of eleven and could memorise scores with extraordinary rapidity. After graduation he became a violinist in the Vienna Court Orchestra, playing under Brahms and Wagner among others, but quickly found that his real talent lay in conducting. Elegant and unfailingly polite, he was loved by orchestras and adored by women. He arrived in Leipzig in 1878 and soon had musicians and public at his feet.

Much of that might suggest Nikisch was a superficial fop, popular because undemanding. In fact with an absolute minimum of words and gestures he galvanised often weary and cynical orchestras into playing their hearts out. Just how he did it was usually a mystery even to the musicians themselves. 'He simply looked at us, often scarcely moving his baton,' an evidently bemused member of the London Symphony Orchestra recalled, 'and we played as though possessed.' That reference to 'simply looking' offers a clue. Rare film footage from 1913 shows

Nikisch conducting, his baton always raised so high and close to his face that the musicians are forced to look into his eyes. And what eyes they are. Even through the shaky old pictures they burn like those of a fanatic – or a hypnotist. No doubt that was the point. Nikisch mesmerised his players. Most good conductors do the same, more or less. Nikisch was special.

So, of course, was Mahler. Well aware of what, or rather whom, he was up against he flung himself into his work with still greater passion. In his very first month, a sticky August when a lot of Leipzigers were still on holiday, he conducted eleven performances of ten different operas including four by Wagner – *Lohengrin* as his début, *Rienzi*, *Tannhäuser* and *Der fliegende Holländer*. He kept up much the same spanking pace for the rest of the 1886–87 year and even increased it in 1887–88 as well as composing 'on the side'. He was determined not to be, as he put it, 'a pale moon circling around the star Nikisch'. Instead he streaked through the Leipzig scene like a meteor, leaving behind a trail of scorched singers and frenzied stage managers as well as wounded instrumentalists from the noble Gewandhaus band who grumbled that 'it's as though we'd been plain daft before Herr Mahler came along from Prague to show us what piano means.'

Not surprisingly, Mahler soon ran afoul of director Staegemann too. Outside the theatre the two men got on well. Mahler was often a guest at Staegemann's house and was full of praise for his two daughters, both talented singers. But when it came to business Mahler, as usual, was tough. In a letter to Staegemann only three months after his début, Mahler offered his resignation because Nikisch was to conduct the whole of Wagner's cycle *Der Ring des Nibelungen*. Mahler claimed that he and Staegemann had 'tacitly agreed' the task should be shared. Evidently the director thought not. At any rate he left the *Ring* in Nikisch's hands and refused to let Mahler go.

That storm blew over mainly because soon afterwards Nikisch caught pneumonia and took extended leave of absence. To Mahler's delight, the *Ring* and much else fell into his lap. 'The latest turn of events,' he wrote to Löhr, 'means that to all intents and purposes I am now on an equal footing with Nikisch and need have no qualms about fighting him for the upper hand, which I am certain to gain if only on grounds of physical superiority. I don't think Nikisch will stand the pace, and sooner or later

[43]

he will decamp.' Unfortunately for Mahler, Nikisch recovered and showed much more staying power than anticipated.

While battling against Nikisch Mahler plunged into another love affair, his most tangled so far. Just when it began is unclear but the scene was set for it soon after Mahler arrived in town. 'I have met a beautiful person here in Leipzig,' Mahler wrote to Löhr (one can almost see the raised eyebrows) in October 1886, 'the sort that tempts one to do foolish things. Do I make myself clear, amice? But this time I mean to be careful, or else I shall be in trouble again.'

Mahler proved unable to keep his good resolution. The 'beautiful person' was Marion von Weber, four years older and married with three children. Carl von Weber, her husband, was a Hauptmann (Captain) in a Leipzig regiment and, what's more, the grandson of Carl Maria von Weber, the father of German Romantic opera. Mahler began to visit the von Webers regularly, wrote songs for the children and, at first with reluctance, took on a composing job from Carl which was to bring him funds and fame. This was the completion of a comic opera *Die drei Pintos (The Three Pintos)* which Carl's grandfather had only sketched. Composers including Meyerbeer had been asked to finish the work but declined. Mahler finally accepted, perhaps because he relished the challenge, perhaps because it gave him a still better excuse for spending more time around Marion.

Just how serious was the affair? There are next to no details about it from Mahler himself but he seems to have unburdened himself years later to Alma. She claims in her memoirs that Mahler and Marion were so deeply in love that they even decided to elope. According to this version, Mahler dreaded the consequences of flight for his career and family but passion got the better of him. He made it to the railway station where he and Marion had agreed to meet but she failed to show up and the train left without them.

Perhaps Alma embroidered the tale. By the time she wrote it she had been through her own intoxicating experience of clandestine romance on rails, although on that occasion Mahler was the cuckolded husband. But a still more striking story comes from Ethel Smyth, the British composer and later suffragette who was in Leipzig at the time. In her memoirs she claims that Carl was aware of his wife's liaison but tried to shut his eyes to it because a scandal would have meant leaving the army. Finally, she writes, he could stand it no longer. 'One day, travelling to Dresden in the company of strangers, Weber suddenly burst out laughing, drew a revolver, and began taking William Tell-like shots at the head-rests between the seats. He was overpowered, the train brought to a standstill, and they took him to the police station raving mad – thence to an asylum.'

Those details may be exaggerated too, although it seems that Carl did indeed have bouts of mental instability and was later nursed at home by Marion. What does ring true is Ethel Smyth's assessment of Mahler as a man who 'in spite of his ugliness' had 'demoniacal charm . . . At the time I am speaking of in Leipzig I saw but little of him, and we didn't get on; I was too young and raw then to appreciate this grim personality, intercourse with whom was like handling a bomb cased in razor-edges.' Ugly, charming, grim, explosive: she might have been describing Mephistopheles or Jekyll and Hyde.

Perhaps the most reliable evidence of how close Mahler and Marion really were came many years later from an unexpected source. In 1907 the Dutch conductor Willem Mengelberg wrote excitedly to his wife of a visit he had paid to Marion, by that time a widow and living in Dresden. Mengelberg knew nothing of the Leipzig liaison, but when the talk turned to Mahler he noticed that Marion's eyes became moist and she trembled. To his astonishment, she finally produced a pile of original manuscripts by Mahler insisting she had shown them to no one else. How many Mahler works Marion really had tucked away is unclear. The manuscripts were later lost, probably during the bombing of Dresden in 1945. But one of them was certainly an early version of the First Symphony, including a sentimental Andante movement called *Blumine* which Mahler later struck out. According to Mengelberg, Mahler had headed the movement *In glücklicher Stunde* (In an hour of happiness). At the end he had written a dedication to Marion on her birthday.

That background helps explain a mystifying note dashed off by Mahler to Löhr in early January 1888. Writing to his friend for the first and last time in red ink, Mahler explained that he could manage only a few lines 'in this trilogy of the passions and whirlwind of life. Everything in me and around me is in a state of becoming! Nothing is! Let me have just a little longer to see it through! Then you shall know all.'

Mahler did not define the 'trilogy' but he was right about the whirlwind. Apart from the affair with Marion, he was embroiled in fraught
preparations to stage *Die drei Pintos*. He had completed the music the previous autumn and done his best with Carl to revise the threadbare
libretto about mistaken identity and amorous high jinks in Spain. Much
hung on the première, set for 20th January. Many leading opera directors
were due to attend, even a representative from the Metropolitan in New
York. Hermann Levi, Wagner's chosen conductor for the première of
Parsifal, would be on hand too as well as the daunting Hanslick, barbed
pen at the ready, from Vienna. A success, surely, would not only boost
Mahler the conductor but thrust Mahler the unknown composer into the
limelight at last. Rather more of the final score may have been by Weber
than Mahler cared to admit, but he had put in a lot of work on it and his
name appeared jointly on the cover.

The piece was an instant hit although it is rarely heard now. After the
triumphant première, it continued to play in Leipzig to packed houses
and within months had also been given in Hamburg, Munich, Dresden
and Kassel. The next year it reached Vienna and later Berlin. Mahler
received an advance of 10,000 marks from the Leipzig publishers and
promptly sent off 1000 of it to his parents, along with a proud account of
how he had been received between acts by the King and Queen of
Saxony. 'I am from today a famous man,' he wrote. The boast seemed
justified but it was premature. Few of Mahler's later compositions drew
such instant cheers – certainly not the First Symphony on which, despite
his other distractions, he was now feverishly engaged.

It is not clear exactly when Mahler got down to work on the symphony
in earnest, but astonishingly he seems to have written the bulk of it in
weeks rather than months. That would have been quick going even if he
had had no other commitments, but on most days he was leading
rehearsals and often conducting in the evenings too. The only respite
came when Kaiser Wilhelm I died and the theatre closed in mourning,
giving the delighted Mahler ten free days to compose. On completing the
first movement, he ran round to the von Webers although it was close to
midnight and played the piece with Marion and Carl on the piano. 'We
were all three so enthusiastic and blissfully happy,' Mahler said later, in
the circumstances a rather macabre remark.

In March Mahler could report to Löhr that his work was finished. 'It became so overwhelming,' he wrote, 'it gushed out of me like a mountain torrent. This summer you shall hear it. At a stroke all the floodgates in me opened. Perhaps one of these days I shall tell you how it all happened.' Whatever Mahler may have told Löhr, he admitted eight years later in a letter to the composer and critic, Max Marschalk, that the symphony had been touched off by a love affair. However, Mahler added, he wanted to stress that the symphony began where the affair left off. 'The real-life experience was the impulse for the work, not its content.'

That may seem like splitting hairs. In fact it is a crucial warning against linking the content of Mahler's works too closely with the circumstances of his life at the time he wrote them. What emerged from Mahler's pen in those first months of 1888 had been welling up in him for years until, as he put it, the floodgates opened. Parts of the first and third movements are built on *Fahrenden Gesellen* songs he wrote for Johanna Richter in Kassel. The *Blumine* movement he dedicated to Marion is based on an excerpt from another of his Kassel compositions, incidental music to a play called *Der Trompeter von Säkkingen*. The trumpet calls and bird-song, the ländler dance and squeaky little band, recall his Bohemian-Moravian origin. As for the flashes of irony and banality, while they might reflect Mahler's anguish over the everyday life of the theatre, the ceaseless tussles with, as he saw it, insensitive musicians and short-sighted managers, that interpretation is altogether too specific. Mahler had many grounds for anguish and no doubt all of them somehow contribute to the teeth-grinding parody of the third movement and the explosive lead into the fourth. As he said after composing his first two symphonies, 'I have written into them everything I have experienced and endured. To understand these works properly would be to see my life transparently revealed in them.'

The love affair, then, served as a kind of bomb which burst the floodgates. But there may have been further reasons, which Mahler did not mention, for the surge of creativity. One of them could have been his work on *Die drei Pintos*, which got him going again on some major orchestration after a long spell of virtual abstinence. Another might have been a wish to show his skill in a field where Nikisch, who was no composer, could not compete.

Nikisch was not Mahler's only rival, not even his most dangerous one. Richard Strauss, an up-and-coming composer-conductor from Munich, had visited Leipzig in October 1887 to give his F minor Symphony. He and Mahler met there for the first time, got on well enough and henceforth were wary friends. Strauss even praised Mahler's work on *Die drei Pintos* in a letter to von Bülow, though he hastily sent a grovelling retraction when von Bülow disagreed. But it was surely not lost on Mahler that Strauss was four years younger and already had two symphonies, concertos, a string quartet and several other compositions to his name. Did that first encounter help spur Mahler to get on with composing something wholly his own? Possibly all these elements combined to produce the critical mass from which the First Symphony erupted.

Not only the First Symphony! No sooner did he finish that work than he began another, a twenty-minute funeral march evidently intended from the start to be the first movement of a symphony. Years later, in revised form, that is what it became. The odd thing is that Mahler should at once have followed up the brassy triumph of the First Symphony's finale with one of his grimmest pieces. All the more so since there is evidence he was at least sketching the new work while still composing the old one.

To Mahler there was no paradox. In his First Symphony, he explained, his hero the Titan is battered time after time by the blows of fate and finally achieves victory only in death. As for the start of the Second, he wrote to Marschalk that 'if you wish to know, it is the hero of my D major Symphony (No. 1) whom I am bearing to his grave and whose life I, from a higher vantage point, am reflecting in a pure mirror. . . . My Second Symphony grows directly out of the First.' Mahler talks about his 'hero' but clearly he means himself. While composing the funeral march, he said later, he had had a vision of himself lying dead on a bier under heaps of wreaths and flowers.

Sceptics may feel that Mahler is trying to establish in words a connection which was not at all so clear when he was actually composing. They would have Mahler at least half on their side. In that same letter to Marschalk, Mahler preceded his comments on the Second Symphony with the confession, 'I know that as long as I can express an experience in words I should never try to put it into music. The need to express myself musically, in symphonic terms, begins only on the plane of obscure feelings, at the gate which opens into the "other world".' In other words Mahler tried to have it both ways. When his work met with incomprehension, or when he feared it would, he tried to 'explain' it in words. Of course he knew the words were inadequate but, at least at first, he felt they were better than nothing. Later he doubted even that.

Still, even sceptics should be wary of rejecting the 'explanation' outright. In 1887, shortly before Mahler got down in earnest to composing his First Symphony, an epic poem called *Dziady (Forefather's Eve)* by the famed Polish writer Adam Mickiewicz was published in a German version in Leipzig. The translation, entitled *Todtenfeier (Funeral Rites)*, was made by none other than Mahler's Vienna comrade Siegfried Lipiner. There is no proof Mahler read it right away but it would have been odd of him not to. It dealt in dramatic terms with life after death, it was a product of a much-admired old friend and it came out on his own doorstep. He certainly knew the work well later and quoted from it.

Did *Dziady* refocus Mahler's mind at a crucial moment in his creative life on issues like salvation and rebirth he had thrashed out with Lipiner years before? Could that be why a few months later, through the unfathomable process in which ideas and emotions are transmuted into music, Mahler simultaneously produced works of victory and death? That would involve no contradiction for a believer (even a wavering one) in eternal life. Quite the contrary.

The theory is unprovable. All we know for sure is that Mahler called his funeral march *Todtenfeier*, like the translation of Mickiewicz's poem, and the Second Symphony which grew out of it he named the 'Resurrection'.

Mahler completed the manuscript of the march in September 1888 in Prague, where he was guest-conducting several performances of *Die drei Pintos*. Apart from that assignment he was out of a job. Four months earlier he had broken with Leipzig in circumstances not fully clear to this day. It is a matter of record that he had a furious argument with the chief stage manager there and submitted his resignation to Staegemann, who accepted it. But Mahler was constantly rowing with somebody and Staegemann was quite used to parrying demands for release from his fiery young deputy conductor. What had changed by early 1888?

One thing had not changed. Despite all Mahler's efforts to budge him, Nikisch seemed set to stay on in Leipzig indefinitely (though, ironically, he left the very next year to take over the Boston Symphony Orchestra). But by this time Mahler clearly felt he was launched, if not yet much heard, as a composer and that his conducting record entitled him more than ever to a top post. Moreover, recently uncovered evidence shows that even before his dispute with the stage manager, Mahler had secretly negotiated his forthcoming Prague appearances in clear breach of his Leipzig contract. Perhaps he deliberately exaggerated the row, or even instigated it, to give himself a firm reason to break free. Perhaps Staegemann got wind of the Prague deal and decided enough was enough.

Whatever the truth, Mahler spent a few anxious months adrift that summer, trying without success to get his First Symphony a hearing and looking for that elusive better job to which he felt entitled. Briefly it seemed that he might stay on in Prague after his *Pintos* performances there but that prospect faded after a fierce, in this case definitely undesired, row with his former sponsor Angelo Neumann.

For Mahler, the uneasy interregnum could hardly have ended more auspiciously with his call to Budapest as artistic director and chief conductor. Evidently he had been pulling strings furiously to get it. We know, for example, that his friend Guido Adler had been plying an influential contact in Budapest with letters explaining why Mahler was easily the best choice. At the end of 1888 the new boss was digging himself into his new job – not yet the Vienna one he craved but a big step closer. In high spirits, he even sent a Christmas package of sausage and paprika to Staegemann along with a chatty letter about the problems he faced now he was a full director – too. Suddenly everything seemed to be going Mahler's way. In fact the next year would turn out to be one of the worst of his life.

Chapter Three

To the Summit

FEW CONDUCTORS can have made a more dramatic début. On 26th January 1889, Mahler had just launched the Budapest Opera orchestra into the subaqueous rumbling which begins Wagner's *Das Rheingold*, when flames began to flicker from the prompter's box on-stage. Mahler tried to press on regardless, grimly determined that his conducting première in Hungary should not, literally, go up in smoke. It was meant to be the start of a full *Ring* cycle given for the first time in Hungarian and Mahler had worked on it virtually since his arrival, getting the text translated and welding together a team of local singers.

The performance finally proved a triumph, though even Mahler had to halt it briefly when firemen arrived to douse the flames. A few faint-hearted souls fled the theatre but most of the audience stayed on to the end to roar approval. On the next night *Die Walküre*, the second of the *Ring* operas, was just as well received by public and critics alike. Even the most fervent local nationalists found it hard to fault all-Hungarian Wagner prepared and conducted with such passion.

Then the blows began to fall. Despite his roving life Mahler had always kept up contacts with his family, but now he found himself shuttling the 250 miles between Budapest and home in Iglau on one crisis mission after another. After years of failing health his parents died within eight months of one another, Bernard on 18th February and Marie on 11th October. His twenty-year-old sister Justine – Justi – tried to run the Iglau household and nurse her mother after Bernard's death, but by September she was close to collapse. Mahler took her to Vienna for a medical check-up and while there also called on his married sister Leopoldine, who had been suffering from splitting headaches for months. Doctors claimed there was nothing seriously wrong with her but Mahler had hardly got back to Budapest when she died, probably of a brain tumour.

While trying to cope with all that and run the opera, Mahler was in considerable pain himself. He had an operation in Munich in July for haemorrhoids but the problem was to recur in later years, once so badly that he nearly bled to death. Shrugging off the operation, he threw himself back into his Budapest duties, taking morphine to 'get through rehearsals'. Mahler rarely let his ailments stop him working although for much of his life he suffered from violent migraines and septic throats as well as his 'trouble in the nether regions' as he called it. 'Illness is talent-lessness' (*Krankheit ist Talentlosigkeit*), he used to say, as though a strong and creative will were enough to see the body through. Most of the time he seemed to be right.

Mahler was now head of the family, or what was left of it. Of his four surviving brothers and sisters he was easily closest to the impractical but devoted Justi and took her to live with him in Budapest. The faithful Fritz Löhr, now married and working as an archaeologist in Vienna, agreed to look after the two youngest children, Otto aged sixteen and Emma, four-teen. That left twenty-two-year-old Alois, the family's 'black sheep', full of silly business schemes and constantly in debt. Mahler naturally paid the bills for the two teenagers but, with 'a slight groan' as he put it, he regularly helped out Alois too.

Mahler's generosity, or at least his sense of duty, did not earn him much joy. His brothers were resentful because Mahler insisted that, like him, they should renounce their share of the family estate to provide their sisters with better dowries. At Mahler's expense, Otto studied music at the Vienna conservatory but shot himself in 1895, perhaps in despair of ever matching his famous brother. He left behind a note saying he was tired of life and was handing back his ticket. Alois left abruptly for America, apparently fleeing his creditors. For years the girls seemed in danger of remaining on the shelf but finally they married the Rosé brothers, two celebrated Jewish musicians in Vienna. Both sisters died in the 1930s, mercifully before the Holocaust. Their families were not so lucky. Emma's husband Eduard, a cellist, perished in Theresienstadt concentration camp and Justine's violinist daughter, Alma, succumbed in Auschwitz where she was forced to play for the SS. Justine's husband Arnold, veteran leader of the Vienna Philharmonic, fled almost penniless to London where he died in 1946.

With family affairs more or less under control, Mahler feverishly began rehearsals in Budapest for a performance he believed could at one stroke transform his career. After the years of emotional turmoil culminating in that burst of creativity in Leipzig nearly two years before, he was at last to conduct the première of his First Symphony. Admittedly, at that stage he called it a 'symphonic poem in five movements', not a symphony. But whatever the name, Mahler felt the performance on 20th November would mark his real début as a creative artist, notwithstanding his hit with *Die drei Pintos* and the few public concerts of his songs. How would people react? Mahler admitted later he had honestly expected a huge success which would let him live on the profits and concentrate on composing. In some ways he was still naïve, despite all his setbacks.

The première was not a total flop. Part of the audience applauded after each movement and a couple of critics wrote comments of real insight: on the whole not too bad for a first night. But the main reaction was one of baffled indignation, especially over the funeral march movement (marked 'with parody' in the score) which no one knew whether to take seriously or not. 'We shall always be pleased to see [Mahler] on the podium,' taunted one newspaper, 'so long as he is not conducting his own compositions.' For the first time, but far from the last, cartoonists reaped a rich harvest from a Mahler symphony. One showed the composer, his hair bolt upright with strain, blowing farm animals out of a huge horn while a friend beat the publicity drum and listeners fell about with fright.

Mahler took it badly, claiming that even his friends avoided him after the performance as though he were 'a leper or an outlaw'. But even he had to admit things were at fault in the work, including some key stretches of instrumentation. That was hardly surprising since until the rehearsals Mahler had never heard any of his orchestral work performed, apart from the special case of *Pintos*. Even the start seemed wrong, a thick, saturated string sound when he had aimed for something as fresh and light as a spring morning. He began to make hefty revisions, initially adding but then rejecting a written programme seeking to explain what the music was all about. It was not until a decade later, in 1899, that the score finally emerged as we now know it. Such was to be the pattern with his later works too – composition, rehearsal, revision, performance, more revision and self-accusations of 'amateurism'. For Mahler improvement always seemed possible, perfection just around the next corner.

To try to ensure that other conductors could be in no doubt about what he wanted, Mahler scattered more instructions across his scores than any composer before or since. Sometimes he inserts an extra few words stressing he really does mean what he says. Players are advised when to pick up their instruments to be in time for an awkward entry, choristers are given hints on how best to reproduce a sound like a bell. Knowing that musicians will probably over-interpret his commands, he tries to get what he is after by cunning. When he wants something played more slowly he tends to write '*nicht eilen*' (do not hurry) instead of *ritardando*; when he wants *accelerando* he writes '*nicht schleppen*' (do not drag). Despite some miscalculations, much of that precision and professionalism is already on hand in the First Symphony. For the fanfares at the very start, for instance, Mahler tells two trumpets to play off-stage in 'the very far distance' (*in sehr weiter Entfernung aufgestellt*) and a third to play only 'in the distance' (*in der Ferne*). The effect is magical if the directions are obeyed. Usually they are not.

Far from 'living on the profits' from his new work, Mahler found himself still busier with opera affairs and with less time than ever to compose. Despite his initial triumphs on the podium and an improvement in the theatre's finances, the nationalist press began to complain that he was not staging enough Hungarian opera and the public started to resent the dwindling number of appearances by foreign guest 'stars'. As Mahler had gone out of his way from the first to boost local talent, he naturally resented the charges. All the more so since the longer he stayed in Budapest the more he yearned to hear German works performed in German again. When Mahler complained about being 'thrice homeless' he meant it mainly geographically, but in Budapest (and later America) he was homesick above all for the language he loved perhaps second only to music. On arrival he had spoken out firmly against the practice, common not only in Hungary, of allowing guest artists to sing in whichever tongue they knew best, no matter what the opera. It would be more acceptable artistically, he wryly told an interviewer, to perform the works without the words. But that rejection of operatic babel did not mean Mahler was personally keen to hear virtually everything sung in Hungarian, from Wagner's *A Rajna Kincse (Rheingold)* to Mascagni's *Parasztbecsuelet (Cavalleria Rusticana)*. He put up with it in the interests of creating a really first-class national ensemble. Now some of his critics were complaining that he had gone too far with his 'Magyarisation' and others that he had not gone far enough. One casualty of hardening attitudes was that projected *Ring*. Despite his initial success with the first two operas, Mahler was never able to complete the cycle in Budapest by staging *Siegfried* and *Götterdämmerung* too.

Mahler felt increasingly sick at heart but as long as he had Ferenc von Beniczky, the even-handed government commissioner for the court theatres, on his side he had little really to fear. Von Beniczky had appointed Mahler, constantly encouraged him and gave him plenty of artistic rein. In the autumn of 1890, though, rumours grew that a fiery aristocrat, Count Geza Zichy, would take over as commissioner early in the New Year. For Mahler the news could hardly have been worse. Count Zichy was a fanatical nationalist and anti-Semite who had been a concert pianist, although he had lost an arm, and fancied himself as a composer. He looked bound to meddle in opera house affairs on artistic and political grounds.

Mahler began to look for another job although his Budapest contract had eight years to run and he was still notching up some big successes. One of the biggest, his *Don Giovanni* with a splendid (in this case largely imported) cast, turned out to be even more important for Mahler than he realised at the time. The crotchety Brahms happened to be in town on 16th December and was invited to attend that night's *Don Giovanni* performance by two Mahler fans who had free access to a box. He accepted with ill grace, noting that at least he could have a good nap there before going on to a tavern. Nothing came of the planned snooze. Mahler had hardly got through the overture before Brahms was giving grunts of approval which turned into cries of 'Quite excellent, tremendous – the deuce of a fellow.' Later the old man hurried on-stage to embrace the conductor and thank him for the finest *Don Giovanni* of his life. Brahms may well not have recalled who had written *Das klagende Lied*, which he and other jurors had turned down for the Beethoven prize nine years before. Although Brahms never really came to terms with Mahler's music, from that December evening he lost no chance to enthuse about his prowess as an opera conductor. That testimonial was to pay off hand-somely for Mahler seven years later when he ran for the directorship in Vienna.

In the mean time, though, he had to get out of Budapest – albeit on the best possible terms. As feared, Count Zichy became commissioner in January 1891 and promptly forced through new regulations giving him the power to intervene directly, even over Mahler's head, in artistic matters. After one blazing row with the new man, Mahler found himself threatened with suspension by the interior ministry. No doubt he felt like storming off there and then but he resisted the temptation. He was deter-mined to leave as soon as possible but he was going to make his employ-ers pay dearly.

Well aware how keenly Count Zichy wanted to be rid of him, Mahler offered in March to exchange his ten-year contract for a new one lasting only another eighteen months. If that contract were not renewed, he was to receive compensation of 25,000 florins in cash. As he expected, Count Zichy could not bear to wait. He told Mahler he could have the 25,000 florins if he would go right away. No doubt he would have been less prodigal had he realised that Mahler already had a firm new job offer in his pocket from Bernhard Pollini, director of the Hamburg Municipal Theatre (Stadttheater). Pollini was a tough businessman but he had had to work hard to get his new man. Letters had fluttered between the two for months, with Mahler haggling over salary and fringe benefits and at one stage threatening to call the whole thing off. By making Pollini believe, and Count Zichy fear, that he was ready to stay on in Budapest for quite a while, he managed to screw advantage from both.

Mahler formally resigned on 14th March, just two and a half years after his début speech pledging to lead the artistic 'pride of the nation' to victory. In a farewell declaration, made through an open letter in the press because he was barred from re-entering the opera house, he said he had 'faithfully and honestly' fulfilled his duty and thanked personnel and public for their support. He still had plenty of fans incensed that their idol was leaving in such shabby circumstances. A few days later, police had to be called to the opera after near-rioting and cries of 'Bring back Mahler' repeatedly interrupted a performance of *Lohengrin*. Later Mahler was to speak fondly of his time in Budapest but that March as he headed north to his new post he felt glad to be 'free at last'. His relief was short-lived although he stayed in Hamburg six years, longer than anywhere bar Vienna.

As a 'free and Hanseatic' city-state, Hamburg was a part of neither the Habsburg empire nor Prussia but considered itself superior to both. Wealthy and cosmopolitan thanks to its booming port, proudly up-to-date with an electric tram system, the Elbe metropolis looked down on Vienna as slovenly and on Berlin as grimly provincial. More important from Mahler's viewpoint, the Hamburg Opera was reputed to be one of Germany's finest, well funded and backed by a keen public. Much of the credit for that went to Pollini, an opera baritone turned impresario, who had already run the house for eighteen years when he engaged Mahler. He had made a small fortune running Italian opera companies in Russia, ploughed much of it into the Hamburg house which he leased from the Senat (city government) and was soon in charge of other local theatres too – hence his nickname 'Mono-Pollini'.

For a time all went well. Mahler initially stayed at Pollini's villa, loved the bracing sea air and roared into his opera work, conducting thirty-five times in the two months to the end of May when the season closed. Fulfilling a long-standing ambition, he gave his first performance of Wagner's *Tristan und Isolde*, arguably the work with which he was henceforth most associated. The critics, abandoning any pretence of Nordic sang-froid, acclaimed Pollini's new find as a 'magician' and 'genius'. Piotr Ilyitch Tchaikovsky was just as dazzled when he visited Hamburg months later for the German première of his *Eugene Onegin*. But the praise which meant most to Mahler came from that same Hans von Bülow who had snubbed him in Kassel seven years before and who now lived in Hamburg. After hearing Mahler conduct Wagner's *Siegfried* von Bülow was almost as blissful as Brahms had been at that Budapest

Giovanni. Later he even sent round a laurel wreath dedicated to 'the Pygmalion of the Hamburg Opera', implying that the Mahler touch wondrously drew life from inert material.

Von Bülow's uncharacteristically generous words were not quite precise. Unlike the Pygmalion of mythology, Mahler in Hamburg was no king. In Budapest he had had virtually supreme artistic control, at least until Count Zichy came on the scene. In Hamburg he was 'only' principal conductor, meaning his employer took the broader decisions on artists and repertoire. Thanks to his background as a singer, Pollini signed up some of the finest soloists in the business but, in Mahler's view, he chose some worthless operas and left stage management in indifferent hands. Influenced by Wagner's '*Gesamtkunstwerk*' concept of a fusion between music and drama, Mahler strove for performances in which every element was equally fine – orchestral playing, vocal and acting ability, production and staging. Even back in the paltry little Olmütz theatre he had had his sights set on that ideal, which he was finally to realise with some consistency only in Vienna. Pollini, on the other hand, strove for profit. To give him his due, he reinvested heavily in the theatre, equipping it with the plush seats, heating and electric lighting which his well-heeled clientele expected. Nor was he unadventurous with repertoire. The decision to stage *Eugene Onegin* by the then controversial Tchaikovsky is a case in point. But Pollini was convinced it was great voices above all which lured the public. Everything else, on which Mahler set such store, was secondary.

Quite apart from this difference of artistic approach, Pollini was a taskmaster who drove even Mahler to the limit of his endurance. In his two Leipzig seasons, seeking to topple Nikisch from the top perch, Mahler had happily taken on all the work he could and conducted more than 200 performances. In his six Hamburg seasons, goaded on by the implacable Pollini, he led 740. Several associate conductors came and went, most unable to stand the pace. One died, apparently of exhaustion. When Mahler delayed his return to Hamburg for the 1892–93 season because cholera had broken out there, Pollini threatened to fine him a year's salary. Later, he took on Mahler's erstwhile student friend Rudolf Krzyzanowski as an associate and, in a show of spite, gave him works to perform like *Tristan* which he knew Mahler was keen to do himself. In his last season, at Pollini's behest, Mahler found himself lumbered with frothy pieces like Carl Millöcker's operetta *Der Bettelstudent* (*The Beggar Student*).

Still, it is never wise to paint Mahler simply as an innocent victim, whether of unscrupulous managers, blockheaded musicians or, indeed, designing women. In his drive not just for artistic perfection but to get to the top of his profession, he had no time for weakness in himself or others. Even close friends were sometimes repelled by his moodiness and tantrums. They put up with it knowing how much more, admirable and lovable, there was besides. Pollini saw only an ambitious, pugnacious conductor – albeit one who was undeniably good for business. When Mahler's initial contract expired in 1894 Pollini renewed it for five years.

It was thanks to Pollini that Mahler paid his one and only visit to London. Sir Augustus Harris, manager of the Covent Garden Opera, planned to give a season of German works including the *Ring* in June–July 1892 and asked his Hamburg colleague for advice on artists. As a result Mahler arrived in England leading more than 150 singers and instrumentalists, most of them from Hamburg, and armed with a dictionary. 'Audience: delighted and much thankfull,' he reported in a letter home written in pidgin English. 'I am quite done up!'

The tour proved such a success that ten extra performances were given. There were a few quibbles all the same. The public was stunned to hear Beethoven's *Fidelio* sung in the original German, not in Italian as had long been the absurd London practice. George Bernard Shaw, deliberately striking a contrast to his ecstatic fellow critics, merely reported after *Siegfried* that Mahler knew the score 'thoroughly' and set the tempi 'with excellent judgement'. As for the German orchestra, Shaw sniffed that Covent Garden's own band could play better if given the chance. The visitors made a far deeper impact on a nineteen-year-old music student who just over a decade later was to compose a First Symphony even more gigantic than Mahler's. Thrilled by Mahler's conducting of *Tristan*, the young Ralph Vaughan Williams staggered home in a daze and for two nights could not sleep a wink.

Mahler should have felt well pleased with a tour which served greatly to raise his international profile. In fact he resented the vacation time lost in England which he could have used for composing, and resolved not to accept such invitations again. He was now thirty-two and had created little since Leipzig because of the twin pressures of career and family. He was also desperate to get out of the opera pit more often and conduct the symphonic repertoire like von Bülow, who gave regular subscription concerts in Hamburg. Mahler often attended them, sitting in the front row where he received bows and winks from his now embarrassingly admiring older colleague. The front row was not enough. Mahler wanted to be on the rostrum.

This was no mere fad but a yearning akin to Mahler's desire to get on with composing. Before arriving in Hamburg, he had conducted hundreds of opera performances but only about a dozen choral and orchestral concerts. The programmes had included the well-received *St Paul* in Kassel and several major symphonies (Beethoven's Fifth and Ninth and Mozart's Fortieth) but were otherwise relatively lightweight. Mahler was simply not widely known, let alone admired, as a symphonic conductor and this rankled. 'You must understand, dear friend,' he told the Hamburg critic Ferdinand Pfohl, 'that an activity such as the opera house demands from its Kapellmeister becomes in the long run insupportable, almost deadly. In the interests of self-preservation and self-respect I have to conduct concerts, to regenerate myself in the concert hall.'

It is a big question, though curiously not one often posed, whether Mahler really managed to regenerate himself on the concert stage – in Hamburg or anywhere else. After von Bülow's death in 1894, Mahler took over the subscription concerts on top of his opera work – thus becoming, albeit briefly, Hamburg's conducting overlord. For the first time he was able not just to give the odd concert or two but to plan and carry through a series of eight in the space of five months. With huge enthusiasm, he put together programmes which cunningly mingled Mozart, Beethoven and Schubert with relatively unfamiliar works like Berlioz's *Symphonie Fantastique*, Edouard Lalo's *Symphonie Espagnole* and Bruckner's Fourth Symphony. Superb virtuosi were engaged too, including the pianist Ferruccio Busoni and the violinist Pablo de Sarasate. However, the series ended with so big a deficit that Hermann Wolff, the concert agent involved, refused to book Mahler for another season, not even for a lower fee.

What went wrong? Mahler had only a 'pick-up' orchestra drawn from three different sources at his disposal, but he had long since proved how well he could bludgeon unpromising material into shape. No, it was not as a rule the playing to which the critics so violently objected. It was

Mahler's interpretations, which were regarded as too often arbitrary, and his 'retouchings' of familiar scores like that of Beethoven's Ninth. Did a mere Kapellmeister know Beethoven's business better than Beethoven, the critics thundered?

In some ways this Kapellmeister thought he did. Claiming that Beethoven had failed to achieve ideal orchestration because he was deaf, Mahler added a clarinet here, a piccolo and a trombone there. For good measure he even placed the wind band in the choral finale off-stage to achieve a sense of distance he felt Beethoven must have had in mind but had not marked in the score. Mahler's 'retouchings', and his explanations for them, did not stop there. He boosted the orchestration of works he felt made too little impact in the huge, contemporary concert halls, and rescored Beethoven and Schubert quartets for massed strings, arguing the music was too powerful to be left to just four instrumentalists. Mahler gave his most comprehensive explanation for taking this approach in a long letter in 1893 to a certain Gisela Tolney-Witt who had written to him from Budapest. He went into fine detail about music history and modern architecture, concluding, 'So away with the piano! away with the violin! They are good for the "chamber", if you are alone or with a friend and wish to conjure up the works of the great masters – as a faint echo – rather the way a copper engraving recalls to your memory a richly coloured original by Raphael or by Böcklin. I hope I have made my meaning clear to you.' Mahler's hope was probably ill founded. Although the evidence is sketchy, it seems the inquisitive Miss Tolney-Witt was only eight years old.

Mahler's 'creative' approach showed up in his choice of tempi too. Already in London, an otherwise well-disposed critic had complained that in a Beethoven overture Mahler had begun an *allegro* too slowly and then speeded up although no *accelerando* was marked. The Hamburg critics were harsher. Unusually flexible tempi in the dramatic context of an opera performance were one thing; in the concert hall they served only to distort the composer's intentions. Mahler was obviously talented but, so the reviewers argued, the concert podium was not the place for him. On the whole the public seemed to agree. Audiences dwindled, perhaps also because they found Mahler's choice of works too adventurous.

This could just have been a case of cloth-eared listeners not recognising genius when they heard it. The conductor Bruno Walter, who was born in Berlin in 1876 and first began to work with Mahler during those Hamburg years, described him nearly seven decades later as 'the greatest performing musician I ever met, without any exception'. Another conductor, Otto Klemperer (born in 1885), differed with Walter on many things but not on this. People praised Toscanini to the skies, he grunted disdainfully towards the end of his life, but Mahler was 'a thousand times greater'. Still, both men were young when they fell under Mahler's spell and Walter, at least, heard his mentor conduct operas far more often than symphonies. Perhaps, after all, Mahler really was at his best in the opera house he claimed to despise. His sworn enemies found it hard to gainsay his achievements there while even his friends sometimes treated his concerts with reserve. Whatever the truth, the dismal outcome of the Hamburg subscription series hit Mahler hard. He would surely have felt still more frustrated but for one thing. In 1893 the creative 'floodgates' opened as they had in Leipzig five years before. Mahler was composing feverishly again, but he had to get far away from the opera house to do it.

Acting on Mahler's instructions, Justi had spent part of spring 1893 combing the Salzkammergut region east of Salzburg for summer holiday accommodation which was quiet and cheap. It had to be big enough for four family members – herself, Gustav, Emma and Otto – plus Natalie Bauer-Lechner, a close friend of Mahler's who wanted to become closer still.

Justi eventually found five rooms with separate kitchen at an isolated hotel called the Gasthof zum Höllengebirge, literally the Inn at the Mountains of Hell. The place was shoddily furnished – the Mahler party had to share a single battered sofa which was pushed from room to room as needed – but otherwise it was far less grim than its name. A white, ivy-clad building with big sun terraces, it stood close to the sleepy village of Steinbach on the Attersee, the largest lake in the Austrian alps. Behind the inn meadows blazing with flowers sloped down to the water's edge. In front of it wooded hills stretched away to north and south, ideal for the long hikes Mahler loved. Only the sheer, grey cliffs of the Höllengebirge towering in the background brought a touch of menace to the scene. It was in these surroundings that Mahler spent four of the happiest and most productive summers of his life. Thanks mainly to

Natalie, who was usually present and made copious notes, they are also among the best documented.

Natalie may just have been the best wife Mahler never married. Two years his senior and a fine viola player, she first felt drawn to him when he was a student at the Vienna conservatory. More than a decade later, after breaking with her professor husband, she turned up in Budapest when Mahler was director there, taking up an invitation he had made in passing to a group of Vienna friends which had happened to include her. Gallantly, or at least circumspectly, Mahler gave up his little flat to her during her stay and retreated to a hotel. By the Steinbach era and thanks to her sheer persistence, Natalie had become almost part of the family but not the part she wanted to be. Mahler treated her like a sister, not a potential spouse. She went hiking and biking with him, swam right across the Attersee with him, carefully noted down what he said about music, especially his own, and only years later gave up hope that he would marry her. 'Mahler became engaged to Alma Schindler six weeks ago,' she wrote in her diary in early 1902. 'If I were to discuss this event, I would find myself in the position of a doctor obliged to treat, unto life or death, the person he loved most in the world. May the outcome of this rest with the Supreme and Eternal Master!'

Thanks not least to that dignified exit, Natalie is often remembered as a worthy but rather pathetic figure wholly lacking Alma's sparkle and daring. That picture is not strictly true. Even allowing for distortion in the accounts of other women (like Alma) who mistrusted her, the young Natalie was anything but self-effacing in her Vienna years. Like George Sand she often dressed in male garb and had a string of men, some married, at her feet. Unfortunately, those she desired most did not recip- rocate. One was Siegfried Lipiner, the other was Mahler. He well knew she was keeping careful track of his remarks as Eckermann did Goethe's and Boswell Dr Johnson's. That was flattering but it could become irksome.

'My God, Natalie,' he burst out during that first summer in Steinbach when she demanded to know how he composed. 'How can anybody ask such a thing? Do you know how to make a trumpet? You take a hole and wrap tin around it; that's more or less what you do when you compose.' He gave her a tip all the same. 'It happens in a hundred different ways. One minute it is the poem that is the inspiration, the next it is the melody,

I often begin in the middle, often at the beginning, sometimes even at the end, and the rest of it gradually falls into place until it develops into a complete whole.'

Although Mahler here is talking about how he wrote songs, he composed symphonies in much the same seemingly haphazard way. That will irritate those who think a serious composer should start with the first bar and plough steadily through to the final apotheosis, but it is a fact. Mahler wrote the first movement of the Third Symphony last and the last movement of the Fourth Symphony first. He dropped the original Andante movement from the First Symphony and was undecided about the order of the two central movements in the Sixth. Sometimes works suddenly poured out of him like the First, the Eighth and much of the Third; sometimes they trickled out painfully like, above all, the Second. It was only when he was tucked away in his room at the Gasthof zum Höllengebirge in 1893 that Mahler began to find a sequel to the *Todtenfeier* movement he had completed in Prague five years before. Oddly enough it was a poem about a sermon preached to fish which helped get him started again.

Mahler had not wholly stopped composing after 1888. Fascinated as ever by the *Wunderhorn* collection of folk poetry, he had again extracted verses from it and written a few more generally lightish songs with piano accompaniment. It was only in 1892 that the pieces began to become more ambitious. On and off from then until 1901, he produced a stream of *Wunderhorn* settings for voice and orchestra, surpassing all that had gone before in subtlety and variety. They are to the symphonies what, say, Tolstoy's short stories are to his novels – lesser works only in length. Mahler held that the naïve and often downright crazy *Wunderhorn* texts concealed 'hidden treasure within' and used every orchestral resource he could muster to bring it to the surface. In '*Wo die schönen Trompeten blasen*' ('Where the splendid trumpets sound'), muted brass set against a gentle ländler tell how the ghost of a dead soldier pays a nocturnal visit to his sweetheart. In '*Revelge*' ('Reveille'), the marching skeletons of men killed in battle are heard in the clickety-click of strings struck with the wood of the bow. Sinister, incessantly repeated jabs from the orchestra form the backdrop to '*Das irdische Leben*' ('Earthly life'), a tale about how bread is brought too late to save a starving child. The accompaniment has all the implacable monotony of the flour mill implied in the song, but Mahler is surely aiming for more. Here the treadmill of life itself revolves, remorselessly crushing what is most worth having. The particular tragedy described in the text becomes a universal one through the music.

Mahler manages a still more striking transformation in '*Des Antonius von Padua Fischpredigt*' ('St Anthony of Padua's sermon to the fishes'), written soon after arrival in Steinbach. On the face of it this is a droll tale and Mahler makes the most of it. With tipsy-sounding clarinet and slithering strings, he vividly portrays the shoals of eel, carp and pike who praise the saint's wise words but swim off again as unenlightened as before. While composing it, he told Natalie, 'I really kept imagining that I saw them sticking their stiff, immovable necks out of the water and gazing up at St Anthony with their stupid faces – I had to laugh out loud!'

This does not look like a promising basis for the Scherzo of a work begun with the black majesty of *Todtenfeier*, but that is how Mahler used it. In the much longer symphonic transformation of the fishy tale, he added odd instruments like the ruthe (a bunch of twigs rattled against the bass drum) and sharpened the irony with a whining trumpet, fierce *pizzicati* and sudden tempo changes. What had previously been a smirk-inducing song became an indictment of all that is meaningless in life, rising near the end to a *fortissimo* outburst of utter disgust. In the symphony's completed form, this anguished third movement leads without a pause into the simple faith of the fourth, another *Wunderhorn* song called '*Urlicht*' ('Primeval light'). It is hard to imagine a more fitting transition but it did not occur to Mahler right away. By the end of the summer he had a lot of music – *Todtenfeier*, a Scherzo, '*Urlicht*' and an Andante based on themes he had sketched as long ago as Leipzig. But apart from *Todtenfeier* at the start it was not clear what piece would fit where, or indeed whether '*Urlicht*' would be used in the symphony at all. Above all, he lacked a suitable finale which would adequately balance the weighty first movement.

It may be thanks to von Bülow or, more precisely, to von Bülow's death, that he got one. Encouraged by their mutual admiration as conductors, Mahler decided in 1891 to give his older colleague a hearing of *Todtenfeier* on the piano. He had not been playing long before von Bülow clapped his hands to his ears. 'Well, if that's music,' he retorted when the ordeal was over, 'then I know nothing about music.' Mahler claimed that 'we parted in a friendly manner' but he must have been deeply disappointed.

Did that bitter encounter create, or at least strengthen, a mental block which stopped Mahler from completing the work until the man behind the trouble was no more? That intriguing theory has often been advanced, notably by one of Freud's early pupils, the psychoanalyst Theodor Reik, in his book *The Haunting Melody*. And indeed, we have Mahler's word for it that the key to the finale only came to him as he sat at the funeral service for von Bülow in Hamburg's St Michael's church (Michaeliskirche) in March 1894. Mahler reported that as the choir in the organ loft intoned a setting of the '*Aufersteh'n*' ('Resurrection') verses by the German poet Friedrich Gottlieb Klopstock (1724–1803), he had the lightning flash 'that all creative artists wait for', and that 'everything became plain and clear in my mind . . . What I then experienced now had to be expressed in sound.' That did not take long. Three months later he sent off exultant letters from Steinbach saying, 'Beg to report safe delivery of a strong, healthy last movement to my Second. Father and child doing as well as can be expected.'

This famous tale begs several questions. Just what came to Mahler because of that 'lightning flash'? It was not the scheme for a choral finale as such. Mahler admits he had long pondered that idea but had so far cried off because he felt he might be accused of imitating Beethoven's Ninth. Did he suddenly realise that the Klopstock text would be ideal for a choral finale if he were to compose one? If so it is odd that he used only two of Klopstock's verses in the finale and wrote the rest himself. Was it, then, simply that for the first time he thought of using the concept of resurrection in choral form to round off the work? Perhaps, but it is very hard to believe the idea had never occurred to him before in the six years since he wrote *Todtenfeier*.

The 'psychological block' theory is problematic too. If Mahler had really been stalled by von Bülow's rebuff, he would surely not have been able to work so productively on other movements of the symphony in 1893 when von Bülow was still alive. More likely, what most blocked Mahler in the years after *Todtenfeier* was lack of time. As soon as he had that wholly free summer in Steinbach he was able to get a lot of work done, including a few (apparently unusable) sketches for the finale. Thus 'run in' again as a composer, he would no doubt have gone on to finish the job the following summer even without that bolt from the blue in St Michael's.

None of that is meant to belittle the way the work was written, let alone the work itself. The marvel is that a symphony composed in so piecemeal a way over so many years should hang together so well. Mahler himself complained that the second movement, Andante moderato, seemed too slight after the tragic first one and asked that conductors make a pause of five minutes between the two, though few of them bother. He may have been too hard on himself. The graceful Andante sets the irony of the succeeding '*Antonius von Padua*' scherzo into sharper relief, just as the '*Urlicht*' setting – 'I am from God and will return to God' – heightens the initial terror of the finale which sweeps it aside. Heaven, Mahler seems to say, is not to be won that easily. When Klopstock's promise of resurrection steals in at last, it has been earned in a titanic instrumental battle ending in the calls of the last trump and the bird of death. Only then is the way clear for a climax in which Mahler's own words 'What thou hast fought for Shall lead thee to God' are hurled out in a joyous triple *fortissimo* backed by organ, orchestra and pealing bells.

'The whole thing sounds as though it came to us from another world,' Mahler wrote in January 1895 after first rehearsals. 'I think there is no one who can resist it.' He thought wrong. Two months later he gave the première of the first three movements in Berlin before a pathetically small, albeit well-disposed, audience and a pack of mainly hostile critics. One fairly typical review accused him of 'cynical impudence'. Undaunted, and backed by cash from generous Hamburg friends, he returned to Berlin that winter to give the first performance of the whole work. Prospects seemed little better than before and free tickets were doled out to musicians and students to help fill the hall. On the night, Mahler had so fierce a migraine that after the last bars he fled pale as death to his dressing-room and collapsed. Behind him, though, applause erupted which grew wilder by the minute. Many of those present were weeping. Walter, who witnessed the scene, claimed that night – 13th December 1895 – marked the true start of Mahler's career as a composer and resolved there and then 'to pledge my future energy to Mahler's creations'.

Walter was soon to get a taste of his mentor's next work. In a buoyant letter the following July from Steinbach, Mahler reported that he was getting on well with a Third Symphony which, like its predecessors, would surely infuriate the critics. 'Everyone knows by now that some triviality always has to occur in my work,' he added cheerfully, 'but this time it goes beyond all bounds.' If Walter had no other holiday plans, why didn't he come and stay?

Keen though he surely was to get to know the symphony, Walter had another good reason to snap up the invitation. He had fallen for Mahler's youngest sister, Emma. After living for years in Vienna, she and Justi had finally joined forces with Mahler at a large apartment in Hamburg where Walter was a frequent guest. In his memoirs, Walter says discreetly little about Emma beyond recalling a talk with her about Dostoyevsky, but it seems that for a time he contemplated marriage. Some accounts suggest, rather implausibly, that Mahler finally vetoed the liaison. Whatever the case, the Steinbach invitation gave Walter an unexpected chance to see Emma in less constrained circumstances before he left, after two seasons at Mahler's feet in Hamburg, to take up a new post in Breslau.

The atmosphere at Steinbach that summer must have been even more highly charged than usual. Apart from the link between Walter and Emma, Mahler was dashing off letters almost daily to Anna von Mildenburg, a temperamental singer from Vienna with whom he was becoming ever more deeply involved. Their relationship had not begun promisingly. When Anna, aged twenty-three, had arrived for her first piano rehearsal in Hamburg the previous autumn, Mahler had shouted at her until she had wept with fright, then forecast that she would stop crying once she had sunk into the 'general theatrical mire of mediocrity'. Anna may have been self-centred, devious and unbalanced as her many (mainly female) detractors complained, but she was never mediocre. Thanks mainly to Mahler's training, she became a dramatic soprano without peer – especially in Wagnerian roles. Within weeks she and Mahler had begun an affair which became the talk of Hamburg and must have deeply worried Justi and Emma. What would happen to them if their brother married? Mahler had similar thoughts. 'My sisters have become so poor,' he confided in a letter to Anna. 'You are right, we must leave it to time – the all-powerful master . . . You and I will surely find the right way.'

No doubt Natalie was even more bothered. Mahler had managed to exclude her from the Steinbach party in 1894 because she got on his nerves, but from the following year she was back in favour. By the summer of 1896 she was only too well aware of her distant, much younger rival and the real reason for Mahler's incessant letter-writing.

Her worries probably increased on one grimly nostalgic outing at the start of August. Her old heart-throb Siegfried Lipiner had married a second time and, by chance, was spending the summer with his new wife just across the mountains in Berchtesgaden. Mahler and Natalie biked a good bit of the way to see them and the four ended the day at a wayside café in teeming rain. To the amazement of onlookers, the two men stood outside in the downpour discussing philosophy and Lipiner's planned new dramatic trilogy *Christus*. Both were gesticulating wildly and Mahler stamped the ground like a wild boar, as he often did when excited. Natalie faithfully noted down the scene but kept her thoughts to herself. She must, though, have recalled how Lipiner had slipped through her fingers more than a decade before and wondered whether Mahler was now going to do the same.

When Mahler went on that excursion he had all but finished drafting the Third Symphony, his longest and perhaps (although there is strong competition) his weirdest. Natalie for one was well aware that something quite extraordinary even by the standards of the 'Resurrection' was being born. Mahler, she noted, was not so much 'up to his ears' in his work that year as 'possessed by a divine madness'. Amazingly, he was not even as disturbed as usual by noises around the *Komponierhäuschen* – the composing hut where he locked himself away each day with his muse and, sometimes, a couple of kittens from six thirty in the morning until at least midday.

This was a revolution indeed. Mahler was so hypersensitive to noise that even the occasional sounds at the lonely inn distracted him. He put up with them for the first summer but insisted that before his return in 1894 a quieter workplace had to be built at the far end of the meadow next to the lake. He loved the hut on sight, calling it fondly his *Schnützelputz-Häusel* after (inevitably) a *Wunderhorn* song about a little house where the mice sing and dance. The single room had sturdy stone walls, double windows on three sides and just enough space for a few pieces of furniture including a piano. Even that spot was not always quiet enough. The ladies were enlisted to shoo away children and pay off passing organ-grinders almost before they could play a note. The bells on nearby cows were muffled and birds kept at bay by a scarecrow dressed in a swimsuit of Justi's, a coat of Emma's and a hat of Natalie's. Mahler tolerated nothing which interfered with his composing, not even the nature he loved.

'Loved' in this context is an inadequate word. Mahler was possessed, intoxicated by nature. Anna von Mildenburg described him 'suddenly standing still in the middle of a walk and, with bated breath and a quiet smile, avidly watching a small animal at work, listening to a bird singing. . . . He always felt the miracle and the mystery, awestruck and with a touchingly childlike astonishment. He could not understand Man's indifference to these wondrous acts of nature.'

That is only part of the picture. Walter came closer to the truth when he wrote that Mahler looked on nature with 'love and fear, rapture and horror. He saw the *bellum omnium contra omnes* (the war of all against all) and sensed its self-destructive forces fighting within his own inner-being.' Alma too tells how Mahler's involvement with nature went far beyond delight in little creatures and pretty views; how even the quiet he yearned for sometimes became unbearable. 'One day in the summer he came running down from the hut in a perspiration and scarcely able to breathe . . . it was the heat, the stillness, the panic horror. It had gripped him and he had fled. He was often overcome by this feeling of the goat god's frightful and ebullient eye upon him in his solitude and he had to take refuge in his house among human beings and go on with his work there.'

Although the incident Alma describes came long after Steinbach, the same atmosphere of sheer fright pervades much of the Third Symphony. That goes above all for the first movement, more than half an hour of it, with its primeval thuds and snorts, its woodwind squealing like stuck pigs, its rabble-rousing march and hurricane sweeping through the strings. Mahler called it *Pan awakes; summer marches in* but admitted that *What the mountains tell me* would do just as well. When Walter arrived by boat that July at the Steinbach jetty and gazed up at the Höllengebirge cliffs, Mahler told him he needn't bother to look because '*das habe ich schon alles wegkomponiert.*' The phrase has sometimes been mistranslated (even in Walter's book on Mahler) as 'I have composed all this already.' It is a crucial error, suggesting Mahler had simply been doing some landscape portraits in sound. What he really said was 'I have already composed that all away,' implying that the mountains were raw material which he had used up in constructing his Third Symphony. Mahler as the Master Builder – or rather as God himself. And yet at times he felt he was just an instrument in higher hands – that 'one does not compose, one is composed.' The remark is uncannily close to one made by Stravinsky after writing *Le Sacre du Printemps (The Rite of Spring)*, another work of elemental power. 'I heard and I wrote what I heard,' he said. 'I am the vessel through which *Le Sacre* passed.'

After that brutal start, the two movements which follow belong for the most part to that side of carefree wonder in Mahler which Anna identified. The first of them, *What the flowers in the meadow tell me*, is like a naïve and playful *Wunderhorn* song without words. With mixed feelings Mahler saw it become an instant hit, performed by colleagues including Nikisch and Felix Weingartner shorn of the rest of the symphony. 'If I ever want to be heard I can't be too fussy,' he wrote wryly, 'and so this modest little piece will doubtless present me to the public as the "sensuous" perfumed "singer of nature". That this nature hides within itself everything that is frightful, great and also lovely (which is exactly what I wanted to express in the entire work in a sort of evolutionary development) of course, no one ever understands that.'

The 'frightful' aspect of nature returns only at the end of the third movement, a scherzo called *What the animals in the forest tell me*. Before that the piece switches in mood from pure fun (a perky little tune taken from a *Wunderhorn* song about a cuckoo and a nightingale) to runaway high spirits, calmed only by the nostalgic sound of a distant posthorn such as Mahler often heard in Iglau days. The *fortissimo* chord with screeching flutes, piccolos and clarinets which puts an end to all this pleasantry has been interpreted in many ways but perhaps 'the veil is torn away' fits best. Torn away to reveal what? Whatever it was in the woods that, as Alma related, sent Mahler fleeing panic-stricken to refuge among people.

It is here that the human voice enters for the first time, at the start of the Adagio fourth movement called *What mankind tells me*. Against a hushed, almost immobile string background rent by desolate oboe *glissandi*, a contralto softly intones Nietzsche's *'Mitternachtslied'* ('Midnight song') – 'O Man take heed, What does deep midnight say?' – from *Also Sprach Zarathustra*. It is music of cosmic loneliness. Even the surge of emotion on the final words, 'But all joy wants eternity, Wants deep, deep Eternity', sinks back into the emptiness from which the piece emerged. At least it seems to. 'Without interruption', according to Mahler's stern (but often ignored) instruction, a fifth movement comes bursting in called *Es sungen drei Engel* (*Three angels sang a sweet song*) and marked 'merry in tempo and cheeky in expression'. A setting for contralto and boys' choir of another *Wunderhorn* poem, it soon whisks away again to the sound of fading bells and leads straight into an extended (about twenty-five minutes) Adagio finale, *What love tells me.*

'When love speaks to me now it always talks about you,' Mahler wrote to Anna in July. 'But the love in my symphony is one different from what you suppose. . . . It is an attempt to show the summit, the highest level from which the world can be surveyed. I could equally well call the movement something like: *What God tells me!* And this in the sense that God can, after all, only be comprehended as "love". And so my work is a musical poem that goes through all the stages of evolution, step by step. It begins with inanimate Nature and progresses to God's love.'

Even some of Mahler's sturdiest backers have expressed doubts as to whether it all hangs together; they are especially dubious about the first movement. Walter with an almost audible sigh of regret wrote that 'In regard to this movement – and this one alone – I must admit that the effort to take it in musically is frequently thwarted by the intrusion of non-musical matter.' Deryck Cooke, a British critic of great insight, called the movement 'a total formal failure' and the whole work 'hardly referable to the true symphonic tradition'. At least he did so in a fine booklet issued by the BBC in 1960 to mark the centenary of Mahler's birth. In a later, expanded version published after Cooke's death the words of disapproval have vanished.

Mahler himself sometimes seemed to share the doubts. In that letter to Anna he calls the Third Symphony a 'musical poem', much as he once did his First Symphony and the first movement of the Second. He even told Natalie in 1895 when he was just getting down to work on the Third that 'my calling it a symphony is really inaccurate, for it doesn't keep to the traditional form in any way'. But a year later he had changed his mind. 'To my astonishment and joy I see now that in this (first) movement, as in the entire work, there is the same framework, the same underpinning – without my having wanted it or even planned it – as one finds in Mozart and, in a more expanded and refined form, in Beethoven; it's the same idea which actually began with old Haydn. There must be profound and eternal laws which Beethoven held to and which I see as a kind of confirmation in my work.'

Mahler's second thoughts came closer to the truth than his first ones.

The first movement does broadly follow a traditional sonata form, albeit on a bewildering scale, and all movements are linked thematically in ways which can fairly be called symphonic. Whether this is enough to put the piece in the 'true symphonic tradition' (a rather hard beast to define) is not worth arguing here. If that tradition does not encompass works with choir, or more than four movements, or 'real life' sounds like bird-song, then even Beethoven does not belong to it either.

The Third is, as Mahler put it, a 'tough nut' but once cracked it turns out to be one of the best balanced and most fully realised of the symphonies. The two huge outer movements are flanked by intermezzi which themselves frame the weightier episodes about 'animals' and 'mankind'. At the very core of the work is that panic-stricken outburst at the end of the third movement. The late Sir John Barbirolli, an English conductor who was an even better interpreter of Mahler than his recordings imply, once said that 'in Mahler's symphonies there are many highlights but only one real climax, which one must discover'. In the Third Symphony that climax surely comes with the 'tearing of the veil' – a last elemental shock before man comes on the scene.

The work can stand on its own terms even without Mahler's 'programme'. You do not have to know about the 'stages of evolution' plan or understand the poems to perceive how the coarse material at the start is refined bit by bit into the final rapt Adagio. Not 'pure music' perhaps but surely 'purified music'. What conclusion you draw, if any, from that progression is your own affair. For Mahler, though, it marked a step in personal faith which went even beyond the 'Resurrection'. He told Natalie that 'the greatest human questions, which I posed and attempted to answer in my Second: "Why do we exist?" and "Will we continue to exist in an after-life?" – these questions can no longer concern me here. For what can they signify in the totality of things, in which everything lives; will and must live? . . . No, one grows confident that everything is eternally and unalterably born for the good. Even human sorrow and distress has no place here any more.'

Mahler very rarely spoke with such optimism and he never wrote a more thoroughly exultant symphony. No doubt the Steinbach landscape played a role, perhaps latterly his love for Anna too. But there was more to it than that. While writing the Third, Mahler was clearly influenced by Nietzsche, not the iconoclast who affirmed that 'God is dead' but the analyst who defined the act of creation and the poet who had dreams of eternity. The symphony's dionysiac first movement (recalling *The Birth of Tragedy*) and the use of the '*Mitternachtslied*' are proof enough of how much Mahler was involved with Nietzsche's world. He was also prone to reading aloud to the Steinbach party from *Zarathustra*, in which the philosopher gives the fullest account of his 'eternal recurrence' theory of immortality. Fechner with his concept of evolution to an 'eternal awakening' was surely an influence too and Lipiner yet another.

To be influenced by ideas about eternal life is one thing, to find them apparently confirmed through one's own work quite another – but that is what happened to Mahler. He composed the Third Symphony hardly less haphazardly than the Second, dropping one movement called *What the child tells me* altogether and shuffling the order of others. For a while he had a mass of music, titles and philosophical concepts but no unified whole. When he hit on his final design, he suddenly found that everything slotted into place and made sense not only as a musical structure but also as a scheme of evolution from 'inanimate nature' to 'God's love'. It was as though the 'profound and eternal laws' he talked about to Natalie applied not just to symphonic composition but to all creation. And he had discovered them – or rather rediscovered them. No wonder he felt 'astonishment and joy'.

Even that splendidly productive summer was not without clouds. Since his first year in Steinbach Mahler had taken to visiting Brahms who spent his holidays 15 miles away in the fashionable spa of Bad Ischl. There was surely at least as much calculation as admiration behind the trips. Mahler knew Brahms was well disposed towards him since that Budapest *Don Giovanni* and could help give a boost to his career. 'I don't mind treating the grand old master with due consideration and forbearance,' he wrote candidly to Anna, 'showing him only the side of myself that I think he finds agreeable.'

The visit in 1896, however, turned out differently. Brahms tried to be especially cordial, even asked Mahler for the first time to send him some of his music. But he tired easily and was feeling the first signs of the liver cancer which was to kill him within a year. When Mahler left in the evening, he looked back down the corridor and saw the lonely figure –

probably the most famous living composer – stooping painfully to pluck a piece of sausage for his supper from the stove. The pathetic scene affected Mahler for days afterwards. 'May Heaven preserve me from ever failing to realise when my works are becoming weaker,' he suddenly burst out to Natalie. 'Far better to be carried off at the height of one's powers, with the promise of still greater and finer things to come.'

The holiday ended in August and the Steinbach era with it. A new innkeeper had taken over the Gasthof zum Höllengebirge and he made such a fuss about arrangements for the following summer that Mahler reluctantly decided not to return. The next year he would leave Hamburg for Vienna at last, winning the directorship he craved but which would make him busier than ever. His composing would be more or less blocked for years and when he falteringly got going again, it would be with a work nothing like the Third. Mahler can have guessed none of that as he left Steinbach but he knew how much he owed the spot. On the last day there he walked up into the hills, looked back at the hut where he had achieved so much in a few short summers and wept like a child.

Chapter Four

Vienna – Digging in

It is doubtful whether Emperor Franz Joseph saw 1897 as a year of revolution, restless though it was. True, his prime minister Count Casimir Badeni had to resign after German-speakers furious over a language concession to the Czechs went on the rampage. Local politics too were becoming more tense and the fast-expanding capital harder to run. Thanks not least to massive immigration by job-seekers, the population of greater Vienna had all but tripled in three decades and was now pushing towards the 2 million mark. A lot of newly rich lived alongside a growing army of desperately poor.

But what were such problems to Franz Joseph who had already ruled around and through a string of prime ministers for nearly fifty strife-torn years? He had put aside personal tragedy (the estrangement of his beautiful wife Elisabeth – 'Sisi', the execution abroad of his brother and the suicide of his son), survived defeats on the battlefield, juggled away one crisis after another between the peoples of his unruly empire and seen the economy bounce back after the great stock market crash of 1873. Undeterred by warnings from 'experts' and groans from many Viennese, he had ordered the destruction of the old fortifications and the building of the Ringstrasse to give the capital a new face. Times changed but the Habsburg dynasty went on and on. Nothing, it seemed, could alter that –

not even the bloody revolt of 1848 which had forced Emperor Ferdinand I to flee Vienna and later to abdicate in Franz Joseph's favour.

In 1897 there was little blood on the streets but revolution was in the air all the same. Conservatives sniggered when youngish artists broke away from the hidebound Künstlerhaus organisation to found an association of their own. But the new Vereinigung bildender Künstler Österreichs (Association of Austrian Fine Artists), better known as the Secession, changed the attitude of a whole generation not just to painting but to architecture and design too. The Secessionists were a motley band; from the explosive Gustav Klimt, the movement's first president whose erotic and sinister pictures scandalised official Vienna, to the aristocratically elegant architect Josef Olbrich; from the back-slapping Carl Moll to the taciturn Alfred Roller (later, respectively Mahler's father-in-law and his stage designer). What united them all was contempt for a generation of artists which had aped the works of past ages and found no style of its own. '*Der Zeit ihre Kunst: Der Kunst ihre Freiheit*' (To each age its art: to art its freedom) ran the Secessionist battle cry, inscribed in gold above the door of the movement's newly built headquarters. For the Secessionist architects the proud new Ring was the city's most obvious abomination, a highway curling from nowhere to nowhere, its buildings a stylistic mess ranging from imitation classical to imitation Gothic. How much better, the young Turks claimed to shudders from traditionalists, were the clean lines and practicality of American skyscrapers.

The Secession had its literary counterpart in Young Vienna, a loosely organised group of writers which collected around Hermann Bahr, an eloquent author and journalist who sprayed out essays and dramas, novels and poems of varied quality in bewildering profusion. Bahr, who later married Mahler's Hamburg girlfriend Anna von Mildenburg, had returned to Vienna after years in Berlin and Paris to find its literary life as backward as its artistic one. When the Secession brought out its magazine *Ver Sacrum (Sacred Spring)*, Bahr was one of the first contributors. Although sheer force of character put him at the centre of Young Vienna, there were other members of the group more gifted – men like Hugo von Hofmannsthal, a master of elegant verse soon to become opera librettist to Richard Strauss, and Arthur Schnitzler, who probed with bitter irony the seamy underside of Viennese life. Schnitzler's insights into psychological and erotic problems were even envied by

Freud, who admitted that he won similar understanding only after painfully long analysis.

Not every talented young writer thought a lot of Young Vienna. The satirist Karl Kraus, born in Bohemia in 1874, was one who did not – but then he scorned most aspects of his age, the modish young around Klimt and Bahr as well as the reactionaries, the abrasive new demagogues in politics and the slovenly system which helped give them their chance. Kraus gave and sought no favours. The state was a travesty, society a charade, Vienna a moral sewer. Arguably he hit out in too many directions, but he used words with a deadly precision few if any of his contemporaries matched. The hundreds of issues of *Die Fackel (The Torch)*, the journal he founded and wrote himself, are proof enough of that.

Kraus and Young Vienna nonetheless had some things in common. For instance they shared the same café, not a matter to be treated lightly in a city where cafés served (and to some extent still serve) as newspaper reading room, club and second home. When Bahr and his crowd got together in the domed and smoke-filled rooms of the venerable Café Griensteidl, they often did so under the piercing gaze of Karl Kraus, naturally seated at a separate table. What Kraus observed there eventually emerged in a bitingly hilarious essay called *Die demolierte Literatur (Demolished Literature)*, which drew a parallel between the café's imminent demise at the hands of city planners – one of the lesser revolutions of 1897 – and the havoc its writer-customers wrought with words.

There was another link. Kraus was Jewish. One way or another many leading members of the Bahr circle (though not Bahr himself) had a Jewish background, including Schnitzler, Hofmannsthal, Richard Beer-Hofmann and Felix Salten. That was only one sign of the Jewish impact on *fin-de-siècle* Vienna, especially its cultural life. The liberal press – newspapers like the *Neue freie Presse*, the *Neues Wiener Tagblatt* and the *Wiener allgemeine Zeitung* – was largely in Jewish hands. Jews were influential in music too, established composers like Karl Goldmark, up-and-coming ones like Alexander Zemlinsky and Arnold Schönberg, violinists like Arnold Rosé and musicologists like Guido Adler. That most Viennese of songs, the *Fiakerlied*, was composed by Gustav Pick, a Jew, and those waltz kings, the Strausses, had a Jewish ancestor. Jewish artists were not prominent in the Secession but Jewish sponsors were. They helped the movement with cash and contact-making, not least through artistic and literary salons like that of Berta Zuckerkandl, daughter of the liberal Jewish editor Moritz Szeps.

This influence was not simply a result of the sharp rise in the overall number of Jews in Vienna, from a few thousand when Franz Joseph came to power in 1848 to nearly 150,000 by the century's end. Even in 1900 Jews made up less than ten per cent of the population of greater Vienna, but they accounted for about one quarter of the students at Vienna university and in some faculties like medicine their share was much greater. Behind this disproportionate impact lay in part the desire of relative newcomers to get on quickly but also a deep yearning to belong to a society which, for all its faults, offered a cultural and intellectual home. Put simply, in their fervid drive for assimilation many Jews became special in a different way. They turned into an influential élite, envied and even hated at least as much as they were admired.

It was against this background that anti-Semitism, never wholly absent, became much fiercer in Vienna in the closing decades of the century. Some of the anti-Semites were Jews themselves. Those who had already gone far to adapt to Viennese life, even converted to Christianity, tended to feel their status threatened by the steady stream of poverty-stricken new arrivals from the far east of the empire. These were the 'Ostjuden' whose dress and habits marked them out right away; who, as the writer Joseph Roth put it, 'have no home, only many graves in every cemetery'. Much more widespread, though, was the growing resentment among ordinary Viennese who felt Jews were gaining far too much clout and blamed them, in particular, for all the nastiness associated with the stock market crash.

Two political movements fed on this bitterness and encouraged it. One was the vicious but still marginal proto-Nazism of Georg von Schönerer, leader of the empire's pan-Germans. The other was the subtler but pervasive anti-Semitism of Karl Lueger and his Christian Socialist party. Lueger would have been a gift to television politics, gravely handsome (he was nicknamed '*der schöne Karl*') and a demagogue with a sure instinct for the ringing but ambivalent phrase. '*Wer Jude ist bestimme ich*' (I decide who is a Jew), he used to say – and indeed, he numbered prominent Jews among his friends. But he used anti-Semitism to draw to his banner the jealous and the disappointed, the artisans and small tradespeople driven from their livelihoods by industrial revolution and looking for a scapegoat. Although Lueger was four times elected mayor of Vienna, Franz Joseph – a strong Catholic but no anti-Semite – refused to confirm him in office. On the fifth occasion, 16th April 1897, the emperor gave way. Lueger took power and decades of liberal administration in Vienna came to an end.

Lueger's election did not bring an instant pogrom but, in its way, it spelt revolution just as the founding of the Secession had done hardly two weeks before. As though underlining the passing of the old order, Brahms had died on the very same day, 3rd April, that the Secessionists issued their declaration of independence. Five days after that an unprepossessing notice of two lines appeared in the *Wiener Abendpost* which heralded revolution too, though it was not widely realised at the time. According to the newspaper, Herr Heinrich [*sic*] Mahler, former director of the Budapest Opera, had been engaged as a conductor at the Vienna Court Opera. The next day the mystified *Neue freie Presse* speculated on the news. 'The laconic brevity of the announcement in the *Abendpost* makes one wonder what position Herr Gustav Mahler will occupy alongside the three conductors who have been with the Court Opera for years – Hans Richter (since 1875), Johann Fuchs (since 1879) and Joseph Hellmesberger (since 1886). Or might Herr Mahler be destined for some other function at the Court Opera? . . .'

The *Neue freie Presse* had put its finger on the key question. The opera had quite enough conductors although both Hellmesberger jun. (the son of Mahler's old foe in conservatory days) and Fuchs were mediocre. On the other hand it clearly did need a new director/chief conductor to replace the veteran Wilhelm Jahn, who had had the job for sixteen years and was starting to go blind. Who would take over? The Viennese were (and are) used to battling for months in advance about top cultural appointments, especially to the opera. The merits and flaws of even unlikely candidates were thrashed out in the press and the coffee houses with an intensity rarely devoted to mere politics. Richter, the most eminent musician in Vienna, clearly stood a good chance although he was no administrator and was often away. Some tipped Felix Mottl, a protégé of Wagner's widow Cosima, others Ernst von Schuch, director in Dresden. Mahler was hardly mentioned. Whatever his achievements in Budapest, he was now 'merely' principal conductor of a municipal theatre and at thirty-six surely too young for the prestigious Vienna post. Besides, he was a Jew. That seemed to settle it. Franz Joseph might be against Lueger and his kind but surely he would not go so far as to put a Jew in charge of the Imperial and Royal Opera. That view was probably right but by April it was outdated. Mahler had converted to Catholicism two months earlier.

Often before, Mahler had displayed the tactical skill of the born careerist but the way he planned and executed his coup in Vienna put all his previous campaigns in the shade. No doubt he had been nursing the ambition to return in glory to the empire's capital ever since he had left it nearly two decades before. While still in that lowly job in Kassel in 1885 he had confessed that 'my ultimate goal is and must remain Vienna'. In Hamburg he constantly joked to friends when the door bell rang that it might herald a summons from 'the God of the southern zones'. It was surely not Italy that he had in mind. He was not just waiting for a summons, he was angling for it. In a passing remark in a letter to Löhr in the summer of 1895, Mahler revealed that he had had a talk in Vienna with Count Josef von Bezecny, the general manager (*Generalintendant*) of the court theatres, including the opera. The chat brought no immediate result, but sometime between then and the autumn of 1896 Mahler realised that the door to Vienna was opening at last. Perhaps it was word of Jahn's failing health; perhaps it was the rumour that a personnel shake-up throughout the court theatres was being planned by Prince Rudolf von und zu Liechtenstein, the lord chamberlain (*Erster Obersthofmeister*) and responsible directly to the emperor for the arts. Whatever the reason, Mahler began to launch an attack on several fronts in Vienna and simultaneously sought reinforcements from further afield.

One of the first to be called into action was Siegfried Lipiner, who apart from having literary renown and a persuasive tongue also knew the ins and outs of the Viennese bureaucracy through his official job as librarian of the Austrian parliament. Sometime in November, he called into von Bezecny's office to argue that Mahler's widespread reputation for arrogance and spleen was quite undeserved. Evidently uncertain that he had dispelled all doubts, Lipiner followed up his visit with a letter arguing that while Mahler had a passionate nature he combined it with 'the greatest self-control and an almost unbelievable patience'. Even Mahler might have felt this was going a bit far.

Natalie Bauer-Lechner was pressed into service too. Not that much pressure was needed since she was naturally keen to get Mahler to Vienna and thus, as she wrongly thought, well away from Anna von Mildenburg. Natalie put Mahler's case before Rosa Papier, a retired opera-star-turned-teacher with immense influence in the Viennese music world. In particular she was a close friend of Eduard Wlassack, the real string-puller behind von Bezecny in the court theatres' office. As luck would have it Rosa Papier had two personal reasons to be well disposed to Mahler. She had sung under him in that fraught but brilliant performance of *St Paul* in Kassel eleven years before, and she knew that Anna von Mildenburg, her finest former pupil, was developing into a great artist under Mahler's guidance. Not that she had any illusions about Anna's faults, including that fierce possessiveness and disposition to 'kiss and tell' which finally cooled even Mahler's ardour.

Mahler later said that it was thanks to 'feminine protection', meaning Rosa Papier's, that he finally got the Vienna job. That is overstating it. The Papier-Wlassack axis played a key role but not the only one. Mahler's summer trips to Brahms had helped assure him support from that vital quarter. The Brahms connection also carried weight with Hanslick, the king of Viennese critics who in any case loathed Mahler's rival Mottl. Influential old friends from Budapest days including Ödön von Mihalovich, director of the music academy, and Count Albert Apponyi, a leading politician, were drummed up to bombard von Bezecny with testimonials. Mahler knew how to use the press too. In Hamburg he stoked up newspaper reports that he was being appointed to Dresden, thus helping put rivals off the scent. In Vienna he confided his plans to Ludwig Karpath, a scheming journalist (and nephew of Karl Goldmark to whom Mahler also appealed), in return for insider tips from court and opera. Karpath later claimed that his behind-the-scenes efforts had 'made' Mahler in Vienna but many others felt they could make the same boast.

Nonetheless, Mahler well knew that his status as a Jew could ruin everything. That clearly emerges from a beseeching letter he wrote to Mihalovich on 21st December, the very same day on which he sent his formal job application to von Bezecny. Asking Mihalovich for support

Mahler's parents: (*Above left*) Bernard
(1827–89) and (*above right*) Marie (1837–89).
'They were as ill-suited as fire and water,' he
said of them. 'He was all obstinacy, she was
gentleness itself.'

(*Left*) The first known photo of Mahler, aged
five or six. Years later he recalled how he had
dreaded the occasion, thinking he would be
whisked inside the camera and stuck on a
piece of cardboard.

(*Above*) Mahler with his eldest sister Justine ('Justi') and friends, visiting the Bavarian spa of Bad Reichenhall in 1892.

(*Right*) Mahler in 1899, two years after becoming director of the Vienna Court Opera. With Justi.

Alma Maria Schindler, aged 19, in 1899 –
the year of her first meeting with Mahler.

Alma with her daughters,
Maria known as 'Putzi'
(1902–07) and Anna as 'Gucki'
(1904–88).

The inn at Steinbach am Attersee, east of Salzburg, where
Mahler spent the summers of 1893 to 1896. To the right, by
the lakeside, is the hut where he completed his Second
Symphony and composed the Third. Behind loom the
'Höllengebirge' – the mountains Mahler told Bruno Walter he
had 'composed away' into his music.

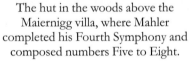

The villa Mahler had built at the village of Maiernigg on the Wörthersee and where he spent the summers of 1901 to 1907. His bedroom was at the top under the eaves, 'like a watchtower.'

The hut in the woods above the Maiernigg villa, where Mahler completed his Fourth Symphony and composed numbers Five to Eight.

Mahler with his daughter Maria at the Maiernigg villa in 1905. She was to die there of scarlet fever and diphtheria two years later.

The farmhouse at Alt-Schluderbach in the Dolomites, Mahler's summer retreat from 1908 to 1910. The town of Toblach (Dobbiaco) is on the right in the distance. Despite his heart trouble, Mahler took to walking there and back every day even in the worst of weather.

The hut Mahler had built a few minutes' walk from the Alt-Schluderbach farmhouse. Here he composed *Das Lied von der Erde* and the Ninth Symphony and began the Tenth.

Mahler (said to be a speaking likeness) with his daughter Anna by the Alt-Schluderbach farmhouse in 1909.

Alma and Gustav strolling in the hills near Alt-Schluderbach in 1909.

'on which the whole pattern of my future life depends', Mahler said his name was receiving serious consideration in Vienna but that his Jewishness told against him. 'As regards this latter point,' he added, 'I should not fail to inform you (in case you are not already aware of the fact) that I completed my conversion to the Catholic faith soon after my departure from [Buda] Pest.'

That was a lie and one which, moreover, Mahler repeated in a letter to Wlassack two days later. He had left Budapest nearly six years before and he had not yet been baptised. But Mahler was growing desperate. His relationship with Pollini was worse than ever and all his hopes were fixed on Vienna. To realise them anything seemed justifiable. A few weeks later he burned his boats in Hamburg and handed in his resignation with effect from the season's end, although he knew he might then be jobless. In a pathetic (and somewhat inaccurate) letter to his Berlin friend Marschalk in mid-January he wrote, 'They need a director in Vienna and have come to the conclusion that I am the right man for the job. But the great stumbling-block – my being a Jew – lies on the road and may well barricade it. I am really half-thinking of settling in Berlin for a while. Do you think I can get pupils for lessons there, or something of the kind?'

Just over a month later, on 23rd February 1897, Mahler removed the block. He was baptised a Catholic, not as is sometimes claimed in that same 'Michel' church where he had the 'lightning flash' of inspiration for the finale of his 'Resurrection' Symphony, but in the nearby Little St Michael's church (Kleine Michaeliskirche). Baptism did not free Mahler from anti-Semitic hostility, any more than it did other Jews who renounced their religion. Once a Jew, the attackers argued, always a Jew. Cosima Wagner for example, despite outward friendliness to Mahler, went on working hard to keep him out of Vienna, though once she had failed she sent him fawning letters pushing the indifferent operas of her son Siegfried. But the conversion did crucially allow Mahler's backers to recommend him not just as the best man for the job but also as a Christian, a word firmly underlined in his personnel file in Vienna.

Despite these circumstances, Mahler's conversion is still judged by some to have been motivated solely or at least mainly by religious conviction. Others suggest Mahler went through with it because he planned to marry Anna, which is just as unlikely. Mahler's Hamburg critic friend Ferdinand Pfohl, on the other hand, admitted that the news made a fatal impression on him. How come, he asked Mahler, that a non-Catholic could be summond to the Vienna post by a strictly Catholic emperor? With a 'peculiar devilish smile on his Lucifer-face', Mahler replied that 'the cloak has been changed'. Pfohl concluded that 'Mahler converted for material gain, forced by neither inner conflict nor inner need. A value we inherit from parents and forefathers is sacred in its own right, the value of a venerable tradition. No, Gustav Mahler was no saint.'

Mahler was more explicit about his conversion in a talk with Karpath. According to the latter's memoirs, Mahler said, 'What particularly offends and angers me is the circumstance that I had to have myself baptised to get an engagement, that's what I cannot get over . . . I do not deny that it cost me a great deal of effort to take an action for what one may justifiably call self-preservation and which one was inwardly not at all disinclined to take.'

Mahler's drive for the empire's musical throne was hardly an act of 'self-preservation' but the rest of his statement rings true. He had not been a zealous Jew before his conversion and he did not become a devout Catholic after it. According to Alma he loved churches, Gregorian chant and the smell of incense. He also believed in some kind of after-life, but none of that proves that he inwardly accepted Christian dogma. Although he used some of Klopstock's 'Resurrection' verses in his Second Symphony, he dropped the reference in the original to Jesus Christ. In his Eighth Symphony he took over the text of the old Latin hymn '*Veni, Creator Spiritus*' but gave the words a massively extrovert musical setting far removed from their liturgical origin. In each case a message specifically Christian was turned into one as universal as Friedrich Schiller's in his *Ode to Joy*, which Beethoven used in his Ninth Symphony.

Mahler's attitude to Judaism was at least as ambiguous. At almost no stage did he show any special interest in Jewish matters, let alone back Jewish causes. Although he and Theodor Herzl, the founder of political Zionism, were contemporaries in Vienna they never seem to have met. Mahler took on Bruno Walter after a few years in Vienna because he knew of his exceptional talent, but in general he did not treat Jewish musicians with special favour. Rather the contrary. In the pre-Walter era he turned down the idea that he should engage Leo Blech, a converted Jew, as a conductor because 'for the anti-Semites, I still count as a Jew despite my baptism, and more than one Jew is more than the Vienna Court Opera can bear.' As for his attitude to the 'Ostjuden', Mahler was as harsh as any of his assimilated brethren in the capital. During a visit in 1903 to Lemberg (Lvov, now in the Ukraine) he wrote to Alma, 'Life here has an unusual look. Oddest of all are the Jews who run around here the way dogs do elsewhere. It is extremely entertaining to watch them! My God, am I supposed to be related to them?'

Mahler did identify with the Jews in some ways all the same. He told Natalie, 'A magnificent symbol of the creator is Jacob, wrestling with God until He blesses him. If the Jews had been responsible for nothing but this image, they would still inevitably have grown to be a formidable people. God similarly withholds His blessing from me. I can only extort it from him in my terrible struggles to bring my works into being.' Telling though that comparison with Jacob may be, it does not imply that Mahler wrote 'Jewish music' or thought that he did. There are traces of Jewish folk-song and dance rhythm here and there, notably in the First Symphony and some of the songs. It would be odd if there were none at all. But there are so many other elements too – Bohemian tunes and mock Viennese waltzes, marchs and ländler, hints of Schubert and Berlioz. To argue, as some do, that the music's transnational character itself makes it Jewish, a product of the diaspora as it were, is over-stretching a point.

Like his music, Mahler's religious affiliation defies pigeon-holing. What Mahler sought throughout his life was something no single faith could give him. Hence his passion for philosophy, physics and oriental mysticism – hence the string of battles, won and lost, that are his symphonies. He was 'not disinclined' to conversion (hardly a ringing declaration!) because he believed that neither side had a monopoly of the truth and his Jewish status had become ever more of a career obstacle. He hated to feel driven to the change all the same. It was an act of opportunism and Mahler knew it.

The man in Vienna who seems to have been least aware of Mahler's ambitions was the one most affected by them, Wilhelm Jahn. Born in Moravia in 1835, Jahn tends to be remembered most for his love of cards and fine wine and for the inglorious end to his career. That hardly does justice to his Vienna record. In his early years as director he acquired and trained outstanding singers and conducted with what the critic Richard

Specht called 'sublime elegance, grace and charm'. The compliment is the more striking since Specht was a great Mahler fan. With Jahn mainly in charge of the French and Italian repertoire, which he adored, and Richter mainly of the German one, Vienna opera-goers were guaranteed evening after evening of magnificent sound. What they rarely if ever got was that vital unity between music and drama for which Mahler always strove. Bit by bit the performances came to seem too cosily out of step with the increasingly restless times. Jahn's health became poor and he failed to weed out singers past their prime. At one stage he got as far as submitting his resignation, apparently as a ruse (one of the few with which he has been credited) to win endorsement of his position. Ruse or not, he stayed on.

Mahler did all he could not to arouse Jahn's suspicions. In his formal application to von Bezecny, he only mentioned wanting a job as 'a conductor' although the handful of Vienna insiders well knew he was after the directorship. He then arranged to be in Dresden on a day when he knew Jahn would be there too so that he could sound him out, 'by chance' as it were. The plan worked. Jahn innocently revealed that he did not dream of stepping down despite his eye problems but that he would probably be needing an extra conductor. If so, he promised, he would think of Mahler. What Jahn thought soon became even more irrelevant. A few weeks after that meeting Mahler was baptised and the Vienna pendulum swung decisively his way. On 4th April he visited von Bezecny and signed a preliminary accord to begin a one-year conducting term at the opera from 1st June. A full contract was quickly drawn up and handed to Jahn for signature eleven days later. In fact Mahler, in consultation with von Bezecny, arrived in Vienna from Hamburg in late April to take up his post a month earlier than planned. An astonished Jahn received the news while in Karlsbad for eye treatment.

In retrospect the rest of the story looks inevitable. Mahler made his triumphant Vienna début on 11th May with *Lohengrin*, prompting Karl Kraus to the comment (applicable to himself as well) that 'you can see in his eyes that he will soon have done with the bad old ways'. Two months later he was appointed deputy director and finally replaced Jahn in October. Initially, however, Mahler was plagued with fears that the top job might still slip through his fingers – all the more so since von Bezecny had unexpectedly announced his resignation, though he finally stayed on into the New Year. Afflicted by a bad throat infection, Mahler took a rare period of sick leave in June and then a long walking holiday during which he kept up the pressure by mail on Wlassack and other string-pullers. When his appointment as deputy was announced in the press, Mahler missed it because he was in the mountains far from newspapers. Ironically, the first he learned of it was from a letter in spidery writing from Jahn.

From then on Mahler felt sure the directorship would really be his but, amazingly, Jahn was still in the dark. When Mahler visited him in late July at his country villa for 'instructions', he was treated with such kindness that he felt pricks of conscience. 'The poor man doesn't seem to have the slightest suspicion that I shall soon be appointed in his place,' he told Karpath. 'I must admit that, from a purely human point of view, I feel terribly sorry for him. But what is the use, for if I do not replace him someone else will.' Mahler the pragmatist! It was finally Wlassack who told Jahn that he had to retire in Mahler's favour. The old man was stunned, then furious, but after a night's sleep he gave in. Decorated by Franz Joseph, he faded out of the picture and died three years later.

Within a year of taking over at the opera Mahler also became conductor of the Vienna Philharmonic Orchestra, thus holding the empire's two top musical posts simultaneously. According to Natalie, Mahler was amazed when a delegation from the Philharmonic proposed in September 1898 that he take the job. He almost regretted saying yes, she added, because he feared his opera work would suffer. That passage alone shows that Natalie's memoirs, invaluable though they are, cannot always be taken on trust. Mahler had told Pfohl years before in Hamburg how desperately he wanted to conduct symphony concerts. His subsequent series there had been a disappointment but in Vienna a far better orchestra was on hand. Indeed, it was virtually Mahler's own since the Vienna Philharmonic was (and is) drawn solely from players in the opera orchestra. There was a crucial difference all the same. In the opera pit the players were employees under the director's (and ultimately the emperor's) thumb; in the concert hall they were jealously independent, running their own affairs and in particular choosing their own conductors. Mahler badly underestimated this difference but it is not surprising that he wanted to combine the two posts. All the more so since as conductor of the Philharmonic he could expect more chances to give his own works a hearing. Just how he got the job, however, only emerged in the 1980s when details from the Philharmonic's archives were made public.

At the opera, Mahler had had to oust Jahn; at the Philharmonic he was up against Richter, on the face of it a tougher challenge. Born in Hungary in 1843, Richter had won renown in both the operatic and symphonic repertoire. As a young man he had become a slavishly devoted friend of Wagner and later a regular conductor at Bayreuth, where 'the master' entrusted him with the first performance of the *Ring* cycle. In Vienna, he had directed the Philharmonic concerts for more than two decades, giving the premières of two Brahms symphonies and (more boldly) Bruckner's Fourth. He lacked Nikisch's power to mesmerise and von Bülow's love of discipline ('Drillmasters belong on the parade ground,' Richter was wont to say); but his performances at their best had a grandeur acknowledged by experts as diverse as Bernard Shaw and Claude Debussy. For the members of the Philharmonic Richter was one of their own, a former orchestral player who had mastered most instruments from violin to double bassoon and who did not believe in having a large number of rehearsals. For the Viennese public, the big, bearded figure with his deliberate gait and firm beat had become an institution. Still, by the century's end many institutions were getting shaky and in the concert hall too a lot of people were ready for change. Behind Richter's back, Mahler and the Philharmonic saw that they got it.

In 1898 the orchestra's business year began predictably enough. At an annual meeting held on 10th May, Richter was unanimously re-elected conductor and thus automatically stayed chairman of the orchestra's organising committee too. That means he should have led the committee's meeting on 28th August to plan the coming season. Instead the chairman was Mahler who promised (or warned) that he would be conducting several works hitherto not heard in Vienna. According to the minutes, committee members noted this statement, no doubt with mixed feelings. In other words, everyone was behaving as though Richter no longer existed. But exist he still did – turning up as chairman at the committee's next meeting on 22nd September. He had sad news. Because of trouble with his right arm, he would be unable to conduct next season

[88]

and proposed Mahler as one possible successor. The members expressed 'the greatest regret' and agreed to ask Mahler to take on the task. Two days later the full orchestra accepted the change with a show of hands.

It is not clear exactly what happened between the annual meeting in May and the committee session in August. Whether Mahler first approached senior members of the orchestra about taking over or they approached him, neither side comes out of the affair very well. If anyone does so it is Richter — 'honest Hans' as Mahler had deprecatingly called him in a letter to Löhr years before. Evidently he got wind of the plot and decided to retreat without making a scene. His 'arm trouble' did not stop him conducting elsewhere, notably in England where he was already popular. He took over Manchester's Hallé Orchestra in 1899 at a better salary than he ever got in Vienna and died seventeen years later — appropriately enough in Bayreuth.

The official record gives no sign that anyone in the Philharmonic raised objections to Mahler's appointment or tried to stop Richter's departure. That does not mean the whole orchestra welcomed the switch by any means. Everyone hoped, of course, that the new man's huge success at the opera would spill over to the Philharmonic and boost takings. But while some players respected Mahler's artistic integrity others, not just the inevitable anti-Semites, deeply resented his demanding work schedules and harsh tone which quickly earned him the nickname of the Duty Corporal (*Korporal vom Tag*).

Things had begun well enough. After his first orchestral rehearsal on arrival in Vienna Mahler had been all smiles, praising 'Austrian musicianship; the vitality, the warmth and the great natural gifts which each man brings to his work'. No doubt he really was happy with the improvement in quality compared with Hamburg and in any case was being diplomatic so long as he did not have the directorship. Still, he was soon complaining privately to Natalie that at close range he found a mass of faults — cellos unable to hold a single note evenly, a general refusal to play softly and sloppy rhythm. 'But I shall drive all that out of them in time,' he promised.

He certainly did his best — or worst. Before long he was scheduling far more rehearsals than Richter or Jahn had dreamed of, even for works the orchestra had played many times before. Schönberg later defended Mahler's perfectionism, claiming that a poor conductor runs out of ideas after three rehearsals and a great one still finds things to improve after nine. No doubt that is true. But many instrumentalists concluded with more exasperation than admiration that what Mahler sought could not be achieved even with infinite rehearsal. Woodwind players were urged to hold soft phrases to the point of strangulation. A kettledrummer was exhorted to produce ever more volume until he broke a drumstick. A cymbal player, repeatedly scolded for weakness, threw all his remaining strength into a single mighty clash. 'Bravo,' Mahler shouted. 'That's the way. And now louder still!'

At least on that occasion Mahler showed some approval. More often he would pick on errant players and give them a dressing-down in front of their colleagues, one of the surest ways to arouse antipathy in any orchestra. Another way is to have one or two spies (usually soon uncovered) among the players who can be pumped on the backstage talk. Mahler used that tactic too. It was almost as though he set out to turn the orchestra against him. Fury, after all, could be productive. When the players began to revolt during a fraught rehearsal of Beethoven's Fifth Symphony, Mahler retorted, 'Gentlemen, if you will save your rage for the performance, we shall at least play the beginning correctly.'

Worse for the players than the tension-ridden extra work was the increased job insecurity. Mahler is often remembered for throwing out ageing singers as Jahn had failed to do, but he was just as tough on the orchestra too. During his decade as director he replaced about eighty instrumentalists including more than thirty wind players – figures which, high as they are, only hint at the true extent of the upheaval. Mahler was much inclined to experiment, taking on new players but dropping them again long before they qualified for pension rights. He would tempt promising aspirants to the opera orchestra with the prospect of lucrative work in the Vienna Philharmonic concerts, although strictly speaking he had no right to do so. He brought in Dutchmen who had mastered the pungent Boehm flute instead of local players of the Vienna flute which he found too soft-toned. Not least, he banned the traditional (mal)practice under which players wanting time off could call in substitutes.

Mahler surely acted not from spite but from the highest artistic motives. He fought, finally with success, to get his players better pay and to boost their numbers from around a hundred to 120. But it is plain enough why many of them saw the Mahler decade as a reign of terror.

Franz Schmidt, a cellist and composer who joined the orchestra in 1896, recalled that 'Mahler burst over the Vienna Opera like an elemental catastrophe. An earthquake of unprecedented intensity and duration shook the entire building from the foundation pillars to the gables. Anything that wasn't very strong had to give way and perish . . . Mahler dismissed and pensioned off so many people in his rage that although I was the youngest in 1897, in 1900 I was already the longest-serving cellist.'

Mahler's spell as conductor of the Philharmonic concerts nearly ended after the first season. At the orchestra's annual meeting in May 1899, his foes proposed that the election of a chief conductor be delayed and Richter asked if he would like his old job back. After a stormy session the motion was carried by fifty-four to forty-one – the first firm evidence that the Mahler era had virtually split the players down the middle. Unfortunately for the rebels, they had failed to find out first whether Richter was prepared to return. He was not. In a letter he thanked the orchestra for its 'flattering request' but said he would be out of town for much of the season. Auguished committee sessions were held in August and September and delegations repeatedly sent to the offended Mahler, begging him to stay on. He agreed at last so long as there was no further 'agitation' against him.

The division in the orchestra was broadly reflected in the press. Some accounts of the Vienna years might lead one to conclude that Mahler faced almost nothing but public attack from knaves, fools and anti-Semites. It is true that he had to contend with plenty of vitriol, some of the worst of it in anonymous letters to the press which clearly came from among his own disgruntled musicians. Usually Mahler did his best to ignore it though once he managed to get hold of one of the original letters and employed a graphologist to track down the culprit. But there were plenty of knowledgeable and often enthusiastic critics about too including Max Kalbeck of the *Neues Wiener Tagblatt*, Richard Heuberger of the *Neue freie Presse* and the young Max Graf of the *Neues Wiener Journal* (though he turned against Mahler later). Even in the anti-Semitic *Deutsche Zeitung* Theodor Helm managed to slip in praise for Mahler now and again, calling him (no doubt to the fury of his editor who took reports from a more bigoted critic when possible) a musician of 'intellect and passion'.

As for the fearsome Hanslick who slated Wagner and excoriated

Bruckner, he gave Mahler a very fair run. 'All's well that starts well,' he wrote in the *Neue freie Presse* after Mahler's first concert with the Philharmonic in November 1898. Hanslick noted that the programme – Beethoven's *Coriolan* overture, his 'Eroica' Symphony and Mozart's Fortieth Symphony – was one which the orchestra could play in its sleep. But thanks to Mahler's 'painstaking rehearsals' the works emerged with 'living spirit and complete dedication' as a quite new experience. About Mahler's own music given in later concerts Hanslick was less complimentary. He rejected the First Symphony as 'crazy' and had doubts about giving simple *Wunderhorn* folk-songs so sophisticated an orchestral setting. Still, he added, 'Mahler has accomplished this hazardous enterprise with extraordinary subtlety and masterly technical skill.'

In other words, more often than not criticism of Mahler's performances was based neither on personal vendetta nor racial prejudice but on real differences of taste and sometimes of principle. The huge dynamic contrasts and clarity of inner parts which Mahler fought for in rehearsal came as a revelation to some listeners reared on Richter but seemed exaggerated and mannered to others. Even the usually well-disposed Kalbeck wrote after a performance of Schubert's 'Great' C major Symphony that 'too many dynamics are just as objectionable as none at all'. Mahler, Kalbeck went on, 'thinks he will save himself from misunderstandings by emphasising every point on which he differs from general opinion, and in the end he breaks up the work of art into a number of salient points.' Viennese and German critics were not the only ones to express this view. After a Paris concert under Mahler, the critic Pierre Lalo (son of the composer Edouard Lalo) complained that while the French gave too little study to a score 'the Germans' gave far too much. 'They discover some intention in every note, emphasise every detail and end up by overcomplicating the structure and destroying the plan of a composition.'

In a thoughtful essay, Max Graf concluded that Mahler was at his remarkable best in music of extremes, whether of passion or serenity. 'It is at these frontiers that his talent explodes at its most brilliant, most powerful, most astonishing. The middle register of his genius . . . seems to me less striking, the way you often hear violins whose E and G strings have a magnificent tone, while the middle strings are duller and less vibrant. Here Hans Richter, with more roast beef and fewer nerves in his body, is the stronger man.'

None of that can now be verified since Mahler (unlike Nikisch) just missed the era of orchestral recording. What can be verified, because the evidence is still available, are his reworkings of other composers' scores. Sometimes the instrumentation was more or less extensively retouched, as in symphonies by Schumann and Beethoven; sometimes works were wholly transcribed, like the rearrangements of Schubert and Beethoven quartets for full string orchestra. Whatever it was, most critics in Vienna (like their Hamburg colleagues) did not approve.

Mahler's main argument, that he was simply adapting works written for smaller halls to performance in much bigger ones, was neither wild nor new. Nikisch and von Bülow were among those to use it too. But it stuck in the gullets even of critics who usually followed Mahler through fire. In his report after a performance of Mahler's retouched version of Beethoven's Ninth Symphony, a clearly anguished Heuberger compared 'this aberration, this barbarism' to the painting-over of an old master's picture. 'We are among the most genuine admirers of Director Mahler,' Heuberger wrote. 'All the more reason why in this case we must loudly and clearly call a halt.' Even Mahler's musicologist friend Guido Adler, now professor of music history at Vienna university, was uneasy. 'Since the original of Beethoven continues to be inviolably preserved, no lasting detriment can result from this,' he hedged. 'Whether interpretation can or should go so far is a question in itself.' It still is.

Audiences too were often infuriated but never bored. Unlike Mahler's Hamburg concerts his Vienna ones remained well attended, so much so that a plan was briefly afoot at the start of the 1899–1900 season to double their number. It came to nothing, probably because of overwork and scheduling problems. Besides, the orchestra had been invited to perform at the World Exhibition in Paris in June 1900, its first ever foreign tour. Some players feared the cost would be too high and the Paris hotel full of bed-bugs, but the majority felt the honour of Austrian musicianship was at stake and the tour went ahead. Despite some critical praise it proved a flop. Advance publicity was poor (posters spelled Mahler's name 'Malheur' or 'calamity'), attendance was sparse and the acoustic in the vast Trocadéro hall was abominable. Takings were so far below expectations that Mahler had to beg for funds from the financier Baron Albert Rothschild to pay for the orchestra's trip home.

The cheers Mahler got from the players when he told them at a Paris banquet that he had raised the cash marked the high point in his relations with the Philharmonic. A few months later he and the orchestra were again in dispute and in April 1901, after a bad illness, he gave up the conductorship. Many of the players sighed with relief but not for long. The elegant mediocrity they elected as successor, Joseph Hellmesberger jun., known as 'der fesche Pepi' (the dashing Pepi), failed to draw the public and his brief reign ended amid scandal. Soundly thrashed in public by the father of an under-age ballet girl with whom he was having an affair, Pepi lost his job and the orchestra went over to a guest conductor system which (with breaks) it has broadly kept ever since. That way it can avoid having to tolerate fools and geniuses for long.

Mahler had been conductor of the Philharmonic for barely three years (though he returned until 1907 as an occasional 'guest'), during which he performed nearly eighty works. About one third of them were by Beethoven (in part 'arr. Mahler') but there were also novelties by composers like Franck, Goetz, Kienzl and Perosi and pieces such as Berlioz's *Symphonie Fantastique* (1830) which to Viennese ears still sounded outlandishly modern. Along with all the rehearsals, that concert activity alone made for quite a heavy schedule but on top of it Mahler shouldered a huge burden of opera work. In the four years between his arrival in Vienna and his break with the Philharmonic, he conducted some 370 opera performances including nearly thirty premières. For comparison's sake, in his five and a half years (1956–62) as Vienna Opera director, Herbert von Karajan led just 168 performances – and he was no slouch.

If Mahler had only been the opera's principal conductor, as in Hamburg, he would still have had a hectic life. But in Vienna, as – on a smaller scale – in Budapest, he was in charge of a house with several hundred musicians, dozens of technical and office staff, 2500 seats and an annual budget of around 3 million crowns. Much as he loathed paperwork, Mahler spent longer hours than his predecessor behind his desk arguing with singers on contracts and leaves of absence, negotiating better conditions for stagehands or fighting for more cash for scenery and costumes. These administrative battles would have been no push-over even if the amenable von Bezecny had stayed on as general manager of the court theatres, but he was replaced in early 1898 by Baron August Plappart, a nit-picking busybody. At the same time the formerly helpful Wlassack turned hostile, outraged that Mahler, now in office, no longer called on him or wrote him obsequious letters. Crucial aid came instead from Prince Alfred Montenuovo, deputy to the lord chamberlain, who had an aristocratic disdain for bureaucrats and admired Mahler's often high-handed defence of his principles. Without Montenuovo's sturdy support, Mahler would hardly have kept his post for a decade.

Opera-goers were soon smarting under the new regime too. Mahler declared war on the claque (fans noisily backing their favourite singers), insisted that the house lights be dimmed for performances and that latecomers be barred entry. On stalking into the orchestra pit he would flash a furious glance around the auditorium to petrify anyone even thinking of whispering or rustling a programme. Usually he need not have bothered. Like schoolchildren in dread of a choleric headmaster, people quickly learned to be quiet the moment Mahler appeared. 'Is music such a serious business?' the emperor asked in wonder on hearing of these innovations. 'I always thought it was meant to make people happy.'

Many Viennese thought the same. Mahler was out to teach them that good music, 'light' or 'heavy', always had to be taken seriously. That meant every night's performance had to be approached as if it were a première. It meant as much care had to be lavished on an operetta like Johann Strauss's *Die Fledermaus* (which Mahler conducted in his first month as director in the presence of its delighted composer) as on a tragic drama like *Tristan und Isolde*. It meant Wagner's *Ring* had to be given without cuts, as it never had been in Vienna until Mahler's day. It also meant ploughing through the many new scores sent in by hopeful composers, picking out the rare plums, filleting the possibles and reject-ing the duds.

The score-sifting gave Mahler endless trouble. Most painful was his encounter after long estrangement with his former student friend Hugo Wolf, a great lieder composer who had written an uneven opera called *Der Corregidor (The Mayor)*. No sooner was Mahler in Vienna than Wolf showed him the manuscript and felt he extracted a promise of early performance. Whatever Mahler may have said first he prevaricated later, worried that the work for all its fine melody lacked dramatic conviction. A heated scene in Mahler's office ended when Wolf, who had long been mentally unstable, raced off into town proclaiming he had been made new opera director. Confined to an asylum, he died in 1903. A year later Mahler finally staged *Der Corregidor* in two versions, one which he reworked himself and the other Wolf's original. The critics panned both.

Less tragic but just as time-consuming were Mahler's struggles with two wholly unlike composers, Ruggero Leoncavallo and Siegfried Wagner. Mahler found himself landed with Leoncavallo's *La Bohème* (not Puccini's finer work of the same name) as one of the last commitments from the Jahn era. The composer proved to be a menace, seeking to dictate Mahler's cast, interfering at rehearsals and bringing pressure to bear via a lawyer and the Italian ambassador. Mahler regarded the work as 'rubbish' but he gave it his usual punctilious preparation. To his irritation it proved quite popular, at least with the public if not the critics.

So did Siegfried Wagner's first opera *Der Bärenhäuter (The Lazybones)* but only after Mahler made some drastic cuts in it. Cosima Wagner, who regarded her son's flawed piece as the finest comedy since her late husband's *Die Meistersinger*, told Mahler his action was 'inadmissible'. He stood his ground, explaining his reasons and noting that he had restored the cuts usually made (not least by Richter) in the *Ring*. Cosima was in any case mystified that Mahler should be staging the work, not Richter who at that time (1899) was still at the opera. 'I am witnessing in Vienna a strange conflict,' she wrote to a friend. 'Mahler and Richter, the Jew and the German. The conflict represents in miniature what is happening on a grand scale in our world: the casualness of the German means that the Jew – if one is to be just – appears the more worthy.'

Singers were at least as difficult to handle as composers (or their mothers). Mahler ruthlessly got rid of the hopeless cases but he played dictator, coach and wet nurse to the worthy ones. Infuriated by the on-stage fidgeting of the great baritone Theodor Reichmann, Mahler taught the man to keep still by binding his limbs in rehearsal. Yet when Reichmann complained that he was being sidelined by a rival singer, Mahler wrote a long reply praising him for his 'masterly interpretations' and signing off with 'your faithful admirer'. He similarly soothed the lachrymose Danish tenor Erik Schmedes, one of the finest Tristans, who wrote begging Mahler to 'be kind' to him.

On the whole the women showed more mettle. When Mahler demanded during a rehearsal of *Die Zauberflöte* that the soprano Elise Elizza repeat '*Stirb, Ungeheuer*' (Die, vile monster) for the umpteenth time, she turned on him in fury and spat the words into his face. Another soprano, Marie Gutheil-Schoder, pushed Mahler out of her dressing-room when he told her to change the wig she planned to wear for that night's performance. She wore it all the same and despite (or because of) her spirit became one of his favourites. So much of a favourite, in fact, that rumours soon spread of an affair. Tongue-waggers linked Mahler with yet another high-spirited singer, Rita Michalek, too. Since he had also hauled Anna von Mildenburg to Vienna from Hamburg, despite almost hysterical opposition from Natalie, Mahler began to win (ill) repute in Vienna too as a Don Juan.

At least in these three cases the Viennese scandal-mongers were probably wrong. Mahler's letters to Anna before she left Hamburg show that he keenly wanted her for the Vienna company, but only on a professional basis. There are plenty of signs that for some years she did not inwardly accept that deal, but Mahler seems to have kept her pretty much at arm's length all the same. As for Gutheil-Schoder and Michalek, if firm evidence ever existed that Mahler had affairs with them it has not survived. What do survive, on the other hand, are the passionate letters he wrote to Selma Kurz, a brilliant and beautiful soprano who made her Vienna début in September 1899 at the age of twenty-four. Four months later she gave the Vienna première of some of Mahler's orchestral songs and by Easter 1900 the two were snatching secret meetings together between rehearsals. The affair seems to have deepened during a brief holiday in Venice, though rather inconveniently Justi and Natalie came along too. Soon afterwards Mahler was urging his 'dearest Selma' by letter to 'believe in my love, that it is something unique in my life and will remain so! Always remember that we are at the beginning of a long road that we should travel fresh and unwearied.'

By summer the relationship had cooled. Selma feared that a lengthy liaison or even marriage with Mahler could spell the end of her career. Mahler may have grown wary again, recalling the complications of his Hamburg affair with Anna. Besides by the end of June he was worn out after another heavy year at the opera and the fraught Paris concerts with the Philharmonic. The wonder is that he found time for any private life at all or, indeed, that he had not long since collapsed. He had had his usual bad throats, migraines and, in 1898, another operation for his old haemorrhoids problem; but thanks to his toughness and resilience none of that had stopped him for long.

Things could not go on that way. On 24th February 1901 Mahler had an even heavier schedule than usual. In the early afternoon he gave a concert with the Philharmonic which included Bruckner's massive Fifth Symphony and in the evening he conducted the 110th anniversary performance of *Die Zauberflöte*. That night he suffered a haemorrhage so bad that he lost more than two litres of blood. A doctor was called, then a surgeon who finally staunched the flow, but Mahler had come close to death and he knew it. The prospect of dying, he told Natalie, had not frightened him at all. Indeed, while hovering between life and death he had wondered whether it might not be better to expire there and then and have done with it.

If Mahler really felt, even momentarily, that he had so little to live for, he was soon to change his mind. In the audience at *Die Zauberflöte* that evening was the twenty-one-year-old Alma Schindler. She later wrongly recalled the work in question as *Die Meistersinger* but she remembered Mahler's appearance clearly enough. 'He looked like Lucifer,' she wrote, 'a face as white as chalk, eyes like burning coals. I felt sorry for him and said to the people I was with, "It's more than he can stand."' A year later she and Mahler were married.

Chapter Five

Alma

On 7th November 1901, Berta Zuckerkandl gave a supper party for her
sister Sophie Clemenceau who was passing through Vienna. Even for a
skilled society hostess like Berta, it was an unusually brilliant affair. No
doubt she felt it had to be. Sophie was married to an engineer brother of
Georges Clemenceau, the French statesman, and had a thriving salon of
her own in Paris. Frequent guests there included the sculptor Auguste
Rodin and the up-and-coming composer Maurice Ravel. The ambitious
Berta, a pungent writer and conversationalist with a thick address book,
was not to be outdone. Among those seated around her supper table that
evening were the Secessionist artists Gustav Klimt and Carl Moll, the ex-
director of the Burgtheater Max Burckhard, and – Berta's biggest coup –
the Court Opera director Gustav Mahler.

Mahler almost never went to such gatherings and when he did so his
presence proved a mixed blessing at best. He would insist on frugal fare
including *Grahambrot* (wholemeal bread) and apples, although he wolfed
apricot dumplings at home when Justi was doing the cooking, and spent
much of the time in gloomy silence. He had been known to jump up
from the table before the meal was over and stride into an adjoining
room, snapping to his anguished hostess that he wished to be alone.
Well-disposed guests put this behaviour down to a sudden burst of

creative inspiration; others saw it as evidence that Mahler, perversely, was bored by them. Probably it was a bit of both.

Berta may well have worried in advance about how Mahler would fit into her group but she must have been proud to get him to come at all. As it happened, she had her sister to thank for the contact. Mahler had met Sophie and her husband Paul the previous year during the Vienna Philharmonic's ill-starred visit to Paris, had got on well with them and promised to pass on their greetings to Berta when he got home. Thanks to that Paris meeting Mahler also got to know two notable Frenchmen who, rather unexpectedly, became fervent fans – Paul Painlevé, a mathematician and future prime minister, and Colonel Georges Picquart, who was made war minister in Georges Clemenceau's cabinet in 1906. Indeed, Picquart learned of his appointment while in Vienna to hear *Tristan* under Mahler, and to his fury had to leave for Paris before the end of the performance.

There is another twist to the tale. It was Picquart who, initially at great cost to his career, had stood up for Alfred Dreyfus, the French officer of Jewish descent sentenced to life imprisonment in 1894 on the trumped-up charge that he had betrayed military secrets. The '*affaire Dreyfus*' became one of the most notorious examples of anti-Semitism in Europe and helped convince Theodor Herzl, who went to Paris from Vienna to report on the trial, that the Jews would have to seek a homeland of their own. Yet Mahler seems never to have discussed the implications of the Dreyfus affair with Picquart, although he met him quite often over the years and called him a man of 'integrity, exceptional class'. Evidently even this infamous case and the close Picquart connection were not enough to draw him out on the fate of a people whose faith he had now forsworn.

Also present at Berta's supper, albeit reluctantly, was Alma Schindler. At least Alma later claimed to have been reluctant. At the start of her *Gustav Mahler – Erinnerungen und Briefe (Gustav Mahler – Memories and Letters)* she tells how several days earlier she had bumped into Berta and her husband Emil, a famed anatomist, on the Ring. They spontaneously invited her to supper that evening to meet Mahler but she, just as spontaneously, refused. On the face of it, this was a very odd rebuff. In her book, Alma explains that although she admired Mahler as a conductor she had heartily disliked his First Symphony, performed in Vienna the previous year, and was put off by gossip about his affairs with singers. So much so, in fact, that she had 'purposely and with considerable difficulty' avoided meeting him that summer.

The Zuckerkandls rarely took no for an answer. Mahler found that, after all, he could only come on a later evening and again Alma was invited. This time she gave way, admitting that she was drawn by the promised presence of Klimt and Burckhard, both of whom adored her. She sat between them and they made up such a 'merry trio' that Mahler, further down on the other side of the table, kept shooting envious glances in their direction. After the meal Alma reported that she and Mahler got into a furious row over a ballet by Alexander Zemlinsky, her music composition teacher. She accused Mahler of breaking his pledge to stage the work. When he countered that he could not understand it she boldly offered to enlighten him. Mahler laughed and instead invited her, along with Berta and Sophie who had just joined them, to an opera rehearsal next day. He also proposed taking Alma home but she refused. Afterwards she claimed to have been unhappy about her outspoken behaviour that evening which she felt had put her in a false light.

Such is Alma's account of what she called her 'first meeting' with Mahler. It has long been taken as broadly accurate although it differs here and there from the version in her bulky and sometimes almost illegible diaries, which have never been published in full. For instance, Alma writes there that she hardly exchanged two words with Klimt the whole evening. So much for the 'merry trio'. She also notes, as she does not in her book, that she went to the supper with Moll, her stepfather, which casts doubt on her later claim that Mahler offered to see her home. Still, those are details. Other evidence suggests that her account has more serious flaws.

Within two months of Berta's supper, Alma and Mahler became engaged. The news that the dictator of the opera was to marry a glamorous Viennese girl nearly half his age was naturally a gift to the gossip-columnists. Indeed, so much exotic 'background' was published about the couple that it was easy to miss a relatively restrained piece which appeared in the *Fremden-Blatt* on 29th December. According to this report, Alma and Mahler had first met during the summer holidays two years before near the Hallstätter See in the Salzkammergut. They had been introduced to one another by a young professor from the Vienna conservatory, the *Fremden-Blatt* said, and later became reacquainted 'at a musical evening in the salon of an outstanding Viennese physician'.

This report would have remained ignored had it not been for the contents of an ancient postcard in Mahler's handwriting made public only in 1995. Postmarked 5th July 1899, in the Salzkammergut spa of Aussee, the message reads, 'Sole genuine signature, protected by law: Gustav Mahler. Beware of imitations.' The card is addressed to 'Frl. Alma Schindler, H.6, Stammback [*sic*] bei Goisern.' Both Stambach, where Alma spent that summer with her family, and Aussee are close to the Hallstätter See. Evidently the *Fremden-Blatt* was on the right track after all. At least it is unlikely that Mahler would have bothered to send such a tongue-in-cheek message at the request of a girl he had never met. No doubt their encounter was only fleeting but Alma was impressed enough to seek an autograph.

The apparent confirmation of that meeting, nearly a century later, throws new light on an account given by Berta herself of the origins of that famous supper. In a volume of her memoirs called *Österreich intim (Intimate Austria)*, Berta writes that one day her husband received a phone call from Anna Moll, Alma's mother. Anna complained that Alma looked pale, was losing weight and – most worrying of all – had even stopped playing the coquette. A doctor had diagnosed anaemia but Anna thought that rubbish. The only clue she could give was that Alma went every night to the opera, returned in tears and spent hours at the piano. Emil Zuckerkandl gave his verdict. Probably the magnetism of 'this musician' (i.e. Mahler) had caused the so-called anaemia. Anna should send Alma round to a supper party he and his wife were planning and perhaps on that evening a cure could begin.

That version has been widely discounted, partly because Berta is often slapdash with her facts but mainly because it contradicts Alma's far better known one. If Alma had really been trying to avoid Mahler and had her 'first meeting' with him almost against her will, as she claimed, then Berta's account makes no sense. It only does so if Alma had already been strongly attracted to Mahler, perhaps ever since that summer meeting shortly before her twentieth birthday. Assume that and another oddity falls into place. In her book *Mein Leben (My Life)* Alma recalls going to a party, nearly two years before Berta's supper, at which she first meets Zemlinsky. The two of them soon agree that all the other guests are deplorable and wonder, sadly, if there is anyone at all of whom only good can be said. Simultaneously they cry the same name – Mahler. No doubt by the time she wrote that Alma had forgotten how initially stand-offish she had claimed to be in her much earlier *Memories and Letters*.

Why didn't Alma admit the truth? It is hardly a crime for a young woman to fall for the most powerful musician in town – a man of great personal fascination and a bachelor to boot. But then Alma was no ordi-nary young woman, particularly not in her own opinion. She was, as she states at the start of *Mein Leben*, the daughter of a 'great monument'. Her father, Emil Jakob Schindler, was not only the finest Austrian landscape artist of his day. At least as important to Alma, he lived as she believed a true artist must, boldly devoted to his dreams and heedless of mundane matters like money. When his only pair of shoes needed repair, the young and poverty-stricken Schindler simply ordered a carriage for a few weeks to spare the leather until he could sell a picture. Although still short of funds he took his wife Anna, a former operetta singer, and two little daughters to live close to the Vienna woods in Schloss Plankenberg, a fifteenth-century castle crowned with an onion-shaped clock tower. There Alma grew up, wandering through the overgrown gounds, trem-bling at night as she scuttled by a candlelit altar set (just for show) in the great stairwell, watching for hours as her father worked in his studio.

Even when Alma was not at her castle home, much of her early life passed in a romantic haze. When she was eight years old, the Schindlers spent several months sailing along the Dalmatian coast while Emil painted scenes for a book commissioned by Crown Prince Rudolf, the emperor's son. They ended up spending half the winter on the Greek island of Corfu. An upright piano was brought to their villa and Alma, already able to play a bit, began to compose. Music became her passion. Naturally she wanted riches too but only, she argued, to help smooth the path of (other) creative people. She dreamed of having a huge garden in Italy filled with white studios to which she would invite oustanding artists. She saw herself being rowed about in a gondola with red velvet draperies trailing astern.

Then her father died. Aged only fifty, he succumbed in 1892 to an intestinal complaint while holidaying with the family on the North Sea island of Sylt. Alma recalled how, full of foreboding, she ran weeping across the dunes with her sister to be met by Moll, Schindler's ever-present disciple. 'Children,' he told them, 'you no longer have a father.' It was arguably the worst blow of Alma's life and she had many fierce ones. At the age of twelve she had, as she put it, 'lost my guide. All my ambition and vanity had been satisfied by a twinkle of his understanding eyes.' Three years later, to Alma's boundless contempt, her mother married Moll, at thirty-four a notable painter in his own right albeit hardly an Emil Schindler. Moll was just 'a pendulum', Alma wrote bitterly (and unfairly), 'but my father had been a mainspring.'

Plankenberg was abandoned and the family eventually moved to Vienna, first to an apartment near the city centre (curiously enough in the very building where Mahler's brother Otto took his life) and later to a villa on the Hohe Warte, a hilly suburb which was gradually becoming an artists' colony. For Alma neither spot had the enchantment of her beloved castle, nor did Moll's visitors from the arts world match up to her memory of her father. All the same she flirted with the pick of them, almost invariably far older than herself. Burckhard, for instance, was already in his forties, a lawyer by training but by instinct a revolutionary in literary matters. Selected by the unsuspecting establishment as a safe choice to run the venerable Burgtheater, he instead introduced shocked but intrigued Viennese audiences to the social realism of modern drama- tists like Ibsen and Schnitzler. He gave Alma two laundry baskets full of books, including works by Nietzsche whom she idolised, and took her on outings chaperoned, needlessly as it happened, by Anna Moll. When Burckhard's interest became less paternal Alma laughed in his face. Physically he meant nothing to her.

Klimt was a different story. Alma was for a time bewitched by the provocative ringleader of the Secession, twelve years her senior, with his outrageous grin and wild (though thinning) hair. The feeling was mutual. When Alma toured Italy with the Molls in the spring of 1899, Klimt trailed along too. He and Alma managed to snatch a kiss in Genoa and a clandestine meeting in Venice during which they swore eternal love. Alas for the two of them, Anna Moll peeked into Alma's diary and learned of the kiss. After some furious finger-wagging by Carl Moll, Klimt agreed to end the fledgeling affair, apparently less worried about losing Alma than about antagonising his artist colleague.

Alma felt doubly betrayed – by her mother, which came as no sur- prise, and by Klimt, which did. In *Mein Leben* she recalled feeling suici- dal. Still, she soon had other men on her mind. That summer, evidently,

[104]

she met Mahler and the following year began composition lessons with Zemlinsky, who rapidly became infatuated. Only seven years older, he was already renowned as a composer, conductor and teacher. Schönberg was one of his pupils and an admiring one at that. Alma felt much more than admiration. Although she wrote of 'Alex' as a 'hideous gnome . . . chinless, toothless, always reeking of the coffee house' she fell into his arms when he played part of 'Tristan' to her on the piano. She yearned to go much further (and so, without doubt, did he) but, like a 'stupid goose' as she put it, she feared flouting convention by losing her virginity before marriage. Besides, there was Mahler on the horizon. From late 1901, he was actually within grasp though even then she did not wholly drop Zemlinsky. It was a hard choice. 'What if Alex becomes great and powerful?' she agonised in her diary nearly a month after Berta's soirée.

What was it about Alma which proved so irresistible, especially to men of genius or close to it? After all, the short list of those who later fell for her too includes the Bauhaus architect Walter Gropius, the artist Oskar Kokoschka and the writer Franz Werfel. She was often called 'the most beautiful woman in Austria' but several of her contemporaries were described in the same way, including at least one of Klimt's many liaisons. Besides, photos hardly bear out the claim. Early ones show a handsome rather than stunning teenager, thick dark hair piled fashionably high, dress drawn firmly almost to her chin. In snapshots from the Mahler era Alma seems, more often than not, sad or nervous. Later in life she looks, frankly, gone to seed with corrugated hair and sack-like clothing to help hide her bulging figure. Yet her conquests even then included a Roman Catholic priest young enough to be her son.

Her daughter Anna held that no photos did Alma justice, not even those few which caught the intensity of her startlingly blue eyes. Such was Alma's magnetism that people hardly noticed 'all the nonsense' (Anna's words) she talked. When she walked into a crowded room as like as not there would be a moment's hush. When she leaned forward to listen, as she usually had to because from youth she was slightly deaf in one ear, her interlocutors felt they were deeply and instinctively understood. That is, most of them did. A notable minority, including the writer Elias Canetti, who fell in love with Anna, and Richard Strauss, found Alma eminently resistible. The rest seem to have felt much like Werfel,

Alma's third and last husband, who called her 'one of the very few great sorceresses of our time'.

Sorceress or not, Alma was at least a superb actress who entered into the role of goddess and muse with utter conviction. Her boldness took men by storm – especially, in her youth, older and gifted ones who unexpectedly found themselves put on the defensive. 'Do you think that someone as extraordinarily creative as I am could still not have heard your opera?' was her opening gambit with Zemlinsky. At Berta's supper it was Alma's fiery defence of Zemlinsky, at least as much as her good looks, which captivated Mahler. He told Burckhard during a walk afterwards that at first he had thought Alma just 'a doll' but soon realised there was a lot more to her. Didn't Alma expect, or at least hope for, just that reaction? Was she really unaware that her 'outspokenness', which she later claimed to regret, was one of her biggest assets? Had she in fact been put off (rather than intrigued) by the chit-chat about Mahler as a 'Don Juan'?

It is hard to believe, like so much else in Alma's two books which have long served as basic source material about Mahler. Not that either volume was ever taken wholly at face value. From the first it was clear that Alma had been careless with facts and figures which she could fairly easily have checked. Obviously, too, her accounts were subjective. What else could they be? No reasonable soul expects a widow's description of her life with a genius to be a piece of dispassionate research. But bit by bit more about Alma has emerged to cast still greater doubt on her published work. Her diaries, held since her death in an American university library, have been studied more closely. New details have emerged from those who knew her well, like Gropius her second husband. Letters from Mahler to her have come to light in a more complete form than she chose to reveal. It is now plain that Alma did not just make chance mistakes and see things 'through her own eyes'. She also doctored the record.

Given her background, that is not really a surprise. The 'monument' of a father she adored had lived up to his dreams. Alma was surely determined to live up to hers – and up to him. That involved some truly breathtaking flights of fancy. Before her marriage to Mahler she told her diary that she would have to stir herself to ensure she got her artistic due because 'he thinks nothing at all of my art and a lot of his – I think nothing at all of his art and a lot of mine. That's how it is.' Her sense of self-importance went far beyond art and easily outlived Mahler. On the outbreak of the First World War she noted, apparently in all seriousness, 'I sometimes imagine I am the one who has caused this whole catastrophe.'

The person who wrote that was hardly likely to admit to the world that she had entered Mahler's life as an autograph hunter – one, moreover, whom Mahler apparently failed to remember when they met again at the Zuckerkandls'. Nor would she aim to publish Mahler's letters to her for the sake of historical accuracy alone. If the text offended Alma's self-esteem or predilections then it had to be 'corrected' with some judicious deletion or insertion before the world could be allowed to see it. Many of the alterations are quite small but cumulatively they count, and nowhere does Alma indicate that she has made them. 'Answer . . . if you are able to follow me,' Mahler exhorts Alma in pre-marriage letters outlining what he expects of a partner for life. 'Answer . . . if you are willing to follow me' is how the text appears in the selection Alma made for her *Memories and Letters*. The suggestion that Mahler doubted her ability, rather than her readiness, clearly seemed to Alma too degrading to leave unchanged. Out, too, went references to presents Mahler bought or offered her (she claims he gave her next to none), to plentiful housekeeping money (she says she was often short), and to people like 'Carl and Anna' (Moll) for whom he had a lot more sympathy than Alma did. They were, after all, about his own age.

In sum, of 159 letters to her from Mahler which Alma made public, she left only thirty-seven unaltered. She chose not to publish at all close to another 200 of his letters, telegrams and notes to her, some admittedly of little interest. As for her letters to him, it seems that after his death she destroyed all she could lay hands on. At any rate the text of only one is known to survive.

Alma thus went to considerable pains to cover her tracks and, in doing so, to shift the blame for what went wrong in the marriage. The more her efforts have been exposed the more they have boomeranged against her, making it easy to see her alone as the guilty party and Mahler as an innocent victim. It is a role which rarely fits him and it does not do so here. Alma was frequently flighty, jealous and deceitful but Mahler was moody and authoritarian at least as often. 'Moody' in this case is a poor word to describe those split-second leaps from a laugh to a snarl and back again so characteristic of Mahler – and his work. Even Natalie, who worshipped Mahler and his music, found living under the same roof with him a strain. In one telling passage about her time with him at Steinbach, she writes how 'it's like being on a boat that is ceaselessly rocked to and fro on the waves. You have to get away from it, to find your feet and yourself again.' If Natalie went through that on a vacation visit, then Alma – who was, she imagined, bound to Mahler for life – must often have felt desperate. Her mournful diaries, filled with outbursts of rage and self-pity, make that even plainer than her books. But then she had wanted a genius. She got one. And geniuses are not known to be much comfort about the house.

Mahler fell head over heels for Alma at the Zuckerkandls'. Soon afterwards he sent her, anonymously, a love poem, fluttered round her when she came to the opera, and took to visiting her on the Hohe Warte. An evening walk together through the snow was followed by a kiss in Alma's bedroom. But passion did not make him uncritical, let alone blind. His early letters to her are dotted with schoolmasterly admonitions to 'learn to ask', 'learn to have a dialogue', and (repeatedly but vainly) to 'write clearly'. In one twenty-page epistle sent from Dresden on 19th December 1901 – hardly a month and a half after their meeting at the Zuckerkandls' – he tells her that she is too young to have a real personality and that men flatter her for her beauty, not her intellectual pretensions. 'My little Alma, we must agree in our love and in our hearts – but in our ideas? My Alma, what are your ideas?' He caps this remarkable document, naturally one of those Alma did not publish, by demanding that she stop composing if they are to marry. 'You have only one profession from now on: to make me happy.' After reading the letter Alma, credibly in this case, says she wept all night – then agreed. But her resentment smouldered for years, perhaps for life.

Mahler was not only brutally frank to Alma, he was clear about the pros and cons of his own position. In a letter to Justi at about the same time, he argues that he has much to bring to the marriage but asks whether it is right 'to chain spring to autumn, to force it to pass over summer'. For a time, Mahler ponders, things will go well enough, 'but what happens when my fruitful autumn gives way to winter?' No doubt Justi saw the problem just as well but she was not inclined to add to her brother's doubts. Apparently without Mahler's knowledge, she had long been having an affair with Arnold Rosé, leader of the Vienna Philharmonic. Now aged thirty-three, she was still acting as Mahler's housekeeper and was not prepared to leave him in the lurch. But if he were to marry then so could she.

According to Alma, Mahler was so shocked when he finally learned of the affair with Rosé that he refused to speak to Justi for weeks. This unlikely claim is one of many in her books with which Alma seeks to draw Mahler as a prude. He 'feared women', she writes, and right up to his forties had had next to no sexual experience. Alma puts this down, at least in part, to the impact of a violent love-making scene Mahler witnessed as a boy at a house where he was staying in Prague. Presumably Alma got the tale from Mahler himself. It has been much touted ever since as a vital clue to his psychology, like that famous 'barrel organ' incident when his parents were quarrelling. Whether Mahler was really as shocked by the Prague incident as Alma suggests is another matter. At any rate his romantic entanglements in nearly every town he stayed in, up to and including Vienna, hardly suggest a fear of women. That need not imply that he 'slept around'. Mahler was no doubt wary of catching syphilis, then a widespread scourge which brought madness and ultimately death to several of his friends, including Hugo Wolf. Even so it is hard to believe that his affairs were very largely platonic, including the lengthy one with the passionately demanding Anna von Mildenburg.

Whatever Mahler's sexual expertise when he met Alma, hers was by her own admission next to nil. Bold flirtation was one thing, kicking over the traces altogether quite another. Still, once she and Mahler were engaged she decided her virginity need not be preserved until her wedding night after all. According to a glum account in her diary on New Year's Day, 1902, their first love-making proved a flop. The disappointment did not last. A succeeding entry of just three words – '*Wonne über Wonne*' (Bliss upon bliss) – speaks for itself. By the time they married two months later, Alma was pregnant.

January turned out to be a memorable month. Immediately after Alma and Mahler began sleeping together she got down to alienating his old friends. Some sort of showdown was inevitable. Alma was well aware that many of those close to Mahler disapproved of her, especially Siegfried Lipiner who raised his eyebrows and called her 'my dear girl' whenever she gave an opinion. The feeling was mutual. Used to being idolised by the most talented men in town, Alma found many of Mahler's friends dull and unimportant. Several of them were also Jewish which, in Alma's view, made things worse. Burckhard, intensely jealous, had already tried to put her off Mahler by telling her she was throwing herself away on a 'rachitic, degenerate Jew'. Alma snubbed him but that kind of talk was not lost on her. Although she twice married Jews (Mahler and Werfel), she often revealed a strong strain of anti-Semitism to her life's end. That may have been all she had in common with Moll, later a convinced Nazi; that and the readiness to make an exception in Mahler's case.

Small wonder that when Mahler arranged a cosy supper at his flat to get his fiancée and in-laws together with some of his friends, the evening turned into a fiasco. He hardly improved its prospects by inviting Anna von Mildenburg too. Naturally, she and Alma soon clashed. When Anna asked what she thought of Mahler's music, Alma said she disliked what little she knew of it. Jaws dropped. Anna Moll blushed. Only Mahler seemed amused. As for the other guests, Alma generally ignored them or mocked their remarks, especially Lipiner's on painting and philosophy. At one stage she and Mahler retreated for a cuddle and were gone so long that Justi, trapped with her fiancé Arnold in the dreadful circle, desperately went looking for them.

Alma writes about the evening in her *Memories and Letters* with some relish as though it were a triumph. For her it was. Not least it led to an estrangement between Mahler and 'dearest Siegfried' which lasted for years. Lipiner was so appalled by the evening that he wrote to Mahler immediately afterwards, unwisely calling Alma heartless, foolish and affected. Alma got her own back in her book, calling Lipiner 'a bogus Goethe in his writing and a haggling Jew in his talk'. She had never, she said, 'encountered such aridity in a human being – if he was a human being'.

Forced to choose between Alma and Lipiner, Mahler of course took Alma. But other friends dropped largely out of sight too, including 'old faithful' Fritz Löhr. Emil Freund, a lawyer, kept in Mahler's good books despite Alma's disapproval because his advice was invaluable. Bruno Walter too, who had become a conductor at the Vienna Opera in 1901, was one of the few in Mahler's old circle who managed to stay in the new one. Alma sniped at him from time to time, calling him later in life when both were in exile in America a 'pseudo-Mahler-Pope'. But he handled her with diplomacy and, despite occasional tiffs with Mahler too, remained one of his closest confidants.

As for Justi, Alma's diary shows that initially the two women got on well, understandably since both had marriage interests in common. Not much of that warmth, though, comes over in Alma's memoirs. There Justi is not only drawn as intensely jealous, triumphantly telling Alma that 'I had his [Mahler's] youth, you have him now he's old.' She is also described as so extravagant that Mahler, on marriage, turned out to have debts of 50,000 gold crowns which Alma says she was able to repay by careful budgeting.

Justi was certainly poor at handling money, no better in fact than her brother was even before he began funding the family after his father's death. But there is no evidence that her shortcomings drove Mahler as deeply into the red as Alma maintains. After all, the sum mentioned is far more than his gross annual income as opera director, salary and fringe benefits combined. He had indeed borrowed part of his sisters' patrimony not long before to help finance the building of a country house, but Alma claims the 50,000 crowns owed was over and above that. Probably this slur on Justi is another of Alma's efforts to belittle the role of almost everyone in Mahler's life before he met her. The same could go for her claim, rarely challenged, that Mahler did not bother to attend Justi's wedding although it was held only a day after his own. Perhaps it is true. If so it is wholly out of character with Mahler's sense of duty to his family and his affection for Justi in particular. He and Alma were married in St Charles's church (the Karlskirche) in the centre of Vienna on 9th March 1902. Justi and Arnold followed suit in a church nearby on 10th March. At least there is no doubt about that. According to Alma, she and Mahler left by train on the 9th for their honeymoon in St Petersburg.

Exactly three months later, on 9th June, Mahler conducted the first complete performance of his Third Symphony at a festival in Krefeld, a provincial town on the fringe of Germany's industrial Ruhr area. Conditions were far from ideal. The orchestra was a pick-up one, albeit dragooned into shape by Mahler. The weather was stiflingly hot and the public was starting to wilt after hearing several other modern works on previous evenings. Would people walk out or nod off during Mahler's hundred-minute philosophical epic, finished in Steinbach six years before and since then gingerly offered at concerts only a movement or two at a time?

They did neither. No sooner had the final Adagio echoed through the hall than the audience rose to cheer. Some enthusiasts rushed towards the stage, others waved handkerchiefs and Mahler was recalled at least a dozen times. Alma, hitherto cool at best to Mahler's work, admitted that the concert that evening put her in 'an indescribable state of excitement. I cried and laughed softly to myself and suddenly felt the stirrings of my first child.' Even the critics were favourable. Most agreed it was the key event of the festival and one felt it might well usher in 'a new stage in the development of German music'. Not that reviewers were always so friendly about the Third. One in Vienna walked out of a performance of it growling that '*Für so was verdient der Mann ein paar Jahre Gefängnis*' (For stuff like that the man deserves a few years of prison), a comment which for some odd reason has often since been attributed to the writer Felix Salten. In fact Salten quotes the remark, made to him by an (unnamed) critic after the concert, in his book *Geister der Zeit (Spirits of the Age)* to show the kind of 'howling' Mahler faced on his home ground. Poor Salten. He was not just a man of catholic tastes whose writings range from the children's tale *Bambi* to the erotic saga *Josefine Mutzenbacher*. He was also one of Mahler's sturdiest supporters.

All in all, the Krefeld festival gave Mahler his biggest triumph so far as a composer. For that he had one person in particular to thank, his old colleague and rival Richard Strauss. Alma records that after the first movement of the Third, Strauss strode through the hall applauding ostentatiously and the public quickly joined in. From then on the concert's success was assured. What Alma does not convey, perhaps did not fully realise, is how much Strauss had already done to get a hearing for Mahler's work in general.

It was fifteen years since that first meeting between the two young musicians in Leipzig, after which (until smacked down by von Bülow) Strauss had praised Mahler's orchestration of *Die drei Pintos*. In 1894 as a conductor in Weimar, Strauss used his influence to get Mahler's First Symphony performed there and a year later in Berlin he did the same for the first three movements of the Second Symphony – their première. Both performances (under Mahler) flopped, at least with the critics, but that did not put Strauss off. He encouraged Mahler to send him his scores and in 1900 asked in a worried letter, 'Don't you compose at all any more? It would be a thousand pities if you devoted your entire artistic energy, for which I certainly have the greatest admiration, to the thankless position of theatre director! The theatre can never be made into an "artistic institution".' Strauss had good cause to know. By that time he was chief conductor at the Berlin Opera. He also gave concerts, taught, steadily composed and, from 1901, chaired the prestigious Allgemeiner deutscher Musikverein (General German Music Association). If anything he had more work than Mahler but he got through it with wry urbanity.

When Strauss learned about Mahler's Third he was keen to have it premièred at one of his Berlin concerts, but the composer's response was hardly encouraging. 'I must insist on having all my requirements fulfilled in performance,' Mahler wrote. 'The acoustics of the Kroll Hall are said to be bad. Is that true? If it is, dear friend, do not do anything of mine there. The orchestra must be tip-top. The rehearsals must be very full – and – my work lasts for two hours – there is no room for anything else on the programme.' Even that did not deter Strauss. 'What a pig-headed fellow you are,' he wrote back. 'But never mind. It's just part of your charm.' He instead earmarked the Third for the Krefeld festival, which was being organised by the Musikverein, and saw to it that most of Mahler's demands were met.

Strauss's efforts on Mahler's behalf were not all selfless. When the two first met, Strauss was easily the better known as a composer but Mahler was in a stronger position as a conductor. On the whole that is how things stayed. From the late 1880s Strauss produced a stream of tone poems like *Also Sprach Zarathustra*, *Don Quixote*, and *Ein Heldenleben (A Hero's Life)* which shocked many delicate ears but soon sailed into the repertoire. His *Zarathustra* was actually completed in 1896 just as Mahler was finishing his Third Symphony partly using the same Nietzsche text. Unlike the symphony, though, Strauss's piece had its première within months. Most of what Strauss produced turned to gold – but not enough of it in those days to allow him to live, as he wished, from composing alone. It clearly made career sense for him to keep in touch with his influential colleague, all the more so from 1897 when Mahler took over in Vienna and Strauss was developing as an opera composer.

Strauss's canniness paid off. His second opera *Feuersnot*, a strong brew of symbolism, satire and sex, had its première in Dresden in 1901 after censors in Berlin demanded changes in its bawdy text. But the Vienna Opera's resources were even finer than Dresden's and Mahler agreed to put them all at the disposal of Strauss's new work. He battled successfully with the censors, supervised the sets and costumes and (as usual) rehearsed singers and orchestra so punctiliously that Strauss, who had planned to conduct himself, happily turned the job over to Mahler instead.

This point, confirmed by the opera house's records, clearly escaped the newly betrothed Alma who attended the Vienna première on 29th January 1902. Mahler did not conduct, she writes in *Memories and Letters*, because he 'had a horror of the work'. Ironically, *Feuersnot* happens to be the only Strauss opera Mahler ever conducted (four times over in Vienna) although he often gave Strauss works in the concert hall. Alma is on firmer ground when she recalls the reaction of Strauss's formidable wife Pauline, who sat next to her in a box. Throughout the performance Pauline grumbled that *Feuersnot* was a shoddy, second-hand piece which only liars could praise. Backstage she then flew at the prematurely elated Strauss, claiming he made her sick and that she would not join him for a supper arranged with Mahler and Alma. Strauss finally turned up at the restaurant alone. He noted that his wife was 'a bit rough sometimes, but that's what I need, you know' and spent the rest of the evening calculating royalties. Mahler was so tormented by this display of materialism, Alma writes, that he hardly said a word.

However, if Strauss is to be believed, none of this is credible. When he first read Alma's book in Switzerland in 1946 he summed it up as a product of the '*Minderwertigkeitskomplexe eines liederlichen Weibes*' (inferiority complexes of a loose woman). Against the account of that Vienna evening he wrote in the margin, '*Alles Schwindel!*' and noted that his wife had always been very fond of *Feuersnot* in particular.

Strauss's comments apart, Alma's claim that Mahler disliked the work and did not conduct it hardly boosts confidence in the rest of her tale. Still, whatever its faults of detail, its general trend may well be right. Pauline, a Bavarian general's daughter who became an opera singer, had a tongue even sharper than Alma's. Her rages and *faux pas* were notorious. She badgered Strauss into composing at regular hours and if she disliked the result (by no means always) she gave him a thorough dressing-down. None the less the marriage held for fifty-five years with no hint of infidelity on either side. Strauss died in 1949 and Pauline a year later.

As for the scene in the restaurant, a letter from Mahler to Alma two days later broadly confirms the account in her book. Strauss was always dreaming of money, he charged, and 'sheds such a blight you feel estranged from your very self. . . . Better, by far, to eat the bread of poverty and follow one's star than sell one's soul like that. The time will come when the chaff shall be winnowed from the grain – and my day will be when his is ended.'

Only half that prophecy has been fulfilled. Mahler's time has come with a vengeance but much of Strauss's work, to the irritation of critics who find it as disposable as Mahler claimed in his letter, remains popular in opera house and concert hall. That apart though, Mahler's harsh words here are in sharp contrast to ones he used about Strauss on many other occasions. Only six weeks before in another letter to Alma, he called him 'a charming fellow. I'm touched by his attitude to me.' Five years earlier he told a critic, 'I number it among my greatest joys that I found among my contemporaries such a comrade-in-arms, such a comrade in creation. Schopenhauer somewhere uses the image of two miners digging a shaft from opposite ends and then meeting underground. This seems fittingly to characterise my relationship to Strauss.'

So did Mahler admire, even treasure, Strauss or despise him? The truth is he felt ambivalent. He was hugely impressed by *Salome*, Strauss's third opera, which he called 'one of the greatest masterpieces of our time'. Indeed, Mahler's failure to persuade the censors to let him stage the work was one reason why he decided to quit Vienna in 1907. Nor did he neglect Strauss's compositions in the concert hall although most of them were tone poems, programme music such as Mahler had flirted with himself but later shunned. He even tried to persuade Strauss that he was going up a 'blind alley' by continuing to write such stuff. 'Blind alley' or not, works by Strauss appeared more often on Mahler's concert programmes than those by Mozart or Haydn, Brahms or Schumann, Mendelssohn or Tchaikovsky.

Up to a point Mahler admired Strauss as a conductor too. He once noted that even after several rehearsals he rarely achieved just what he wanted, whereas Strauss got results in only a couple of sessions. No doubt the remark betrays a touch of envy. Strauss so often seemed to win success without pain, Mahler had to fight every inch of the way. Their very aspect suggested as much; Strauss the tall, elegant German with a firm gait and superior smile, Mahler the short, swarthy Jew with an explosive temperament. But whatever envy Mahler felt was tempered by his sense of Strauss's limitations. Although he acknowledged that Strauss achieved quick results he did not say there was no room for improvement. The implication is that Strauss, for all his great technical skill (or partly because of it), was too easily satisfied. The perfectionist versus the pragmatist! Not that Strauss lacked the spark of genius, either as conductor or composer. But too often it lay buried, as Mahler once graphically put it, like a subterranean fire under a slagheap.

Soon after Mahler died in 1911, Strauss got into a conversation about him with the young Otto Klemperer who owed his breakthrough as a conductor to Mahler's support. Strauss confessed that his late colleague had always baffled him by talking about seeking redemption through music. 'I don't know what I am supposed to be redeemed from,' Strauss said, according to Klemperer. 'When I sit down at my desk in the morning and an idea comes into my head, I surely don't need redemption. What did Mahler mean?'

It is a revealing remark. Strauss knew Mahler on and off for twenty-four years. He helped him, used him and was better acquainted with his work than almost anyone else. Yet evidently he did not realise that for Mahler every symphony was a new struggle to find out 'What did you live for? Why have you suffered? Is it only a vast terrifying joke?' In other words Strauss missed the main point. For Mahler composition was not just an ideal way to earn a living, it was a matter of life and death. In the summer of 1902 Mahler was a married man about to have a family. He was on the threshold of his greatest achievements at the opera. But none of that meant as much to him as creating his own music. Alma may already have had an inkling of that. If not, she was soon to find out.

Chapter Six

Maiernigg

Of all Austria's lakes, the Wörther See in Carinthia seems most readily to spark the inspiration of composers. No doubt the splendour of the site has something to do with it. Flanked to the south by the peaks of the Karawankel range, the last natural barrier before the Balkans, the lake is a sun-trap more than 10 miles long stretching from the Carinthian capital of Klagenfurt in the east to the resort of Velden in the west.

Still, plenty of other spots in the Alps are equally breathtaking, and it is hard to explain what makes this one so special. There is a sense of mystery and drama in the air which somehow survives even the tourist invasion of 'Austria's Riviera' every summer. Perhaps it is linked to Carinthia's ages-old role, of which archaeological evidence abounds, as a crossing-point and battle ground. The Celts were there, who held the mountains sacred and built settlements on their slopes. So were the Romans, as soldiers and traders. So were Illyrian tribes, Goths, Turks and Slovenes. Perhaps, too, the climate plays a role. The muggy heat which builds up around the lake is periodically swept away by spectacular elec-trical storms, sending blue and white lightning crackling over the water.

Whatever the reason, the spot stirs the imagination and evidently it spurs composition. Brahms, for one, claimed that at the Wörther See melodies came to him easily for which he had to struggle elsewhere. He spent several summers near Pörtschach on the northern shore, producing among other things much of the Second Symphony (his sunniest) and his Violin Concerto. Anton Webern wrote some of his earliest music in and around Klagenfurt in the years before he studied with Schönberg. Alban Berg, another Schönberg pupil, composed some of his best work, including his Violin Concerto and part of his (unfinished) opera *Lulu*, in a lakeside retreat near Velden. The concerto proved doubly poignant. Berg dedicated it 'to the memory of an angel' – in fact Manon Gropius, Alma's lovely daughter by her second husband, who had died of polio at the age of eighteen. Soon after completing the work in 1935 Berg was stung by an insect. The wound went septic and he perished within months of blood poisoning.

Tragedy eventually struck the Mahlers at the Wörther See too, but when they arrived there in June 1902 their life had few shadows. The triumph of the Third Symphony at Krefeld was just behind them; more than two months' holiday lay before them in a villa built for Mahler at Maiernigg, a quiet hamlet on the southern shore of the lake. Not that the house itself, which Alma was seeing for the first time, looked ideal for relaxation. A rather forbidding pile of masonry and dark wood, with balconies and verandahs like ramparts on three levels and a footbridge to the front door, it seemed as much castle as holiday home. Inside, Alma found the decoration 'frightful' and clambered about pulling down the fretwork ornamentation from the tops of the cupboards.

There were compensations all the same. All the rooms had splendid views across the lake, especially Mahler's tucked away like a watch-tower under the eaves of the steeply sloping roof. From the garden, steps led down to a private promenade, a boat house and changing-rooms with flat roofs ideal for sunbathing. Later, after their first child was born, Mahler carted in sand for a lakeside playground. Yes, there might be snakes, he admitted to an anxious Alma, but not poisonous ones because they shunned water. 'You can ask any doctor.'

Mahler felt proud of the property, even a little guilty that he owned it. 'It's too beautiful,' he murmured in 1901 on first moving in. 'One can't allow oneself such things.' He was really keener on a far simpler building altogether, his new composing hut set about 200 feet up in the thickly wooded hills directly behind the villa. Every summer on arrival at Maiernigg, Mahler dumped his things and sped away to his refuge up one of the steep paths winding between the fir trees. He would push open the three shuttered windows, drink in the fresh forest air and his Vienna Opera cares would drop away. Even when he got down to composing the windows often stayed open. The bird-song no longer disturbed him as it had done at Steinbach years before and passing ramblers were few.

Mahler spent nearly as many of his waking hours in the hut as he did in the villa. Bigger and more sturdily built than his Steinbach retreat, it had plenty of space for his desk, a piano and lots of books – Goethe, Kant and many volumes of Bach. The place even had a separate toilet cabin close by, misused for nesting by a stubborn owl. One day, Mahler wrote wryly to a friend, a plaque would be put up at his woodland workshop reading 'Here the once so famous G.M. used to sit every morning.' It was to be hoped, he added, that the memorial would be placed on the right building. He need not have worried. Nowadays only the composing hut survives, tastefully restored as a museum.

During all but the last of the six summers he spent with Alma at Maiernigg, Mahler's daily schedule hardly varied. He got up at about 6 a.m. and went to the hut for breakfast carried up to him by the cook, evidently a woman of abnormal stamina and sure-footedness. At least five hours of uninterrupted work followed, sometimes much longer. On descending to the villa he swam and sunbathed with Alma. After a light lunch the two of them would go on strenuous walks during which Mahler would sometimes stop to make notes or beat time in the air. When Alma nearly collapsed from exhaustion, Mahler would tell her, 'I love you', and she would pick up again. The evening was spent reading or making music, sometimes with friends.

'Mahler at that time gave the impression of being utterly healthy,' wrote Alfred Roller, the Secessionist artist who became Mahler's stage designer and who was a regular guest at Maiernigg. His view is worth stressing. Mahler was in his forties. He had several serious illnesses and operations behind him as well as more than two decades of theatrical struggle, not to mention family strains. After that he might well have been a sickly bundle of nerves, as Alma often suggests without putting it quite so crudely. In her *Memories and Letters* she leaves no doubt about Mahler's energy in those days. But she also claims that from the start she felt Mahler's swimming and sunbathing routine at Maiernigg strained his heart, and calls his choice of food 'an invalid's diet'.

Yet Roller's account, written with an artist's eye for the tiniest of details, reveals a man apparently close to prime physical and mental shape. Because of his haemorrhoids Mahler was pernickety about his food, as hostesses like Berta Zuckerkandl sadly discovered. But despite that, says Roller, 'he ate well and derived much pleasure from food. Lots of fruit, especially apples and oranges, plenty of butter, plain vegetables and pasta, very little meat and only from farm animals. . . . He slept splendidly, relished his cigar and in the evening enjoyed a glass of beer. Spirits he abstained from completely.'

Roller found, like Alma, that Mahler walked so fast on his hikes that it was hard to keep up with him. 'He would lean forward, his chin stretched out, and tread firmly, almost stamping. This gait had something stormy, almost triumphant about it.' When he stopped it was often to enthuse even about country scenes which, to people less passionate about nature, were really nothing special. 'Isn't this a wonderful spot,' he would repeat over and over again to his bemused companions. As for Mahler's swims, these 'usually began with a high dive. Then he swam under water and did not reappear until he was far out in the lake, bobbing about comfortably like a seal. Rowing a boat with Mahler was no pleasure. He had a very powerful stroke and pulled too fast; his strength enabled him to keep going for a long time.'

While the two of them were sunbathing, Roller noted that Mahler's body was well muscled with no trace of excess fat. 'In the course of my profession, I have seen a great many naked bodies of all types and can testify that . . . Mahler had the perfect male torso – strong, slim, beautifully made although the total body length was probably not quite seven and a half times the vertical head diameter.' Roller was even reminded of a racehorse in peak condition. This was not a bad comparison. Mahler loved outdoor exercise. But he needed it too to keep in trim and get his works past the finishing post in the summer.

Those who know Mahler's most readily appealing symphony, the Fourth, might well guess that it was written during that summer of 1902 in Maiernigg. The work has about it an ease and grace suggesting a composer for whom most things in life have come right at last. But the guess would be wrong. In 1902 Mahler was completing his Fifth Symphony, a weightier and often anguished piece. The Fourth was already finished (inasmuch as any work by Mahler, the eternal revisionist, can ever be considered truly finished) and had cost its creator no end of trouble. Indeed it was largely because of his problems in settling down to work on it that Mahler finally became a property owner in Maiernigg.

After completing the Third Symphony in 1896 Mahler did little composing for three years. The break was more or less forced on him. In 1897 he was fighting for the Vienna Opera job and in 1898 he had another operation for haemorrhoids which kept him convalescing for much of the summer. He completed two more *Wunderhorn* songs but that was about all. Determined to get down to serious composing again in 1899, he booked a holiday house in a quiet village for himself, Justi and Natalie. But when the three of them arrived on the doorstep in June, they found half the place locked up by the owners and the rest of it unsuitable. Ten days' frantic search followed before they found in the Salzkammergut what seemed a good substitute, a solitary villa set above the spa of Aussee (and Mahler's base when his path first crossed Alma's that summer). Alas, this too proved an unhappy choice. It often rained in torrents and became so cold that Mahler could hardly hold his pen. On trips to the village the '*Herr Direktor*' found himself gaped at by the '*Kurgäste*' (visitors on a cure). '*Kuhgäste*' (cow visitors), Mahler promptly called them. Worst of all, the distracting oompahs of the local band floated up even to Mahler's distant window.

With most of the holiday over, Mahler had written but a single song, corrected proofs of past work and resigned himself to getting little else done. Then, against all expectations, so many ideas for a Fourth Symphony began to course through his mind that he could hardly control them. He even had dizzy spells as, in a desperate race against time and in dread of the next blast from the band below, he tried to get as much as possible down on paper. With the first two movements largely sketched and the third one planned, he had to break off and return to Vienna. He tossed the unfinished score into a bottom drawer and could not even think about it, he told Natalie, without a stab of grief.

Things could not go on that way. Mahler knew he needed a long-term holiday home and in August Justi and Natalie set off on a bike tour to look for one. Still empty-handed and increasingly depressed, they were taking a steamer across the Wörther See when, according to Natalie,

Anna von Mildenburg happened to bump into them. She took them to see an architect acquaintance at Maiernigg who told the house-hunters it would be wiser to build than rent. Within a matter of weeks sites for the villa and hut had been found and Mahler sped down to Maiernigg to sign contracts. The hut was to be ready by the next summer and the house a year later.

So Mahler indirectly owed his holiday home to that chance meeting with Anna, his old Hamburg flame and now part of his Vienna ensemble. It seems a remarkable coincidence but since Anna did indeed come from the region it may be no more than that. At any rate she spent subsequent summers in the neighbourhood too and, once the newly married Mahlers were installed, took to calling in uninvited with what Alma calls 'a mangy dog' trailing at her heels. At least one of these visits was truly spectacular. During a violent thunderstorm which lashed branches of neighbouring trees against the villa, Anna 'playing Valkyrie' dragged Mahler out on to the terrace and called to the pregnant Alma to follow. She refused. Anna, her long hair whipping about her face in the gale, turned triumphantly to Mahler and taunted, 'She's a coward.' Alma was often intensely jealous but sometimes she had cause to be.

In principle Mahler should have had little trouble completing his Fourth Symphony in 1900. He was already well on the way with it, the Maiernigg hut was ready by June as promised and, pending completion of the house, he, Justi and Natalie found a spacious villa to rent nearby. For all that, Mahler at first could get next to nothing done. He began to feel desperate. A year earlier he had gloomily told Natalie, 'In the end I'll have my summer house, my peace and quiet and everything I need for my well-being – only the creative artist won't be there.' The prediction seemed to be coming true.

Mahler's mental block that summer has given rise to some ingenious psychoanalysis. Theodor Reik, for instance, argues that Mahler may have been immobilised by subconscious guilt for not finishing his symphony before 'rewarding' himself by ordering erection of his villa. Mahler's worry about failing creativity has also been linked to a fear of sexual impotence. Possibly Natalie is closer to the mark when she notes that, on arrival in Maiernigg, Mahler was worn out from the tense Paris tour just ended with the Vienna Philharmonic and needed time to recover. Whatever the truth, Mahler finally got the symphony under way again in early July – close to his fortieth birthday – and finished it in roughly a month, albeit rarely composing with the ease he had known at Steinbach. Some of Mahler's later works, especially the Eighth Symphony, still emerged like much of his earlier ones in frenzied bursts of creativity. But the troubles with the Fourth taught him a useful lesson. 'Perhaps it isn't necessary, or even desirable, for a work of art always to spring from a mood, like an eruption,' he told Natalie that summer. 'There should rather be a uniform degree of skill throughout. This is true art, which is always at the disposal of its possessor and overcomes all difficulties, even that of one's not being in good form.'

The Fourth betrays next to nothing of its painful birth. From the jingling of sleigh bells at the start to the ethereal *Wunderhorn* song '*Das himmlische Leben*' ('Heavenly life') at the end, the piece scuds along with a Mozartian transparency and facility. The tortured Mahler who always 'saw the skull beneath skin' seems to have vanished – or almost. In the scherzo second movement a violin tuned a tone higher scrapes away 'as if Death had taken up the fiddle' and the woodwind duly tremble. But the instrusion does not last. The ensuing Adagio (especially admired by Richard Strauss) ends in a *fortissimo* blaze from the whole orchestra which routs any last qualms. As Mahler put it, the basic mood of the work is like 'the uniform blue of the sky. . . . Sometimes it becomes overcast and uncanny, horrific: but it is not heaven itself which darkens, for it goes on shining with its everlasting blue. It is only that to us it seems suddenly sinister.'

That outburst ending the Adagio is one of the few in the symphony. The orchestra is smallish by Mahler's standards, with no tuba or trombones and 'only' four horns (compared with a contrabass tuba, four trombones and eight horns in the Third Symphony) and in performance the whole work usually lasts under an hour. That does not mean it is simple. The first movement is one of the most complex Mahler ever wrote, a miracle of intricate organisation wholly belied by the ease with which it reaches the ear. It begins 'as if it couldn't count to three,' Mahler remarked, 'but then launches out into the full multiplication table, until at last it is reckoning dizzily in millions upon millions.' He also acknowledged that the scoring of one apparently artless theme in it had caused him untold trouble. 'I'm probably still suffering from a lack of strict counterpoint, which every student who has been trained in it would use at this point with the greatest of ease.'

Quite an admission, coming from the director of the Imperial and Royal Opera with three massive symphonies already behind him. It not only confirms that Mahler really did leave the Vienna conservatory lacking a vital technical skill and had to make up for it afterwards with intuition and sweat. It also helps explain why at the Maiernigg hut the only music he had on hand apart from his own was that of Bach, an unsurpassed master of counterpoint. According to Natalie he exclaimed, 'It's beyond words the way I am constantly learning more and more from Bach, really sitting at his feet like a child . . . If only I had time to do nothing but learn in this highest of schools.' Even back in his Hamburg days, Mahler had talked about Bach's work as a cleansing spring in which he could 'wash off the dirt' after returning from another night's grind at the opera. By the Maiernigg era at the latest Mahler's admiration had grown so much that Bach, at least as teacher, had an equal place in his musical pantheon alongside Mozart, Beethoven and Wagner.

Apart from the 'untold trouble' he still claimed to be having with his counterpoint, Mahler set himself a conundrum in the Fourth Symphony which made his task still harder. He had originally composed '*Das himm-lische Leben*' in Hamburg in 1892 and later considered using it as a seventh and last movement to his Third Symphony. After rejecting that scheme, which would have unbalanced and lengthened an already marathon work, he decided to use the song to conclude his Fourth instead. On the face of it writing the rest of a symphony to fit an existing finale might seem no tougher than finding an appropriate equation for a given solu-tion in algebra. But what satisfies in maths does not necessarily do so in art. How could Mahler give a sense of development to his work without dropping into bathos when he came to his naïve, pre-set ending? The key part of a complicated answer is that Mahler solved the problem by embracing it as a solution in disguise. The symphony develops but it does so backwards, gradually unravelling from the complexity of that 'full multiplication table' in the first movement to the straightforward 'two plus two' of the child's vision of heaven in the last. The approach works because the essence of what Mahler wants to get across is that human bliss is attainable only by discarding sophistication for simplicity. 'Except ye become as little children ye shall not enter the Kingdom of Heaven,' he underlines in the last movement – albeit with a *Wunderhorn* text, not a Biblical one. At the very end even the soprano soloist falls silent, leaving *pianissimo* strings and harp slowly to fade into a 'peace which passeth all understanding'.

Not everyone sees the work that way, particularly not Theodor Adorno (1903–69), a German musician and philosopher of great influence although his many nuggets of critical insight are hard to dredge from the slough of his prose. According to Adorno the Fourth Symphony means just the opposite of what it seems to say from the first note to the last. The seraphic sleigh bells at the start are really a fool's bells warning that 'none of what you are about to hear is true'. Paradise is presented in such a way as to 'give notice that it does not exist'. The soprano may promise in the finale that 'all shall awake to joy', but when the music dies away no one knows 'if it does not fall asleep for ever'. Mahler is not expressing faith in the indestructibility of childlike innocence but mourning its irretrievable loss.

If this view is right then the Fourth is indeed, as Adorno puts it, a fairy-tale symphony as sad as any of Mahler's late works. There is some circumstantial evidence which might seem to support the notion. Already with the mock funeral march in his First Symphony Mahler showed himself a master of irony and ambiguity, so in theory he could be up to the same game in the Fourth. Even his specific direction to the soprano to sing the finale 'with childlike and serene expression, absolutely without parody' could be taken, by Adorno-ites at least, as a further sign of his wry cunning. Moreover this was the first symphony Mahler wrote after becoming director in Vienna, a career goal for which he had long struggled and (formally at least) had switched faiths. Yet even after reaching the very top of his profession, the perfection he sought in opera house and concert hall had turned out to be as elusive as ever. Perhaps the Fourth is a disguised acknowledgement that his youthful ideals, at least as a performing musician and possibly in other ways too, would never be realised after all.

If it is, then the disguise is extraordinarily elaborate even for Mahler. So elaborate, in fact, that for most listeners it has proved impenetrable. More likely the piece really is meant to be taken in the spirit in which it seems to be offered and in which Mahler talked about it. Initially audiences were baffled by it, not least because they had come to expect symphonies by Mahler to be very loud and very long. But that was just the point. With his huge Third Symphony Mahler had offered a vision of all creation from the lowest things to the highest. Where could he possibly go from there, musically and philosophically? The answer lay in front of him in the *Wunderhorn* song he had planned to use as *What the child tells me* to round off the Third. Its message of simplicity and innocence could be used as the basis for a new work, smaller in scale but more subtle in content. If it really is a fool jingling those opening bells, as Adorno claims, then it is a holy fool – like Wagner's *Parsifal* or Alyosha in Mahler's favourite *Karamazov*. Or indeed like that childlike aspect of Mahler's own complex character. 'My Fourth will be very strange to you,' he wrote to Alma soon after they became engaged. 'It is all humour, "naïve" etc. It is that part of me which is still the hardest for you to accept and which in any case only the fewest of the few will comprehend for the rest of time.'

Did Mahler notice that there was a parallel between his Fourth Symphony and Beethoven's? Both works are more compact than their immediate predecessors, in Beethoven's case the mighty 'Eroica', and both have an unexpected lightness of touch which makes them easy to underrate. The parallel does not end with the Fourth. When Mahler begins his Fifth Symphony he does so with something very like the 'fate knocking at the door' motif Beethoven used to open his own Fifth nearly a century before. The difference is that Mahler's 'fate' theme is given to a trumpet, not mainly to the strings like Beethoven's and that it is used to launch a funeral march. We are back to the tragic mood of the 'Resurrection' Symphony's first movement. What has become of the eternal bliss of '*Das himmlische Leben*'?

There seems to be an obvious answer. Mahler began composing the Fifth Symphony in the summer of 1901, only a few months after suffering his near-fatal haemorrhage in February in Vienna. No wonder many commentators link the tragic tone of much of the Fifth to that recent brush with death. The case looks all the stronger since a great deal of Mahler's other work during that highly productive summer is gloomy too, for instance the song '*Der Tamboursg'sell*' ('The drummer-boy') about a youth facing execution for an unspecified crime, presumably desertion. It is Mahler's last setting of a *Wunderhorn* poem and perhaps his most bitter, its slow but implacable march rhythm and pattering snare-drum offering not the faintest hope of pardon. A different but no less intense kind of grief haunts the *Kindertotenlieder (Songs on the Death of Children)*, of which Mahler composed three that summer and two in 1904. According to Natalie, Mahler said he felt sorry for himself for having to write the songs and sorry for the world which would one day hear them. For much of the cycle the sparse, sometimes skeletal, instrumentation underlines a sense of parental loss too deep for full expression. It also, incidentally, reflects a new stringency in Mahler's handling of the orchestra in general which foreshadows the austerity of his late works like *Das Lied von der Erde*.

Naturally Mahler's serious illness must have influenced his state of mind and eventually, one way or another, his music too. But it is debatable whether that really accounts for the grim character of so much of his work that same year. How handy (and dull) it would be if the creative process were so easy to fathom. Mahler was badly ill, possibly close to death, in Hamburg in late 1893 yet the following summer he wrote the joyous finale to the 'Resurrection' Symphony. Despite bouts of great frustration in 1899 and 1900 he produced the light-footed Fourth Symphony. The Sixth looks an even odder case. Mahler composed it during the summers of 1903 and 1904 which were two of the happiest of his life – at least they seem to have been so, judging from all we know of his marriage, health and career at the time. Yet the Sixth is the only Mahler symphony which seems to end in unequivocal disaster.

In other words there is so often no apparent correlation between Mahler's physical state and the character of his work that it is wise to be wary when it does crop up. Doubly wary in the case of the *Kindertotenlieder*. No work, except perhaps the Sixth Symphony, has been more misused to sustain the myth of Mahler as tragic prophet. The argument runs thus. Alma reports that when Mahler completed the *Kindertotenlieder* in 1904 she warned him he was 'tempting providence'. Three summers later one of their little daughters died. Ergo: Mahler, displaying supernatural powers as well as grim artistic genius, actually foretold the event in music. Psychoanalytical explanations for the *Kindertotenlieder* are at least more convincing than that. In one of the more elegant of them, the American Stuart Feder argues that Mahler's near-death in 1901 unconsciously spurred him to seek a kind of immortality through paternity. Hence both Mahler's hasty courtship of Alma and his near-simultaneous composition of the *Kindertotenlieder* in which the concepts of birth and death mingle.

Perhaps there is something in that, though if Mahler began the cycle in 1901 because of a longing for children, it is odd that he should have returned to it three summers later when he already had one toddler (Maria) and one infant (Anna, born in June 1904). The answer may have more to do with pragmatism than with the subconscious. In the spring of 1904 Mahler had promised to give the première of one of his works the following season for the Vereinigung schaffender Tonkünstler, a short-lived society founded by Schönberg, among others, to promote contemporary music. By adding two more *Kindertotenlieder* to the existing three, Mahler probably felt he could produce a full cycle which would fit the bill nicely – as it soon did. The complete work had its first performance on 29th January 1905, at an all-Mahler concert in Vienna with the composer conducting.

Clairvoyance here, psychoanalysis there, at least one observation about Mahler in 1901 is indisputable: he had become fascinated by the work of the German poet Friedrich Rückert (1788–1866). Of the eight songs he composed that summer, seven of them – including the three *Kindertotenlieder* – were to Rückert texts. Why Rückert? Although he was a sensitive and prolific poet he was not a truly great one, but in this case that was part of his attraction. Mahler once told a friend it seemed to him profane for composers to set perfect poems to music 'as if a sculptor chiselled a statue from marble and a painter came along and coloured it'. What he found in Rückert, as in the *Wunderhorn* texts (which were not great poetry either), was mood and subject matter to stir his imagination. No wonder he alighted on the *Kindertoten* verses, written by Rückert after his two small children died within weeks of one another. Mahler had lost so many of his own family and his favourite brother, who died aged thirteen, had been called Ernst like Rückert's son.

Of the four remaining Rückert texts Mahler set that summer, none is remotely as grim as the *Kindertotenlieder*. '*Um Mitternacht*' ('At midnight') is a grand rather than painful soliloquy on man's fate. In '*Ich bin der Welt abhanden gekommen*' ('I am lost to the world') Mahler captures the deep sense of peace he felt composing in his isolated hut, dead to 'the world's commotion'. The two other pieces are the delicate '*Ich atmet' einen Linden duft*' ('I breathed a sweet scent') and the whimsical '*Blicke mir nicht in die Lieder*' ('Don't peep into my songs'), often called Mahler's weakest song. Maybe that is true, but it is still fun to hear. So is '*Liebst du um Schönheit*' ('If you love for beauty's sake'), another semi-playful Rückert text which Mahler set for voice and piano the following year as a love-song for Alma. Eager to surprise her, he slipped the newly composed manuscript just inside the score of Wagner's *Walküre*, which she often pounded out at the piano. Surely, he felt, she would come across the song in a day or two. She did not. Finally Mahler's patience gave out. He picked up *Walküre* as though by chance and '*Liebst du um Schönheit*' fluttered to Alma's feet. That same day, she reported, they performed the piece together at least twenty times. Oddly, Mahler never got round to orchestrating it but this was later done by Max Puttmann, a musician and critic in Leipzig. He made such a workmanlike job of it that many listeners mistake the orchestration for Mahler's even now.

Part of the lighter mood of '*Liebst du um Schönheit*' finds its way into the Fifth Symphony, for instance in the fourth movement Adagietto for strings and harp which is doubtless Mahler's most popular work. Not that the Adagietto is generally played as though there were much joy about it. Since its use in 1971 as part of the soundtrack to Visconti's film *Death in Venice*, it has regularly been mistreated as a dirge and a sentimental one at that. To some extent, of course, this is a matter of opinion and taste. If conductors feel the music has intrinsic solemnity then it is up to them to interpret it accordingly. They have Mahler's initial tempo direction of 'very slow', albeit soon changing to 'more flowing' and 'do not drag', to back them up. But there is evidence that the grave approach not only distorts the true character of the piece but also upsets Mahler's symphonic architecture. One of the most intriguing insights comes from Willem Mengelberg, the Dutch conductor mentioned earlier who helped confirm how close Mahler in his Leipzig years had been to Marion von Weber. According to Mengelberg, whom Mahler called his finest interpreter (next to himself), the Adagietto was a declaration of love sent to Alma in manuscript form – probably in late 1901. No words were attached and none were needed. Alma understood the point right away. Perhaps Mengelberg was mistaken, though he claimed to have heard the tale from both Mahler and Alma, but he demonstrably acted on his conviction. His 1926 performance of the Adagietto, at just over seven minutes the fastest on records, has a compelling flow and ardour worlds away from the schmaltz with which the piece often drips nowadays.

Even if Mengelberg did get the story wrong, there is another good reason to keep the Adagietto moving along. Mahler wrote the symphony in five movements but he also divided it up into three, carefully balanced, parts. Part one consists of the first two movements, the funeral march and its fierce albeit shorter successor marked '*Stürmisch bewegt. Mit grosser Vehemenz*' (violently agitated, with great vehemence). The last part begins with the Adagietto which leads straight into the rondo finale, a movement bursting with cheerful polyphony and ending with a triumphant chorale. Mahler had been learning his Bach lessons well! That leaves the third movement, the most elaborate scherzo Mahler ever wrote, as the second part and pivot of the whole work. It is a piece in which, as Mahler put it, every note is charged with energy like a comet's tail. Or nearly every note. There is a ghostly interlude with *pizzicato* strings and croaking bassoon, hinting that the comet may not be so potent after all. Is the music about to sink back into the gloom of the first part or, in a new burst of power, soar away from it for good? The outcome of the whole symphony hangs briefly in the balance. Then the pace quickens and the answer is clear, or should be but for the Adagietto problem.

It seems certain that when Mahler began the symphony, working on the scherzo first, he did not have exactly this construction in mind. As so often he was feeling his way. With respect to the orchestration he went on doing so to his life's end, constantly cutting and revamping in the eternal quest for perfect clarity. Alma even claims that he crossed out nearly all the side-drum part and half the percussion instruments on her advice, though study of the score's various editions does not support this. But orchestration was one thing, structure quite another. Once Mahler had settled on his five movements in three parts he stuck to them. This has consequences, especially for the interpretation of the Adagietto. Take it buoyantly like Mengelberg (and other old-school conductors including Bruno Walter and Rudolf Schwarz), and it plays a natural role as an introduction to the joyful finale. Take it ultra-slowly (at least one modern conductor drags it out to about fourteen minutes) and the piece becomes a sombre intermezzo wholly separated in mood from what follows. The finale is left to supply a convincing resolution of the symphony's whole tormented first part, but on its own it does not have the weight to do so. Many critics who admire the symphony in other respects groan that at the end Mahler proclaims a confidence which has not been wholly earned. Adorno, for instance, offers this as part of the evidence that Mahler was 'no good yes-sayer'. Drag the Adagietto and these complaints can seem justified; take it with spirit and the fine balance of the whole work is decisively revealed.

According to the tidy view of Mahler's symphonic output, the Fifth marks the start of a new phase. The genre of the vocal symphony has been left behind and does not return until the choral Eighth. Quasi-philosophical programmes are abandoned and a new and tauter style emerges, with starker orchestration and more tightly woven counter-point. The *Wunderhorn* years, it is said, are at an end. The music has moved from innocence to experience.

That is not wholly wrong but it needs qualifying, like virtually all firm statements about Mahler. Strictly speaking his style was already changing in the so-called 'last of the *Wunderhorn* symphonies', the Fourth, and in the songs with orchestra composed around the same time. And while it is true that he banished singers from the Fifth Symphony, several of his songs none the less lurk there in light disguise. Two of them are from the *Wunderhorn* collection. The theme of the first movement's funeral march is strikingly like that of *'Der Tamboursg'sell'* and the finale begins with a direct quote from the perky *'Lob des hohen Verstandes'* ('In praise of lofty intellect'), a satire on blockheaded critics. It is also hard to miss the similarity between the main theme of the Adagietto and that of *'Ich bin der Welt abhanden gekommen'*, Mahler's hymn to composing in solitude. The link is so obvious that some authorities take it as proof that the Adagietto cannot be a love declaration after all. Their argument is unconvincing. Is there no similarity between the joy of love and that of creation? Might not Mahler have felt just as much 'lost to the world' with Alma, at least at that stage of their relationship, as he did when composing? Besides, there is even a phrase in the Adagietto uncommonly like one from Wagner's *Tristan und Isolde*, which both Alma and Mahler revered.

So there is not such a firm line to be drawn between the Fourth and Fifth Symphonies after all, with respect to either the 'new style' or the influence of song. Nor is it clear that with the Fifth Mahler suddenly took a different attitude to programme music. True, he all but dropped giving movements explicit titles like *Pan awakes, summer marches in* and no longer produced synopses of what his symphonies 'meant'. He had learned the hard way that this approach was almost always counter-productive. As he exclaimed at a gathering in 1900 after conducting his Second Symphony, programmes simply aroused false impressions. 'If a composer himself has forced on his listeners the feelings which over-whelmed him, then he has achieved his object. The language of music has then approached that of the word, but has communicated immeasur-ably more than the word is able to express.' With that, we are told, Mahler raised his glass and cried, 'Death to programmes.'

Yet a year or so later he marked the first movement of the Fifth Symphony 'funeral march', adding to make the point crystal clear, 'with measured tread, austere, like a funeral cortège'. And besides comparing the scherzo to a comet's tail, he also told Natalie that 'it is a human being in the full light of day, in the prime of his life.' So even now he could not resist hinting that his work had, if not necessarily a fully fledged pro-gramme, at least extra-musical associations. As indeed it generally does, above all religious and philosophical ones. They cannot be pinned down bar by bar but they can very broadly be identified symphony by sym-phony; worldly triumph in the First, resurrection in the Second, panthe-ism in the Third, salvation through innocence in the Fourth. Each piece proposes a new answer to the riddle of life and death but it never starts from scratch. It builds on the experience of its predecessors, musically and philosophically. As the American conductor James Levine puts it, the works 'are all inter-related through the use of direct musical quotes, cross references or ideas hinted at in one symphony only to be fully developed in the next.'

In other words Mahler did not so much compose nine and a half separate symphonies (or ten and a half with *Das Lied von der Erde*) as a single, vast, constantly evolving one. Something of the same could be said of other symphonists, including Beethoven, but there is a closer analogy in literature. Mahler's symphonies are like the chapters of an epic novel, especially the most epic of all – Tolstoy's *War and Peace*, begun three years after Mahler was born. There is a similarly grand conception and bewildering range of incident, held together with technical mastery and developed in an inexorable, often tormented, quest for life's meaning.

Hence the danger of dividing up Mahler's output into neat phases and hence the overlap in this case between the Fourth and Fifth Symphonies.

Mahler even signals the overlap at the very start of the Fifth though it can be hard to identify right away. That initial menacing trumpet call clearly recalls Beethoven's Fifth but where else, one may wonder at first, has one come across it before? The answer is, note for note, at the main climax of the Fourth Symphony's first movement (and, rather less obviously, near the start of the 'Resurrection' Symphony). The difference is that in the Fourth it functions as what Mahler described as a 'little call to muster', easily restoring order to a cluster of jostling themes. In the Fifth it ushers in about twenty-five minutes of *Sturm und Drang* (storm and stress) largely unrelieved until the start of part two, the scherzo. Then the break is abrupt indeed. An almost indecently bright and breezy horn bursts in on part one's last gloomy bars, still hanging in the air like dust after an explosion. The work does not so much develop here as bolt off in another direction.

Although he left few extra-musical clues, there is a plausible answer as to what Mahler is up to. The Third Symphony reaches its musical and philosophical resolution via evolution ('from the lowest to the highest things'). The Fourth Symphony does so via simplification. In the Fifth Mahler presents two stark alternatives. He lays out the bad news first, then abruptly turns around in the scherzo as though to say, 'Mind you, there is another way of looking at all this.' Here the philosopher who comes to mind is not one we know Mahler studied closely, like Nietzsche, but the Dane Søren Kirkegaard (1813–55), whose classic *Either/Or* presents two persuasive but directly opposed views of life. Mahler does the same but, unlike Kierkegaard, he finally makes a choice. For the fifth time in a row (*pace* the Adorno-ites) he finds a credible route to optimism.

Strictly speaking, the *Either/Or* approach of the Fifth Symphony only magnifies a key element of Mahler's personality and work which was present all along. No one was more subject than he to brusque switches of mood for no apparent reason. No composer leaped more abruptly from the major to the minor mode, even within the same phrase, or more often undercut a noble chord with a banality. Indeed, this is a particular hallmark of his music. Bruckner, too, wrote ultra-long symphonies; Berlioz pioneered the orchestral song cycle and a lot of modern instrumentation; Beethoven called up bird-song and a storm for his 'Pastoral'; Liszt wrote programmatic choral symphonies (based on Goethe and Dante). But no composer matches Mahler's relentlessness in putting up and knocking down propositions almost simultaneously. Next to nothing is taken on trust.

That does not necessarily make Mahler what he is often called these days – a 'prophet of the age of anxiety'. But it does brand him as music's most consistent sceptic, especially appealing to those for whom former axioms about, say, religion, nation and family no longer hold. Sceptical though he was, Mahler usually managed to hammer out convincing answers for himself in his symphonies. At least they convinced him at the time. 'My dear friend,' he told Bruno Walter who had just referred to a serene phase of Mahler's life, 'I used to possess certainty, but I lost it again. I will regain it tomorrow and lose it once more the day after.'

Mahler seems to lose serenity most comprehensively in the Sixth Symphony. He began the work in 1903, a year after writing the bouncy end to the Fifth, but in this case there is not even an illness to cite as a superficial reason for the change of mood. It is as though Mahler simply decided that this time he would descend into the maelstrom come what may. Just to see what it was like? In the hope of getting the worst over with once and for all? At any rate a grim sense of purpose controls the work from its opening march to its final *pizzicato*, as bleakly unmistakable as a full stop, around eighty minutes later. Despite its huge orchestra with odd instruments like a celesta, hammer and cowbells, the Sixth is Mahler's most classical symphony – a quasi-traditional four-movement structure centred on a single key. That does not make the piece more comforting. Quite the contrary. The Fifth Symphony begins in the grating key of C sharp minor but ends in the affirmative one of D, an example of how Mahler uses 'progressive tonality' to help usher a work out of sorrow into joy. The Sixth Symphony, on the other hand, stays firmly imprisoned in A minor, a key often linked to the tragic in Mahler's work.

Alma had much to say about the Sixth in her *Memories and Letters* and, as usual, her comments have had great influence. She writes, for example, that Mahler said he had tried to portray her in 'the great soaring theme' of the first movement (its second subject). That could be true, but since the theme soars only briefly before breaking up, the portrait is not over-flattering. More suspect is Alma's claim that in the biting scherzo Mahler 'represented the arhythmic games of the two little children, tottering in zigzags over the sand. Ominously, the childish voices became more and more tragic, and died out in a whimper.' If that is really what Mahler pictured in sound then the two children cannot have been his own. When he wrote the scherzo in the summer of 1903 his first child was only about eight months old and his second one was not yet born.

Alma is at her least persuasive about the three great hammer blows in the finale. Again she may well be right in quoting Mahler as saying that here he portrays 'the hero, on whom fall three blows of fate, the last of which fells him as a tree is felled.' That fits Mahler's directions in the score. He initially wrote that each blow should be a 'short, powerful but dull-sounding stroke of a non-metallic character' but he later added the suggestion 'like the stroke of an axe'. It is also wholly credible that here (as in the First and Second Symphonies) Mahler identifies himself with the hero. But Alma goes further. The Sixth, she writes, is not only Mahler's most personal work but also 'a prophetic one. In the *Kindertotenlieder* and in the Sixth, he "musically anticipated" his life. He, too, received three blows from fate and the third did fell him.'

The 'three blows' Alma means are Mahler's later resignation from the Vienna Opera, the death of his elder daughter and his final heart ailment. Leaving aside for now the question whether the resignation was a disaster at all, Alma naturally fails to mention a fourth 'blow' – her own infidelity. If Mahler was being prophetic he should surely have had that one in too. In fact he ended up with only two hammer blows, deleting the third one after the first performance in Essen in 1906. It is widely assumed that he did so from superstition, trying to avoid his fate as it were by suppressing the *coup de grâce*. That approach is in line with Alma's, but there is a more down-to-earth explanation. After hearing the Sixth in Essen, Richard Strauss complained that the finale was too heavily orchestrated ('*überinstrumentiert*'). Mahler habitually revised his works after their first performances anyway but in this case the criticism from Strauss, the only colleague he would have heeded on the matter, must have acted as an extra spur. That summer much of the instrumentation fell to Mahler's red pencil, the third hammer blow included.

It is hard to say whether the Sixth is really Mahler's 'most personal' work as Alma suggests. There is so much competition for the title. Even if it is, that does not make its message any the less universal or disturbing. In the Fifth Symphony Mahler presents an alternative and comes out smiling. In the Sixth he seems to propose that the answers he found in all his previous symphonies were illusory. It is not just Mahler going down under those hammer blows but mankind itself.

Can any consolation be gleaned from this grimmest of works? Did Mahler do so himself? In a way. During that summer of 1904 when Mahler was finishing the Sixth, Alma invited a student friend of hers, Erica Conrat, to stay at Maiernigg. Happily Erica kept a diary which has survived. She reports that late one evening she was sitting on the terrace of the villa watching a distant firework display across the Wörther See when Mahler came out to join her and see the show. After a bit he began to philosophise. Goethe, he noted, had exalted all those who died in the fire of creativity. Even if one's life was only brief, like a rocket's, it gained meaning if one used every instant of it productively – for posterity.

Mahler was certainly using every instant that summer. He not only completed the Sixth and the *Kindertotenlieder* but, amazingly, he began work on a Seventh Symphony too. Before returning to Vienna he had completed two 'night music' movements, one a spooky piece which lurches along to screeches and flutters, the other a tender Andante amoroso with warbling clarinets serenading away against the strains of mandolin and guitar. It is as if Mahler set out to catch the spirit of the Wörther See at its most sinister and its most easeful. With the Sixth he had faced up to the worst imaginable and now, with hardly a pause for breath, a new work was starting to take shape. Carrying on despite everything – that was what counted.

It seems Mahler mentioned none of that in detail to Erica Conrat but he used Goethe obliquely to help say it for him. After a while he went back inside to the piano in the living-room 'and played a lot of short pieces by Bach, so clear and simple that one could have believed oneself in ancient Greece'. Erica stayed on the terrace watching the rockets soar aloft and plummet into the lake.

Chapter Seven

Triumph and Tragedy

IT WAS THE closest Mahler had yet come to realising an almost impossible dream. For more than two decades in some of Europe's best and seediest opera houses he had striven for performances in which music and drama fused perfectly. In spots like Laibach and Olmütz the task had been hopeless from the start; even in Budapest and Hamburg some missing elements still marred the greatest triumphs. At last in Vienna, in the première of a new production which made operatic history, virtually everything came together – singing and playing, acting and décor worthy of the composer's conception. The work was Wagner's *Tristan und Isolde* and the date 21st February 1903.

Even decades later, those lucky enough to be present that evening still spoke of it with awe. Erwin Stein, an Austrian musician who later fled before the Nazis to London, was bowled over by the intensity of Mahler's conducting. There was 'something feverish, even delirious' about it, he recalled, which matched the moods of the three acts – 'unrelieved yearning, white-hot passion and violent suffering'. And yet Mahler never lost control. The most shattering climaxes of all were carefully reserved for the rare pivotal moments of the drama – like the drinking of the potion in the first act and Isolde's appearance before the dying Tristan in the last. Stein's point is the more striking since Mahler was suffering so piercing a migraine that he all but collapsed in his dressing-room after the second act.

Anna von Mildenburg was already a fine Isolde but with Mahler conducting, at the première and on most succeeding evenings, she gave the performances of a lifetime. What little she lacked in strength of tone (her voice was rather weak at the very top), she more than made up for with acting of tragic grandeur. According to Stein, who surely spoke for many, Mildenburg was and remained unmatched in the role. No one else so tellingly put over all Isolde's conflicting emotions – her love and hate, gloom and rage, tenderness and spite. Her Tristan was the Danish Heldentenor Erik Schmedes, greatest in the tortured monologues of the last act. Perhaps there most of all Schmedes had cause to identify with the part. He had first clapped eyes on Mildenburg in a train years earlier while on his way to Vienna for an audition and had promptly fallen for her. She seemed to reciprocate at the time. Asked much later what happened then Schmedes claimed 'nothing', although he often partnered Mildenburg in romantic roles on-stage.

True or not, it is quite credible that in those *Tristan* performances Anna felt much closer to the conductor than to her stage lover, and that Mahler, a year after his marriage, still felt more than pride for the great singing actress he had begun to create in Hamburg almost from scratch. Certainly he felt a very special bond with *Tristan und Isolde* which may not have been due to the music alone. Increasingly often he would turn over other operas to his deputies, Bruno Walter and Franz Schalk – *Tristan* almost never. Of twenty-seven performances of the new production between 1903 and his resignation in 1907, Mahler conducted all but six.

Apart from Mahler and Mildenburg, it was Alfred Roller's sets and lighting which made the new *Tristan* so special. In the first act aboard ship, an orange-yellow sail towering above the sickly green radiance and shadows of a divided stage suggested the suppressed passion of the doomed couple. In the second act love duet, flaming red torchlight and the glinting of a myriad stars gave way to the sulphurous yellow clouds of dawn – and betrayal. When the curtain rose on the last act the audience could not suppress an 'ah' of wonder. In a scene suffused with grey but searingly brilliant light, the dying Tristan lay dwarfed by the walls of his castle and encircled by the roots of a huge lime tree. What one saw, Stein reported, perfectly matched what one heard.

Stein's comment applied to almost all the operas, more than a score of them, on which Mahler and Roller collaborated. The two seemed made for one another. Both were much the same age and came from the same area (Roller was born in 1864 in Brno, the Moravian capital); both were uncompromising idealists, snatching the chances Vienna offered but contemptuous of its shallow ways. The artist's eyes complemented the musician's ears. Yet oddly it remains a mystery how the two got together. Of the various versions Alma's is the best known. She says that Mahler met Roller at the Molls' house on the Hohe Warte in 1902 and began to talk about *Tristan*, then still being performed with the tired old designs. Roller, director of the Vienna School of Arts and Crafts, said he loved the music but could not bear to look at the scenery which ruined everything. He outlined his own ideas to Mahler who told Alma on the way home, 'that's the man for me.'

On the face of it that account looks plausible. It is usually claimed that Mahler and Roller first worked together on the new *Tristan* of 1903 so an encounter between them in 1902 seems to fit. The tale is also in line with Alma's view that it was thanks to her influence and contacts that Mahler at last began to develop a sense for the visual arts. However, tucked away in the archives of the Austrian National Library are sketches by Roller of sets for Wagner's early opera *Rienzi*, apparently for a new production Mahler staged in January 1901. There may thus have been a fledgeling start to the collaboration a couple of years earlier than is widely thought and more than a year before Mahler's marriage. The final proof is lacking. The records do show, however, that it was definitely Roller who designed the costumes (though not the décor) for a new production of Weber's *Euryanthe* premièred in January 1903 – one month before *Tristan*.

Whatever the truth about when the two first met, their partnership was the outstanding feature of the second half of Mahler's Vienna reign. To howls of fury from stick-in-the-muds and of delight from the rest, especially the young, Mahler and Roller went back to basics and re-created a stream of works most opera-goers thought they knew. The traditional presentation of Beethoven's *Fidelio* was one case in point. Roller felt much of it dramatically and musically absurd, especially the way in which an entire chorus of prisoners would march from the cells and line up on a brightly lit stage to burst into '*O welche Lust! In freier Luft den Atem leicht zu heben!*' (Oh what joy, in the open air to breathe with ease).

He felt the inmates should struggle up from the depths in twos and threes, feeling their way like 'poor, earthen, suffering worms' and only gradually winning the strength to sing. Mahler quite agreed, although the new scheme gave him cueing problems, but he had to fight it out with minions who whined that the chorus was being robbed of its star turn. 'What you theatre folk call your tradition,' Mahler snorted, according to Roller, 'is nothing other than your comfort and slovenliness' (*Was ihr Theaterleute euere Tradition nennt, das ist nichts anderes als euere Bequemlichkeit und Schlamperei*). The remark has often since been shortened and quoted out of context as the well-nigh meaningless 'Tradition is slovenliness' (*Tradition ist Schlamperei*). What Mahler really meant is clear enough. He and Roller got their way – and collected a few more foes.

The *Tristan* and *Fidelio* examples alone show Roller's versatility. He was designer and lighting expert, creative artist and handyman rolled into one. Just as fussy as Mahler, he would flit for hours from darkened auditorium to stage revising the tiniest details and brooding on the results. Yet like most revolutionary concepts, Roller's were often so simple it seemed odd that no one had tried them before. Contemporaries like the Swiss producer Adolphe Appia and the Englishman Gordon Craig had similarly bold ideas, but thanks to the Mahler connection Roller got the chance to apply his own consistently to the operatic stage. In Mozart's *Don Giovanni*, for instance, he for the first time placed two broad, semi-permanent pillars in the front corners of the stage. Easily adaptable with, say, windows or balconies, to fit different sets, the so-called 'Roller towers' aided the kind of quick scene changes which are nothing special now but were rare then. In Gluck's *Iphigenie in Aulis* in 1907, the last and perhaps finest Mahler-Roller production, the most sparse of décor and subtle of lighting intensified the drama by eschewing all superfluous effect. Nearly fifty years later Wieland Wagner was to adopt much the same approach in Bayreuth, initially to cries of outrage at the 'novelty' of it all. No doubt Roller's ghost had an ironic laugh.

It is easy to see why the Mahler decade, especially its second half, is called 'the golden age of the Vienna Opera'. That rather hazy description can mislead all the same. Even the most splendid era has drawbacks. Although Roller learned quickly, his initial inexperience with the sight lines between auditorium and stage meant part of the audience missed some of his best effects. Mahler's passion for singers who could act finely, admirable in itself, brought trouble too. He surely did not build an 'ensemble of disagreeable voices' as some ill-disposed critics claimed, but from time to time he gave artists roles they could play well although their voices were not strictly suitable. Perhaps there is also something in the claim that his productions rarely settled down because he constantly fiddled with staging and casts. No doubt now and then he would have done better to 'let well alone' but that was not in his nature. As Mildenburg said about him, one had the feeling that he was always on an endless voyage of discovery. She was talking about Mahler the theatre director but her remark applies equally to the composer.

If Mahler's addiction to experiment really was a flaw then it was one on the right side. More pertinent is the criticism that although he showed his re-creative genius with several revivals his choice of new works was far from unerring. True, he introduced Vienna to masterpieces like Verdi's *Falstaff*, Tchaikovsky's *Eugene Onegin* and *Pique Dame (The Queen of Spades)* and Smetana's *Dalibor*. But he also took on a string of novelties which flopped at the time and have hardly been heard of since; works like Leo Blech's *Das war ich (That was me)*, Josef Reiter's *Der Bundschuh (The Laced Shoe)* and Camille Erlanger's *Le Juif polonais (The Polish Jew)*. Weightier, at least more pretentious, than these trifles was *Die Rose vom Liebesgarten (The Rose from the Garden of Love)* by Hans Pfitzner, a neo-Romantic German composer who long pestered Mahler to stage the work. Mahler finally gave way, not least under pressure from Alma to whom Pfitzner made half-rebuffed advances for years. Once he had taken on *Die Rose* Mahler typically became keen on it, saying it had the best first act since Wagner's *Walküre*, a verdict posterity has not endorsed.

Sadly, Mahler conducted no opera by Berlioz, the French genius to whom he was surely closest. He was interested in Debussy's *Pelléas et Mélisande* but did not get round to it and he had something of a blind spot for Puccini. Sadder still, through little fault of his own, two of the century's finest works narrowly passed him by. One was the tragic *Jenůfa* by the Moravian composer Leoš Janáček. Mahler was unable to attend the 1904 première in Brno but was keen enough to ask for a piano version of the score with a German text. Janáček could not oblige and the contact faded. The other missed chance was Strauss's *Salome*. Mahler fought long and hard to put on the work but the censor would not budge, arguing that 'the representation of events which belong to the realm of sexual pathology are not suitable for our court stage'. In 1907, two years after that refusal, Vienna heard *Salome* anyway but not under Mahler. A visiting company from Breslau gave the work in a theatre not subject to the court censor.

The world première of *Salome* (like that of Strauss's *Feuersnot*) went to Dresden which was having something of a 'golden age' of its own. So was La Scala, Milan, under Arturo Toscanini, no less a perfectionist than Mahler and seven years younger, whose *Tristan* in 1901 brought gasps of delight from Siegfried Wagner. So was New York, which could muster singers (if not productions) even more outstanding than Vienna's. All the same, Vienna was matchless in one respect. Under Mahler and Roller, it stripped Mozart's operas of their Rococo trappings and revealed a depth and drama hitherto only hinted at. Astonishingly, in the pre-Mahler era the works had rarely been taken as seriously as they deserved. Half a century later Bruno Walter recalled that in his youth opera managements everywhere would hedge about staging Mozart, claiming 'better pieces' would draw the crowds.

Mahler in Vienna changed that, first with sporadic performances, then with new productions in the 1905–6 season of the five major operas (*Le Nozze di Figaro, Die Zauberflöte, Don Giovanni, Così fan Tutte* and *Die Entführung aus dem Serail*) to mark the 150th anniversary of Mozart's birth. Roller designed the sets and costumes, Mahler conducted with what Stein called 'the exceedingly subtle rubato that is implied in Mozart's melodies and does justice to both the high degree of their organisation and the perfect balance of their phrases'. It was a skill which, for all his majesty in much other repertoire, Toscanini never mastered in Mozart. The Viennese flocked in, at last convinced there were no 'better pieces' than these. For once Alma was perfectly correct when she noted that 'Mahler gave the signal to the whole world for the Mozart renaissance'.

During the winter of that Mozart cycle Alma and Mahler took a short break at Semmering, a sunny mountain resort south-west of Vienna. The trip was a big success. They took sleigh rides through the thick snow, drank grog and sang the great quartet from *Die Entführung aus dem Serail* with unflagging gusto. According to Alma, Mahler complained a lot about Mozart's widow Constanze whose speedy remarriage he found unforgivable. No doubt Alma had another view. She does not say.

Alma did not often record interludes in her life with Mahler as joyful as that one. Perhaps they really were few and far between. She clearly became quickly bored by Mahler's routine, no less stringent in Vienna than it was 'on holiday' in Maiernigg. Their flat in the Auenbruggergasse, which Mahler had shared with Justi, was spacious but nothing special. Mahler was up promptly at seven, snatched breakfast brought by the maid and worked until nine, revising or orchestrating his summer's compositions. The opera house was about fifteen minutes' walk away. Mahler spent the morning there, then raced back at 1 p.m. punctually for lunch. He rang the bell on the ground floor and when he got to the flat on the fourth the soup had to be on the table. Afternoons – brisk walks, often in the park of the Belvedere palace nearby; evenings – opera again, even when Mahler was not conducting; late night – supper usually at home, talk on the sofa, and so to bed. Alma and Mahler had separate bedrooms at opposite ends of the flat.

Alma was not just bored, she was deeply frustrated. Her diaries reveal that far better than her books. On 13th December 1902, nine months after her marriage and five weeks after the birth of her first child Maria, nicknamed 'Putzi', Alma noted that 'I feel as though my wings have been clipped. Gustav, why did you bind to you this splendid bird so happy in flight, when a heavy grey one would have suited you better? There are so many heavy ducks and geese who cannot fly at all.' There were also, to remain with the imagery, some entrancing songbirds around as Alma well knew. A month later she shook with jealousy on spying Mahler and some of his divas after a rehearsal for *Euryanthe*. 'Gustav let those whores drink out of his glass,' she scribbled. 'He disgusts me so much that I dread his coming home. Playful, charming, cooing, like a young man he danced around Mildenburg and [Lucie] Weidt. My God! If only he never came home again. Not to live with him any more! I'm so agitated that I can scarcely write.'

When Mahler returned that evening and tried to embrace her, Alma pushed him aside. 'The next day we had it out in the Stadtpark. He said he felt clearly that I did not love him. He was right. After what happened, everything in me was cold.' Yet in the very next sentences Alma adds, 'But suddenly my feelings were all there again. Once more, I know how much I love him. I am determined to be calm.' Alma's switchback moods were no less vertiginous than Mahler's.

The baby was no help either. Alma was about the last person to find fulfilment caring for an infant. It had been a breech birth (i.e. bottom first) and that appealed to Mahler's sense of humour. 'That's my child,' he teased on hearing the news, 'showing the world straight off the part it deserves.' Alma was not amused. She noted in her diary that Maria's birth had cost her dreadful pain. 'I don't yet love her as much as I should.'

Alma's attitude did not change. Even her memoirs (let alone her diary) suggest admiration rather than love, as though she were recalling someone else's daughter. In a way she was. Maria, she wrote, was 'entirely' Mahler's child. 'Very beautiful, defiant and unapproachable, she promised to become dangerous. Black locks, great blue eyes.' The little girl would go into Mahler's study each morning and emerge later, usually smeared with jam from top to toe. 'They held long conversations there together,' Alma wrote. 'Nobody has ever known what about. I never disturbed them.' She became closer to her second child, Anna, but it was a slow process. Decades later, after Anna showed great skill as a sculptress, she recalled Alma telling her, 'If I had known you as I know you now, I wouldn't have treated you so miserably.' Talent always impressed Alma.

Above all else, at the start anyway, Alma missed her music. According to her diary, new works welled up in her so strongly that she felt them behind her every word and could not sleep at night. She told Mahler but, not surprisingly, he brushed her complaints aside: he had warned her from the first that there could only be one composer in the family. 'My God,' Alma wrote bitterly, 'how hard it is to be so mercilessly deprived of everything, to be mocked about things closest to one's heart. Gustav lives his life. My child has no need of me, I cannot occupy myself only with her! Now I'm learning Greek...'

There were some compensations. From time to time the Mahlers had fascinating guests. For instance Alma's old flame Alex Zemlinsky would turn up with Schönberg, then aged around thirty, who initially spurned Mahler's music but gradually became a disciple after hearing the Third Symphony in 1904. Mahler, on the other hand, recognised Schönberg's quality the moment he came across the early (1899) string sextet *Verklärte Nacht (Transfigured Night)*. He later had trouble with Schönberg's swing away from tonality but defended him all the same, arguing, 'He is young and perhaps he is right.' At the première of the radical First String Quartet in February 1907, he almost came to blows with one of the scandalised members of the audience who were hissing the performance. Not that he always took Schönberg's part during those evenings at home with Zemlinsky and Alma around the piano. Schönberg would be provocative, Mahler haughty and the sessions often ended in storm. Mahler would thunder that the two should never darken his door again, but he soon relented and back they came.

Other visitors tickled Alma's intellect less but that was not everything. Pfitzner tended to call when Mahler was not present, sick with desire for Alma. She was less ardent. His brief embraces gave her an all-too-rare 'prickling of the skin' but when he was not there she did not pine for him. Gustave Charpentier, a French composer in town because Mahler was staging his opera *Louise*, made for a pleasing diversion too. He sent bouquets of flowers every day to 'Madame Mahler, gracious muse of Vienna from the grateful muse of Montmartre' and squeezed her knee during a performance of *Tristan*. On the street, Alma noticed 'with yearning and joy' that a young man was following her. Later she wrote, 'In my heart I was unfaithful to Gustav – only in my heart. But he knows it.'

No doubt Mahler did know but his hundreds of letters to Alma do not show it, at least not until much later when she abandoned flirting for a serious affair. Sometimes he ticked her off for moaning, telling her in essence to snap out of it and 'keep a stiff upper lip'. Sometimes he seemed to lose patience with her jealousy, once exploding on-page with a meaningless but expressive '*Himmelherrgottkreuztausenddonnerundhagelsappermentnocheinmal*!' over Alma's renewed suspicion that he was carrying on with Mildenburg. But even that outburst was rounded off with 'See you again the day after tomorrow, my sweet Almscherl, silly little sausage. Warmest kisses. Your Gustav.'

Many of the letters were playful and loving like the ending of that last one, full of queries about Putzi and Gucki (Anna) and regrets that Alma did not come more often on business trips. There were a lot of them. After the breakthrough in Krefeld with the Third Symphony in 1902, Mahler and his music were in growing demand. As a guest conductor he criss-crossed Europe giving concerts in more than a score of cities from St Petersburg to Trieste, Berlin to Strasbourg, Basle to Breslau. The interminable train journeys gave Mahler no pleasure but his growing recognition did, especially in Holland. Mahler fell for the country immediately, bubbling to Alma about 'these long straight canals converging from all sides and shining like streaks of silver, these houses and over it all a grey-blue sky with countless flocks of birds. It's so lovely.' At the Rijksmuseum in Amsterdam he stood transfixed before Rembrandt's *The Nightwatch*, later linking it with the first 'night-music' movement of his Seventh Symphony. He really was learning to use his eyes at last.

Mahler was still keener on the Dutch musicians and public. At the first rehearsal for his Third Symphony with the Amsterdam Concertgebouw Orchestra in October 1903, he confessed himself 'quite stunned. It's really breathtaking. The orchestra is excellent and has been very well prepared.' For that he had Mengelberg to thank who, along with a couple of other Dutch conductors, had been present at the Krefeld première and became a fan straight away. On returning, he laid the basis for a Mahler cult in Holland unbroken (but for the Nazi occupation) to this day. During that first visit Mahler conducted his First as well as his Third Symphony and, overwhelmed by the jubilant reception, could not resist boasting to Alma, 'Everyone tells me there has been nothing like it in human memory. Strauss is very much in vogue here, but I'm now head and shoulders above him.' A year later he was back again conducting his Second and Fourth Symphonies, the latter twice over in the same concert (not, as Alma claims, sharing the concert with Mengelberg). He could hardly have risked repeating the Fourth like that elsewhere, certainly not in Vienna, although even there audiences were warming to some of his music. When he gave his 'Resurrection' Symphony at his last Vienna concert in November 1907, it was greeted with 'a hurricane of applause'.

Alma was present on some key occasions in distant parts but more often than not she stayed at home. In view of her boredom there that may seem odd. Sometimes she pleaded illness, more often lack of cash and the need to look after the children. At the very start funds may well have been tight but surely not for long. Mahler's growing post-Krefeld fame meant not only that he could earn at least 2000 crowns for each guest concert, in addition to his opera salary and perks. He also signed a contract in 1903 with C.F. Peters, a celebrated Leipzig publisher, bringing him 20,000 crowns for the Fifth Symphony alone – big money for Mahler, albeit less than the kind of sums Strauss was getting for his work.

As for Alma's housework, she had a maid and an English nurse to help her in both Vienna and Maiernigg. It is not clear how much house-keeping money she was getting in her first years of marriage. But a post-card from 1905 shows that at that time Mahler was paying her 1000 crowns monthly (equivalent nowadays to more than 8000 Deutschmarks or 3000 pounds sterling), one of the points Alma deleted from her edition of her husband's letters. All in all, what is known of the family finances suggests Alma could have afforded many more trips had she wished. Perhaps she hated being cooped up in railway carriages even more than Mahler. More likely she simply did not want to hear his music that often. Although she helped copying the manuscripts in the summer and temporarily fell under the spell of some of the works, she was never really converted. Her pre-marriage outburst about disliking the few Mahler works she knew was meant to shock, and did, but it was no lie. As she admitted in her diary four years after Mahler's death, 'Gustav's music was strange to me. For a short time, with the utmost effort of will, I got closer to it but now it is strange again and it will stay strange.'

Despite squabbles with Alma, mini-crises at the opera and tediously familiar sniping in the press, Mahler was riding high in 1906. For one thing the Mozart cycle turned out to be a financial as well as artistic success so that the opera almost kept to its budget for the year as a whole. In 1905 it had overshot badly and Mahler had come under fire even from his usually staunch ally Prince Montenuovo. Thanks to Mozart and a rise in seat prices, takings were up in 1906 and Mahler managed simultane-ously to cut costs.

Not that the result was even close to a profit. Then, as now, no opera house could make ends meet without a subsidy of some kind. Mahler's court employer always specified in advance the 'tolerable deficit' which it expected to have to make good for the coming year. For 1906 the pro-jected figure was 200,000 crowns. The real shortfall turned out to be 209,000 crowns. That result was of course seized on by critics of ill will to show how Mahler and his spendthrift stage designer were driving the opera into the red. For the rest it indicated, on the contrary, that Mahler had his house under control despite his regular leaves of absence to conduct his own works. In May the première of his Sixth Symphony in Essen drew only lukewarm applause, but the faithful Dutch were already taking up the initially unpopular Fifth. No sooner had Mahler given the work in Amsterdam in March than Mengelberg repeated it there and took it on tour to four other Dutch cities.

Back in Maiernigg in that summer of 1906, Mahler seemed wholly recovered from the 'composer's block' which had tortured him a year earlier when he had settled down at his hut to complete the Seventh. Two of the middle movements were already written by 1904 but in 1905, after a year's break, the rest of the symphony stubbornly refused to be born. Mahler vainly struggled for a fortnight to get the work going again, then fled for a few days to the Dolomites hoping for inspiration. Nothing happened and he headed sadly home, sure his summer would be wasted. He was saved on the very last stage of the journey as he was being rowed back to the villa across the Wörther See. 'With the first stroke of the oar,' he wrote later to Alma, 'the theme (or rather the rhythm and the type) of the introduction to the first movement came to me.' The dam broke and the rest of the Seventh poured forth.

In 1906 the opposite happened. It was as if Mahler's next work, the massive Eighth Symphony, had been waiting in the woods to overpower him. Four years later he recalled that 'on the first day of the holidays I went up to the hut at Maiernigg with the firm resolution of idling the holidays away (I needed to so much that year) and recruiting my strength. On the threshold of my old workshop the Spiritus Creator took hold of me and shook me and drove me on for the next eight weeks until my greatest work was done.' With its eight soloists, choirs, orchestra and organ the so-called '*Symphonie der Tausend*' ('Symphony of a Thousand') is Mahler's largest composition. At its Munich première in 1910 it brought him the biggest popular success of his life. Whether it is really his greatest work as he several times claimed is another matter. At any rate that summer Mahler was in ecstatic mood, reporting to Mengelberg in mid-August, 'I have just completed my Eighth . . . Just imagine that the universe is beginning to sound and ring. It is no longer human voices, but circling planets and suns.'

All in all, it is hard to think of another year which went better for Mahler than 1906. Yet by the end of 1907 he had abandoned the Vienna Opera (and the Maiernigg villa) for good and gone with Alma to New York. Many have argued that he was driven from his post an almost broken man. That is a myth although it is true that after deciding to leave for America, literally to seek his fortune, he suffered a couple of bitter personal blows. Two events in 1906 which are easy to overlook give some clues as to what really happened.

In May the Mahlers joined Strauss in Graz, a provincial but artistically bold little town, for the Austrian première of *Salome*. According to Alma, on the day of the performance they all went for a trip in the country which proved so enjoyable that Strauss was reluctant to return to Graz to conduct. He budged only when Mahler finally threatened to go and do the job himself. Alma suggests Strauss may have been covering up inner tension under a show of frivolity but acknowledges that the performance that evening was 'a great success'. The next morning at breakfast Strauss laid into Mahler for taking everything, like the opera house, too seriously. He should look after himself better. No one would thank him for grinding himself to bits. 'A pigsty that won't even perform *Salome*. Not worth it, I tell you.'

For once Alma quite agreed with Strauss. She does not say how Mahler reacted at the time but the remarks could hardly fail to strike home. He was nearly forty-six years old and more than half his life had been spent in the opera business. Even in Vienna his vision of ideal performance was often shattered by routine and intrigue. The Mozart festival was all very fine but, unlike Bayreuth, Vienna could not live from festivals alone. Strauss was right about *Salome* and, Mahler must have thought, might well be right about other things too. He was always going on about money but he was clear in his aim, to become independent of the opera house as soon as possible and devote himself to composing. Wasn't that what Mahler really wanted too, that and the chance to conduct his works even more often? For all the careful instruction he wrote into his scores, Mahler acknowledged that his music remained for its interpreters 'a book with seven seals'. If he did not establish a tradition of correct performance then no one would.

Even if Strauss's comments that May were not decisive they must at least have acted as a catalyst. For in August Mahler let slip to Bernard Scharlitt, a music critic, that 'I shall depart in the next year from the Court Opera because in the course of time I have become convinced that the idea of a permanent opera company directly contradicts modern principles of art.' There is no evidence that when Mahler made that forecast he already knew just how he could win more time for creative work without taking a cut in income. But that autumn an answer began to emerge by an unexpected route.

In October the great Italian tenor Enrico Caruso made a guest appearance in *Rigoletto* at the Vienna Opera, an event preceded by much haggling over fees with Heinrich Conried, Caruso's manager. The Austrian-born Conried had gone to New York as an actor, managed several small theatre companies with aplomb and in 1903 burst to stardom as director of the 3600-seat Metropolitan Opera House. He did not know much about music but he could pick talent and he had a head for figures. He was also without scruple. Although Wagner and later his widow had forbidden performances of *Parsifal* outside Bayreuth, Conried staged it anyway and fought off the resulting litigation. He reckoned that, if nothing else, *Parsifal's* curiosity value would make it a success in New York. He was right.

It is not clear when Conried began bidding for Mahler but he probably had his eye on him by the end of 1906. Shortly after that Vienna *Rigoletto*, which had brought the first albeit distant contact between the two directors, Conried suffered two serious setbacks. In November Caruso, his ace, was arrested in New York and fined for molesting a woman in the monkey house of the Central Park zoo. There were signs the affair was a put-up job, meant to create a bad press for Caruso which in turn would harm his employer. In any case it did. A month later Conried's life became tougher still when Oscar Hammerstein, another canny impresario, set up his Manhattan Opera House to rival the Met. Conried badly needed to hit back. The weapon he chose, and finally obtained, was Mahler.

The New World had had Mahler in its sights before. As early as 1887, when he was struggling for supremacy against Nikisch in Leipzig, Mahler had been invited to replace the conductor Anton Seidl in New York. Later there were rumours, which he denied, that he was going to Boston. There is no doubt, on the other hand, that he seriously considered the offer of a dual post as a conductor and director in New York made to him in 1898, the year after he took over in Vienna. At least he got as far as seeking advice about the kind of fee he should demand. It seems amazing that he was ready even to think of leaving Vienna so soon after getting there, but clearly the 'land of unlimited opportunities' (and matchless earnings) was already hard to resist. Plenty of Mahler's colleagues felt the same, not least Strauss. In 1904 he gave more than thirty highly lucrative concerts in America, including two performances of his *Sinfonia Domestica* before cheering crowds in Wanamaker's New York department store. Pauline Strauss went along too to perform her husband's lieder and was regularly showered with lavish bouquets. Word of this triumphant, if at times artistically dubious, tour can have escaped neither Mahler nor Alma.

In other words, in seeking to hire Mahler Conried was pushing at a half-open door. Even so he found the negotiations tricky. At one stage Mahler seemed ready to pull out of them, asking his agent about prospects of a deal with Conried's arch-rival Hammerstein instead. Perhaps that was merely a ploy to extract better terms from Conried. Mahler's whole career shows that he was no innocent when it came to bargaining. Finally the skirmishing stopped and on 21st June 1907 the two signed a contract covering the four years 1908–11. Under it, Mahler was to get 75,000 crowns each year for three months' conducting (January to April), plus all expenses paid for first-class travel and lodging. The sum was thus more than double Mahler's total annual earnings in Vienna of 36,000 crowns (basic salary of 14,000 crowns plus perks), for which he not only conducted but ran the opera house too. It was a good deal by any standards, even Strauss's. When he read its details in Alma's memoirs in 1946, Strauss penned a pungent *'Na also!'* (So there we are!) in the margin.

Against that background, it is hard to justify the claim that Mahler was run out of town. It is true that there were further personnel upsets at the opera in early 1907 and renewed newspaper attacks, some blatantly anti-Semitic. Howling that Mahler was 'neglecting his duties', the weekly *Die Zeit* carried a cartoon series showing him either obsessed with his own compositions or resting in his office after a taxing holiday. Mahler still had plenty of allies all the same, not just in the press (which broadly hailed the new *Iphigenie* in March) but well beyond. The names under a public declaration of support for him in May read like a *'Who's Who'* of culture in Vienna – Klimt and von Hofmannsthal, Schnitzler and Schönberg, Bahr and Burckhard to name just a few. Touchingly, old Julius Epstein signed too, the professor who had helped Mahler enter the conservatory more than three decades before. If Mahler had really wanted to stay he could have done so and he knew it. The truth was he wanted to leave. Some of his friends including Guido Adler, who had hatched a plan to keep Mahler in Vienna as head of a wholly reorganised conservatory of music, hinted that Alma was the real driving force behind his decision to go. In this case they probably do her an injustice. She surely jumped at the prospect of a more luxurious life in a new and exciting city, but Mahler needed no persuading.

He could not simply walk out on his Vienna job all the same. The emperor had to approve his request for release from his duties and simultaneously name a successor. A suitable one, good enough for the opera but not too keen on conducting elsewhere, would not be easy to find. So when Mahler left in late June for his usual Maiernigg holiday, he was already locked into his contract with Conried without knowing exactly when he would formally cease to be director in Vienna. Still, there were several months left to sort that out. In the event an answer was found in October with the appointment of Felix Weingartner from Berlin (who kept the job just three years).

Mahler soon had far worse things on his mind. A few days after arrival in Maiernigg his elder daughter, the adored Putzi, went down with scarlet fever and diphtheria. Little Gucki had caught the same illness in May but recovered. Putzi did not. For nearly a fortnight, while the usual summer storms rumbled around the Wörther See, she lay at the villa fighting for her life. Towards the end when she threatened to suffocate the doctor tried to relieve her with a tracheotomy, cutting into the windpipe to her lungs. During the operation Alma fled weeping to the lakeside. Putzi survived, choking, for one more day. She died on 12th July, not yet five years old. Mahler ran to and fro sobbing. Alma's mother came and all three of them, dreading to be left alone, slept in Mahler's room. Later, when a hearse took the coffin away, both women collapsed.

That account of those dreadful weeks is taken from Alma's memoirs. It is the only first-hand one available but there is no good reason to doubt its details thus far. What Alma wrote next, however, helped create a pernicious legend still widely believed. She says that after she and her mother broke down the local doctor came. 'Mahler, thinking to make a cheerful diversion and distract us from our gloom said: "Come along, doctor, wouldn't you like to examine me too?" The doctor did so. He got up looking very serious. Mahler was lying on the sofa and Dr [Carl] Blumenthal had been kneeling beside him. "Well, you've no cause to be proud of a heart like that," he said in the cheery tone doctors often adopt after diagnosing a fatal disease. This verdict marked the beginning of the end for Mahler. . . . [He] went to Vienna by the next train to consult Professor [Friedrich] Kovacs, who fully confirmed the verdict of the general practitioner; hereditary, although compensated, valve defects on both sides.'

The way Alma presents all that suggests Mahler was virtually given a death sentence. He was not. The diagnosis of 'compensated' defects (curiously omitted from English editions of Alma's book) meant he could live with the problem if he took care. It is hardly material whether he was really born with it, inheriting his mother's weak heart, or gradually acquired it, for instance through youthful bouts of rheumatic fever. Evidently he had had it for a long time and it had not stopped him leading a hyperactive life. The doctors were now telling him to take things easier. To that extent his impending departure from the Vienna Opera was splendid timing.

Even if the diagnoses were no death sentence, Mahler might have taken them as such – although a letter he wrote to Alma on 30th August showed he well understood what he was being told. In it Mahler said he had been for an inoculation to a Dr Franz Hamperl in Vienna who had examined his heart at the same time. 'He found a slight valvular defect, which is entirely compensated, and he makes nothing of the whole affair. He tells me I can certainly carry on with my work just as I did before and in general lead a normal life, apart from avoiding over-fatigue. It is funny but in substance he said just what Blumenthal said, but his whole way of saying it was somehow reassuring.'

That letter was long thought to have been written in March, implying that Mahler was already under scrutiny for heart trouble at an early stage and that his condition had worsened by the summer. The true date of 30th August is now beyond doubt. But yet another letter, this one to Alma from Mahler in January, has caused much confusion too. In it Mahler wrote, 'You see Almschi, one does not die of it – look at Mama with her heart – one goes full speed ahead and suddenly comes the crash.' That extract seems to indicate Mahler is talking about his own health, and it has been widely taken that way. But Mahler goes on to urge Alma to look after herself and pledges that when he returns to Vienna he will take her on a cure. In other words she is the one with a complaint which,

Mahler assures her, is not fatal. His diagnosis was right. Alma had all sorts of aches and pains but she lived on until 1964.

The lightish tone of that August letter does not mean Mahler had simply shrugged off the events of the summer. He hated the idea of dropping his habitually violent exercise, as the doctors advised. Above all he suffered deeply from Putzi's death though he bottled up his grief. As for Alma, 'She seems to take it better,' wrote Bruno Walter to his parents, 'with tears and philosophising.' It was an acute observation. Thirteen years later Alma briefly referred in her diary to Putzi's death. It is a chilling entry, oddly little noted, in which she reflects on how often ill has befallen those on whom she has wished it.

On one occasion, Alma recalls, she and Mahler had driven by their house and seen Putzi pressing her 'endlessly beautiful dark curls' against a window pane. 'Gustav gave her a loving wave. Was that it? I don't know – but suddenly I *knew*: this child must go . . . *and at once. In God's name.* Away with the thought! Away with the accursed thought. But the child was dead a few months later. Freud explains these desires as perverted fear . . . Gustav's death too – I wanted that. I once loved another and he was the wall over which I could not climb.' When she later went over the typescript of that entry, Alma wrote in a few changes. The only one of real substance was the smallest. After the sentence 'Gustav's death too – I wanted that' she inserted a question mark.

On 15th October 1907, Mahler conducted at the Vienna Opera for the last time. It was his 648th performance there in not quite ten and a half years. The work was *Fidelio*. On 7th December, in a farewell message to the whole company, he wrote, 'Instead of the whole, the complete creation, that I had dreamt of, I leave behind something piecemeal and imperfect – as man is fated to do. It is not for me to judge what my work has been to those for whose sake it was done. But at such a moment I am entitled to say of myself: I was honest in my intentions, and I set my sights high. . . . In the throes of the battle, in the heat of the moment, neither you nor I have been spared wounds, or errors. But when a work has been successfully performed, a task accomplished, we have forgotten all the difficulties and exertions; we have felt richly rewarded even in the absence of the outward signs of success. We have all made progress, and so has the institution for which we have worked.' The message was pinned up on a notice-board. Later someone tore it off and scattered the pieces on the floor.

Two days afterwards Mahler and Alma took the early morning train for Paris, *en route* for Cherbourg and the liner to America. Around 200 friends and fans gathered at the station to see them off. Bruno Walter, Alfred Roller and Arnold Rosé were there of course, so were singers like Erik Schmedes and Marie Gutheil-Schoder as well as the avant-garde triumvirate Schönberg, Berg and Webern. Mahler had wanted no fuss but he was touched and went round warmly shaking hands. Many of those present were in tears. 'It had all been arranged overnight,' wrote Paul Stefan, a music critic. 'No official personages had been informed. There was not a scrap of artificiality: just an urgent desire to see him once again, this man to whom we owed so much. . . . The train moved off. And Gustav Klimt gave voice to what we all felt and feared: "It's over!"'

Chapter Eight

America

Turn-of-the-century New York, according to the American writer Theodore Dreiser, offered 'glory for those who enter its walls seeking glory, happiness for those who come seeking happiness. A world of comfort and satisfaction for all who take up their abode within it.' Well, not quite all. Dreiser admitted there were 100,000 or so poverty-stricken New Yorkers – among them Greeks, Italians, Russians, Poles, Syrians, Hungarians and Jews – whose children grew up in conditions like those of a slum in Constantinople. But that bitter aspect apart, New York was 'an island of beauty and delight'.

It was also a huge building site. The main railway stations were under construction and the first subway lines were being opened. Gas lights were being replaced by electric ones, making of Broadway a 'great white way' in which vehicles fluttered about like 'jeweled flies' (Dreiser). The tallest skyscrapers were yet to come but already the Manhattan skyline looked bold enough to thrill new arrivals, especially those slowly approaching by liner after days at sea. Gustav and Alma Mahler were no exception. When they sailed into New York harbour on 21st December 1907, aboard the SS *Kaiserin Augusta Victoria*, the sights and bustle took their breath away.

As he disembarked, Mahler was pounced on by reporters wanting to know when he would replace Conried as director of the Metropolitan. It was an open secret in New York that Conried's days in the top job were numbered, partly because his health was poor (he died in 1909), partly because his often outlandish tactics had alienated the Metropolitan's all-powerful executive committee. To most interested parties it seemed obvious that Mahler was the coming man: after all, he had taken over as a mere 'conductor' in Vienna exactly ten years before only to become director there a few months later. At his dockside press conference Mahler firmly denied any plans to step into Conried's shoes. That was certainly true. He had not cast off a director's burden in Vienna only to shoulder one again in New York. Whether his denial was believed is another matter.

The Mahlers had been promised first-class accommodation in New York and they were given it. Their suite on the eleventh floor of the Majestic hotel had a giant salon, two bedrooms, two bathrooms, two pianos and a fine view to the east over Central Park. They had hardly begun to unpack when an emissary arrived to take them to lunch with Conried, in the circumstances a rather delicate meeting. It was also a very odd one. 'The super-God Conried', as Alma called him, reclined on a divan set under a canopy supported by convoluted pillars. In one corner of the room stood a suit of armour with red lights glowing from within. The Mahlers could hardly hide their mirth over Conried's 'utter innocence of culture', and burst out laughing once they were back in the street.

Otherwise they had little to laugh about. It was Christmas time, Putzi was dead and Gucki had been left behind with the Molls in Vienna. According to Alma, Mahler stayed half the time in bed 'to spare himself'. She spent sleepless nights walking up and down the suite, then sitting on the stairs in the early morning straining to catch some sound of human life below. On Christmas Eve a well-wisher called and took them out to dinner but the relief was short-lived. Some actors and actresses joined the party, one of them a 'raddled female called Putzi'. Gustav and Alma fled back to the Majestic.

So began Mahler's time in America. It has generally been judged harshly, even as a failure, and part of the reason is clear enough. Accept the legend that Mahler left Vienna all but broken under the 'three blows' of fate and the rest follows. A man brought so low is unlikely to make a comeback anywhere, let alone in an alien continent far from his colleagues, friends and remaining child. Alma's account of that first Christmas, which there is no reason to doubt, seems to fit well into that grim picture. Mahler surely was grieving over Putzi, concerned about his health and dismayed by the ructions at the Met, but he had proved his resilience often enough before. When he arrived in New York he was down but very far from out. Although his subsequent American career had troughs, above all in its second half, it was a greater success than is often supposed.

Mahler was no exile in America. By his own choice, he spent several lucrative and initially not very strenuous periods there each year. Not surprisingly he suffered bouts of longing for Europe, as well as bursts of enthusiasm for the exuberant and refreshing New World, but he hardly had to wait long to see 'home' again. His four American seasons up to the spring of 1911 lasted, all in all, not quite twenty months. That is less, for example, than the time Mahler's Bohemian contemporary Dvořák spent away from his roots as director of New York's National Conservatory of Music in the three years 1892–95. And Dvořák strayed well beyond the 'more European' east coast, getting as far as Iowa and Nebraska. Mahler went no further from New York City than the 470 miles to Cleveland, Ohio (for a one-night stand during a concert tour). Most of his time was spent in Europe, mainly composing and conducting his own works. That certainly kept him busy, arguably it over-strained him, but that is what he had always wanted to do.

There is another, more complex, reason why Mahler's American time has tended to be undervalued. It has less to do with Mahler himself and more with the mingled awe, envy and ignorance with which Europe and America viewed (and in part still view) one another. Plenty of Europeans saw America as *the* land of opportunity and big money but also as a cultural desert in which New York was hardly distinguishable from the Wild West. The very phrase 'Mahler in Manhattan' had about it a ring almost as incongruous as, say, 'Beethoven in Bombay'. Alma's snide little sketch of the (Austrian-born!) Conried with his ridiculous divan and illuminated suit of armour was bound to meet with knowing nods and winks in many European salons.

Naturally Americans resented this patronising attitude and had long been hitting back. In *The Innocents Abroad* (1869) Mark Twain debunked the superficially attractive but decadent culture he had seen (through) on a tour of Europe. In his novels, Henry James (1843–1916) often pitted American heroes and heroines bursting with moral integrity against corrupt and devious Europeans. Such salvoes rather overshot the mark but in the circumstances they were not surprising. Nor was the pique, especially among the critics, over European ignorance of musical life in America, including New York. After all, the New York Philharmonic Society had been founded as early as 1842. That meant its orchestra was as old (if admittedly not as good) as the Vienna Philharmonic, and older than similar bands in Berlin, Amsterdam or London. The rival New York Symphony followed in 1878, founded by the German-born Leopold Damrosch and later taken over by his son Walter. By 1900 cities including Philadelphia, Chicago, Pittsburgh and Cincinatti had fine orchestras too and Boston had the finest of all, thanks not least to a four-year spell under Mahler's old rival Nikisch. Mahler well knew of the Boston Symphony's excellence. He turned down an offer of the directorship himself but warmly recommended the job to Mengelberg, albeit without result.

Opera was not widespread but it had been a firm feature of the scene in New York at least since 1854, when the Academy of Music opened there with the world's biggest stage and room for an audience of 4600. Despite claims to the contrary, New York opera was never a matter only for the 'upper crust'. But it is true that its financing ultimately depended on the rich and that a box at the Academy, and later at the Met, was a much sought-after status symbol. Indeed it was largely because the Academy had too few boxes in which top people could put their wealth and beauty on show that a group of millionaires founded the Met in 1883. The new house had two rows of boxes nicknamed the 'Golden Horseshoe' (later consolidated into a still more exclusive 'Diamond Horseshoe'), held by families whose total wealth was estimated at around 540 million dollars – equivalent to many billions today.

Initially everything at the Met, even Italian opera, was given in German and there was a heavy diet of Wagner spiced with singers tempted over from Bayreuth. Later even box-holders, who anyway tended to arrive late, leave early and chatter most of the time, rebelled against this Teutonic excess and French and Italian works began to be heard in the original. Merely reading through the cast lists, with names

[159]

like Emma Calvé, Nellie Melba, Marcella Sembrich, Pol Plançon and the de Reszke brothers, is enough to turn most modern opera buffs green with envy. When Hammerstein set up his rival Manhattan house in 1906 he produced the startlingly nimble Italian tenor Alessandro Bonci as his 'answer' to the Met's Caruso, along with stars like John McCormack, Luisa Tetrazzini and Mary Garden. The gibe that New York loved voices more than music no doubt has some truth in it – but what voices they were, their strength and beauty still evident even now through all the vagaries of primitive recording.

Box-holders might be show-offs and the general public mainly dote on high Cs, but broadly speaking New York's music critics knew their stuff. There were plenty of them, indeed a real flood by today's standards. The greater New York area at the turn of the century had more than thirty newspapers, many of which ran music reviews on a regular basis. Leading critics included Richard Aldrich of the *Times*, which even then had a daily circulation of more than 200,000; William Henderson of the *Sun*, author of several opera libretti; Reginald de Koven of the *World*, also a prolific composer; Henry Finck of the *Evening Post*, who had studied music and philosophy and been present at the first Bayreuth *Ring* in 1876. Arguably the most influential and certainly the most pugnacious was Henry Krehbiel, who remained critic of the *Daily Tribune* for about forty years. His fierce glare, bull-neck and jutting chin seemed to equip him more for the boxing ring than the concert hall. But he was scholarly too, among other things editing and publishing an English-language version of Alexander Thayer's classic work on Beethoven. Krehbiel over-estimated himself as the supreme arbiter of musical taste in America, but he was well informed and a master of pungent prose.

Mahler thus faced a powerful band of critics which above all knew its Wagner. It was all the more striking, therefore, when he won virtually unanimous acclaim for his début performance at the Met on New Year's Day 1908 with *Tristan und Isolde*. Characteristically, Krehbiel could not resist a spot of American flag-waving, claiming that 'Herr Mahler . . . is a newcomer whose appearance here, while full of significance, is not likely to excite one-half the interest in New York that his departure from Europe did on the other side of the water.' But even he went on to admit that Mahler was 'a master of his art' who 'did honour to himself, Wagner's music and the New York public'. Aldrich, who with Finck became one of Mahler's most consistent backers over the years, noted in the *Times* that the voices were 'never overwhelmed . . . they were allowed to keep their place above the orchestra and to blend with it always in their rightful place. And yet the score was revealed in all its complex beauty, with its strands of interwoven melody always clearly disposed and united with an exquisite sense of proportion.' For the young Samuel Chotzinoff, a Russian-born musician who later became a close associate of Toscanini, the performance was a revelation. 'Now at last I knew how Wagner should sound,' he wrote in his memoirs half a century later. 'Wagner could be as clear, as understandable, as lucid as *Aida*.'

In some ways *Don Giovanni* about three weeks later was a still bigger hit. That was partly because Mahler had at his disposal voices which even he found 'almost unsurpassable'. His *Tristan* cast had been fine enough, led by the Munich Heldentenor Heinrich Knote and the Swedish-born American soprano Olive Fremstad making her début as Isolde. But for *Don Giovanni* he even had the legendary Sembrich in the relatively modest role of Zerlina and, as Leporello, the Russian-born Feodor Chaliapin, a giant bass-baritone of unsurpassed dramatic skill. Antonio Scotti sang the title role; Bonci, Don Ottavio; Johanna Gadski, Donna Elvira; and Emma Eames, Donna Anna. Casting from strength indeed! But in striking proof that you can never please everyone, the *Tribune* carried a letter from an 'indignant subscriber' demanding that Chaliapin be barred from the Met because of his 'coarseness and vulgarity'. Krehbiel did not think much of Chaliapin either but he waxed almost lyrical over 'Mr Mahler's treatment of the orchestral part. The Metropolitan's walls have never echoed to anything as exquisite as last night's instrumental music. . . . The effect was ravishing.'

On the whole Mahler's success continued with *Die Walküre* and *Siegfried* in February. Critics raised occasional question marks over his 'unusually flexible' tempi and regularly pilloried the clumsy productions and sets, for which Mahler was not responsible. Nor did the public flock to the Met for Wagner, even under a masterly interpreter, as it always did for Caruso. But all in all no conductor could realistically have hoped for a better reception. There was much comment too, usually favourable but sometimes tinged with regret, that Mahler was proving to be no ogre after all. Advance reports had claimed that he would find conditions at the Met so impossible that he would throw a tantrum, pack his baton and take the next boat back to Europe. For the sensation-mongers it would have made a rousing start to the season. In the event, as the *New York Herald* reported in wonder, Mahler 'has handled his singing and orchestral forces so deftly here that, instead of finding him a dictator, they are eager to do his bidding'. That was a remarkable feat, the paper noted, 'for everyone knows that singers and snakes cannot be charmed too easily'.

This really did seem to be 'a new Mahler'. Alma commented on it too, writing that Mahler not only accepted the cuts in Wagner's works which were usual in New York but actually made new ones. This is a surprising claim but one which press reviews, not least of *Tristan*, show is well founded. On the other hand Alma goes too far when she writes that Mahler 'was merely amused, too, by lapses in the sets which in Vienna would have roused him to fury'. He spent the first couple of months in New York abortively trying to get Roller over from Vienna to revamp the Met's rotten scenery. But in general he was more tolerant in the opera house than he used to be.

Was he simply resigned? Hardly, or he would not have produced performances which so quickly won over critics not easily impressed. Alma suggests that 'the death of our child and his own personal sorrow had set another scale to the importance of things' and that sounds plausible. But Mahler had already 'set another scale' when he decided to drop his director's duties in Vienna in favour of more money and time for his own work. His whole approach in New York was in line with that decision. Soon after his arrival he was, as the press foretold, offered Conried's job but he turned it down, despite a salary 'that would sound fantastic in Vienna – 300,000 crowns for six months plus some extras'. Five years earlier, he wrote to a Vienna friend in February, 'I should not have been able to resist such an alluring offer. The climate, the people and the extremely generous conditions suit me extraordinarily well.'

Now Mahler had other priorities. At the Met he had fine singers and a passable orchestra, and he was constitutionally incapable of conducting half-heartedly. But it was time for someone else to grind himself down in the director's office. And if the New Yorkers wanted cuts then cuts they would have. In Vienna Mahler had groaned that he constantly banged his head against a wall, but that finally it was the wall which gave way. In New York he was determined that there would be no more banging, at worst a few sharp taps. The advice of his doctors the previous summer must have confirmed him in this approach, but even without it he would not have treated his job at the Met very differently. The truth is that in his attitude to the opera business he had become uncommonly like the pragmatic, even phlegmatic, Richard Strauss.

It was *Fidelio* more than anything else which changed the course of Mahler's New York career. Mahler had always lavished special care on Beethoven's opera and, despite his general rule to take things easier, he did the same at the Met. He scheduled a large number of rehearsals, intervened in the production and insisted that Roller's famous Vienna sets be duplicated in New York. The première on 20th March 1908 was a triumph which put even Mahler's previous Met successes in the shade. On the face of it that is a surprise. Dramatic though it can be, *Fidelio* lacks the orchestral subtlety of *Giovanni* and the vocal allure of *Tristan*. Moreover Mahler was wont to tinker with the score, retouching the orchestration here and there and inserting the overture *Leonore* No. 3 (which Beethoven decided not to use in the opera after all) as a prelude to the final scene. All of that seemed likely to bring censure, especially from Krehbiel who was all for cuts in Wagner but cherished every note by Beethoven, his God.

In the event, although Krehbiel complained about some of the singing and liberties with the text, he was bowled over by the 'power and splendid eloquence' of Mahler's interpretation. Other critics agreed that the Met had heard nothing as fine for years. But the most prescient comments came on 25th March from the *Musical Courier*, a weekly which loved baiting musicians and other critics, especially Krehbiel. It used Mahler's 'magnificent' performance of *Leonore* No. 3 as an excuse to praise New York's orchestral players and as a stick to beat their usual conductors. 'After hearing that,' it declared, 'can anyone blame the *Musical Courier* for paying no attention to the orchestral concerts given in this city by men like [Wassily] Safonoff and [Walter] Damrosch?' Those two gentlemen were, respectively, conductors of the New York Philharmonic and the New York Symphony.

Damrosch, then aged forty-five, may well have been a poor conductor. Contemporary judgements vary on that. But there is no doubt that he put together adventurous programmes and that he was a Mahler fan of long standing. As a young man he had been enthralled by a performance of *Die Meistersinger* under Mahler in Hamburg and in 1904 he had given the

American première of Mahler's Fourth Symphony. In principle the two should have been allies and so they were – at first. When Damrosch learned in 1907 that Mahler would be coming to the Met he wrote to him proposing a concert or two with the New York Symphony. It seems a plan was even mooted for Mahler to give the world première of his Seventh Symphony in New York during the 1907–8 season.

Nothing came of all that, apparently because Conried felt orchestral concerts would distract Mahler too much from his opera work. But neither Mahler nor Damrosch wanted to give up. On 16th March, four days before his hit with *Fidelio*, Mahler wrote to Damrosch regretting his 'superior's lack of understanding' but adding, 'I would however like to make good this omission during next season . . . and am asking you whether you will require my services.' Damrosch certainly did. He visited the Majestic on 22nd March and later reported that a verbal accord was reached under which Mahler would give three concerts, including his 'Resurrection' Symphony, with the New York Symphony at the turn of the year. Mahler stressed that he needed a formal go-ahead from the Met but would certainly get it or he would refuse to renew his contract for the next season. Damrosch was delighted. He was also flattered when, a day later, he gave a concert with the New York Symphony in Philadelphia to which Mahler unexpectedly turned up, afterwards going backstage to meet the players.

Then things started to go wrong. On 26th March Damrosch received a letter from Mahler saying that 'a few difficulties have unexpectedly arisen, which I hope to overcome but which now cause me to ask you to wait a little, before we conclude our business.' Mystified, Damrosch phoned Mahler and was told the problems involved the opera contract but would be cleared up shortly. On the face of it they were. Damrosch happened to bump into Otto Kahn, chairman of the Met's executive committee, at a dinner and was told Mahler's right to give concerts next season had been conceded. Hence Damrosch's shock to hear from Mahler soon afterwards that 'It is true that Kahn has given me the all-clear; but that only clears up the matter for the Metropolitan, since I must now forfeit 3000 dollars of my salary to be released. I must therefore now see where I can re-earn the amount. . . . I have proved that I would soonest be associated with you. But you will understand that under such circumstances I must now contemplate other points of view.'

The full explanation emerged in a letter to Damrosch, dated 1st April, from a New York lawyer called Dave Morris. The text was polite but the message brutally clear. Morris represented a 'committee of ladies' which had approached Mahler about giving concerts the following season. Mahler had had to give a 'certain concession' to the Met to obtain this concert privilege, Morris noted, 'and I understand from him that he was willing to make this concession on account of the proposition made by the committee of the ladies . . . which proposition he has accepted in writing, and a contract has been duly entered into.'

Damrosch felt double-crossed. Only about a fortnight earlier Mahler had been offering 'his services' and giving Damrosch to understand that the sole problem lay with the Met. Now, without warning, Mahler had done a deal with someone else which could well result in dangerous competition for the New York Symphony. The 'committee of ladies' (which included four men) was no ignorable little group with a passing fad, although Damrosch later tried to dismiss it as such. Led by the formidable Mrs Mary Sheldon, a banker's wife and veteran concert-goer, it had powerful financial influence and a burning desire to see the city get an orchestra at least as good as Boston's. That meant finding a conductor of peerless skill as interpreter and trainer. At the latest after hearing *Fidelio*, Mrs Sheldon and her friends agreed their search was at an end. They approached Mahler just as he was about to seal his accord with Damrosch.

Mahler did in fact conduct the proposed concerts with the New York Symphony after all, but by then the damage was done. Damrosch had become a bitter foe. Arguably he over-reacted but his rage at the coup by the 'ladies' committee' was no doubt intensified by the caustic comments made about him simultaneously in the *Musical Courier*. Mahler (not for the first time in his career) had not played quite straight, but he felt he had been made an offer he could not refuse. As he wrote excitedly to Anna Moll at the end of March, '*Fidelio* was a total success, completely altering my prospects from one day to the next. I am moving, or rather "things" are moving, towards the formation of a Mahler orchestra entirely at my disposal. . . . Everything now depends on the New Yorkers' attitude to my work. Since they are completely unprejudiced I hope I shall here find fertile ground for my works and thus a spiritual home, something that, for all the sensationalism, I should never be able to achieve in Europe. A tree needs such ground if it is not to die.'

This was a change indeed. Only a month earlier Mahler had told Roller in confidence that 'I do not intend to stay here long; but at least for next season, if I am still in good health.' Now he was starting to see a long-term future in New York with a 'Mahler orchestra' and a better chance to give his works a hearing. No wonder he was in buoyant mood – too buoyant as it proved.

Meanwhile, a successor had been found to succeed Conried at the Met. When Mahler refused the job Giulio Gatti-Casazza, director of La Scala, Milan, was signed up instead and with him La Scala's explosive maestro Toscanini. Gatti-Casazza had already been approached by the Met 'informally' (i.e. behind Conried's back) the previous summer but he had hedged, stressing that he would take the job only if Toscanini came too. The pair had worked well together for years at La Scala and Gatti-Casazza was canny enough to see that he would need some tried and trusted support from the outset in New York. In early 1908, with Mahler out of the running, he got his way – beginning an association with the Met which was to last until 1935. In principle Toscanini looked a fine catch too, especially to beat off the fierce competition from Hammerstein's Manhattan Opera in the Italian repertoire. Still, Otto Kahn for one was worried about how Toscanini would get on with Mahler. At Kahn's request, Gatti-Casazza sounded out Toscanini who replied, 'I hold Mahler in great esteem and would infinitely prefer such a colleague to any mediocrity.' Mahler, for his part, referred to Toscanini as 'a very well-thought-of conductor' who, he at first assumed, would take over only the Italian side of things at the Met.

Mahler deceived himself. Toscanini, who revered Wagner and had fought (unsuccessfully) to give the Italian première of Strauss's *Salome*, did not dream of renouncing German opera. A collision between the two conductors was hence inevitable. But that does not mean that Mahler was more or less driven out of the Met by an 'Italian juggernaut', a legend to which Alma contributes in her memoirs. She writes that during the winter of 1908–9 Mrs Sheldon and a lady-friend 'determined to put an orchestra at Mahler's disposal and within a few days they collected a hundred thousand dollars. This came in very opportunely for Mahler. His relations with the Metropolitan were no longer very good. Conried was at death's door. Gatti-Casazza . . . had brought Toscanini over with him. The glorious days of German supremacy were over.'

In fact, Mahler had accepted the Sheldon committee's offer well before the Italians arrived on the scene. True, he had also renewed his contract with the Met, which meant that for another season he would be involved in opera as well as a growing amount of orchestral work. But in the longer run he certainly did not aim to go on doing both. That had not worked in Vienna, even before his doctors had warned him not to overstrain. Mahler did not get on with Toscanini, who later called his former colleague 'a crazy man' and conducted none of his music. But when he left the Met it was due neither to the new Italian regime nor (another legend) to hostile critics. He went, as so often before, because he saw a more attractive post. At least it seemed so.

When Mahler sailed with Alma on 23rd April 1908 to spend seven months in Europe he had good cause to feel satisfied. The New York gamble, for such it was, had paid off handsomely so far – not least financially. After conducting just twenty-seven opera performances (twenty in New York and the others on tour in Boston and Philadelphia), he was 100,000 crowns better off. Although his original contract with Conried had specified a salary of 75,000 crowns for the season, Mahler received 25,000 crowns more because he arrived in New York a month earlier than first planned. After arguing with the Met he also won an increase in his living allowance, yet another sign of his negotiating skill. On top of that he had received 20,000 crowns severance pay from the Vienna Opera and had been granted an annual pension of 14,000 crowns, the latter (thanks to the generosity of his former court employer) more than he was strictly due. Mahler called all this 'stocking the larder' for Alma and Gucki. Already by the spring of 1908 he had provided well for both – and taken a big step towards that financial independence which would allow him to concentrate on composing alone.

Storm clouds were gathering that summer all the same. For one thing, the Met proposed in July that Toscanini conduct a few *Tristan* performances 'in the Milanese *mise-en-scène* familiar to him' at the start of the next season before Mahler began work. By this time Mahler had conceded that Toscanini could have a share of the German repertoire, but he had specifically excluded those works he had already rehearsed and conducted in New York. That applied, above all, to *Tristan*. In an indignant letter of reply Mahler noted that 'I took very special pains with *Tristan* last season and can well maintain that the form in which this work appears in New York is my spiritual property. If Toscanini . . . were now to take over *Tristan* before my arrival, the work would obviously be given an entirely new character, and it would be quite out of the question for me to resume my performances in the course of the season.' He won his point. Toscanini made his Met début on 16th November 1908 with *Aida*. He got round to *Tristan* only the following November. By that time Mahler had left the Met though he returned briefly as a 'guest' in March 1910 for the first performances in America of Tchaikovsky's *Pique Dame*. He never conducted opera again.

Potentially more worrying during that summer of 1908 was the war of words being waged in New York over the proposed 'Mahler orchestra'. According to a report in the *Tribune*, Damrosch had sneered at the plan as the product of 'two or three restless women with no occupation, and more money than they seem to know what to do with'. The *Musical Courier* pounced on this outburst with glee, noting that it too was restless and so were thousands of other musical New Yorkers. It was only thanks to such 'restless elements', the weekly said, that a worthy orchestra was at last going to be 'devised and organised and a renowned conductor like Gustav Mahler put at its head'.

In a side-swipe at Krehbiel, the *Courier* also stressed that the music critic of the *Tribune*, which had carried the 'restless women' report, was 'an associate of Mr Damrosch'. Was Krehbiel in fact in league with Damrosch, as the *Tribune* implied, or even in his pocket as some claimed later? It is true that Krehbiel taught at the Institute of Musical Art (later the Juilliard School), founded and directed by Damrosch and his brother Frank. And it was only after Mahler left the Met for full-time concert work, in competition to the New York Symphony, that he came under really fierce fire from Krehbiel. Those attacks on Mahler in the *Tribune* naturally suited Damrosch down to the ground but it is not clear that he instigated them. Krehbiel later had a pressing reason of his own for turning against Mahler.

In the mean time, though, Krehbiel was going out of his way to be fair. That emerges above all from his review of the 'Resurrection' Symphony with which Mahler, back in New York since 21st November, made his American début as a conductor of one of his own works. After the concert at Carnegie Hall on 8th December, a clearly puzzled Krehbiel acknowledged that 'Beyond all doubt Mr Mahler was deeply in earnest when he wrote this music, and of the beauty and insight of certain episodes there can be no doubt.' He concluded, with rare modesty, that it was not possible to give a final judgement on so large a work after a first hearing. Nonetheless, it was 'a pleasure to record the quick and evidently sincere expression of a New York audience . . . in its favour.' Other reviewers were at least as positive apart from the sour Lawrence Gilman in *Harper's Weekly* who complained that the work lacked 'original, potent and noble musical ideas'.

The 'Resurrection' formed the second of Mahler's three long-planned concerts with the New York Symphony. On the whole the others, which included symphonies by Schumann (the First) and Beethoven (the Fifth), were well received too but Mahler thought nothing of the orchestra. 'Completely inadequate', he called it in a letter to a friend in Europe and bitterly complained that the musicians drifted in and out of rehearsals as it suited them. Even so the *New York World* noted that the Symphony had played 'much better than usual, with so much more precision, sonority, colour and unity of orchestral feeling' – hardly a flattering reflection on its usual conductor, Damrosch. Later the New York Symphony Society issued a statement saying that it did 'not expect to repeat in the future its experiment of inviting European guest conductors'. The experience with Mahler, it claimed, had been 'rather unsatisfactory'. Mahler cannot have been much bothered by the snub. The Symphony was not *his* orchestra. The one he aimed to forge would surely be far better.

By this time, though, the project of the 'ladies' committee' was looking rather different. Back in the spring of 1908 the aim had been to form a wholly new orchestra. At least that is what Mahler (and the press) expected and in April a committee statement seemed to confirm it. It said that during the coming season Mahler would conduct a series of concerts with musicians whom he would select, and that this was to lead to the foundation of a 'Greater New York Orchestra excelled by none other'. There was no mention of revamping the existing New York Philharmonic, hitherto run on a loose self-governing basis. No doubt the Sheldon group considered this but initially balked at the difficulties. Reorganising the New York Philharmonic meant reforming the sixty-six-year-old Philharmonic Society, a daunting enterprise. But by the end of the year this option was looming largest and it was finally the one chosen.

Backed by cash pledges from a string of philanthropic millionaires including J.P. Morgan and John D. Rockefeller, Mrs Sheldon and her friends issued what amounted to an ultimatum to the Philharmonic Society in February 1909. Their aim, they said, was to organise an orchestra 'of the highest order under the exclusive direction of a fine conductor' for at least twenty-three successive weeks a year. The corporate frame of the Philharmonic *could* be used but if it were then it had to be brought up to date. In a nutshell, the Society would no longer run itself but be under the thumb of a guarantors' committee which would have the final say on everything which mattered, including choice of conductor and management. In return all players would get a regular salary (many hitherto were part-time) and any deficits would be made good by the guarantors for at least the next three seasons.

The offer proved irresistible. Much as the Philharmonic prized its independence, it had been steadily losing players to the greater financial security of the Met and the Manhattan Opera. If a new orchestra offering attractive conditions were created, as the Sheldon group implicitly threatened, then still more players would drift away. The Philharmonic caved in and by the end of February the guarantors' committee, chaired (inevitably) by Mrs Sheldon, was hard at work.

Although ultimately accountable to the committee, Mahler was given sweeping powers to raise the average strength of the orchestra to around a hundred players, weed out the incompetents and choose programmes. Hence it could be argued that he as good as got the scope to form his 'own orchestra'. But there is all the difference in the world between selecting the best applicants for a new team and revamping an old one. Removing the luckless Safonoff, who had conducted the orchestra for three seasons, proved the least of the problems. He gave his last Philharmonic concert in March and was sent on his way with a laurel wreath and a diamond watch fob. Dealing with the players was a far trickier proposition. A lot of them (rightly) feared dismissal or demotion from first-chair jobs to the rank-and-file, and even those in favour of the Philharmonic's new structure could not be sure it would survive.

If Mahler realised that he was walking into a minefield he gave no sign of it, at least not at first. Probably he did not care much about details of corporate structure so long as he had a free hand, above all to pick the best possible musicians. But he soon found out he was less free than he thought. Even before formal confirmation of his Philharmonic post he had begun to prospect for players in Europe, especially Vienna. Evidently he did not then know of the daunting obstacles the American musicians' union placed in the way of employing foreigners. By the summer, though, he had become painfully aware of the problem. In a letter to the Philharmonic from Europe, Mahler announced that 'after unbelievably difficult negotiations' he had engaged Theodore Spiering, 'a native-born American and a member of the Chicago Union', as concert-master. He added, almost plaintively, that since the union had given him the go-ahead to import a foreign concertmaster and he had found an American instead, then surely it would not object if he imported a flute player and signed up a timpanist from a town other than New York.

Union resistance notwithstanding, Mahler finally got most of what he wanted and by the winter nearly half the players had been exchanged. But when he gave his first two concerts with the Philharmonic before leaving for Europe on 9th April 1909, the orchestra did not yet differ much from Safonoff's. Not surprisingly, with so many players facing dismissal, both occasions proved rather fraught. After the first one (Schumann, Beethoven, Wagner) on 31st March the *New York Sun* reported that 'it would be misleading to regard this concert as a correct indication of what is to be expected of Mr Mahler hereafter. The orchestra of next winter will without doubt not be that which has been heard during the last three years . . . Mr Mahler may perhaps discover the long-lost wind players. Heaven send that he may, for the Philharmonic sadly needs them.' After the second concert, a performance of Beethoven's Ninth on 6th April, Mahler was chided by several critics for his interpretation and retouching of the score. Krehbiel was still fairly restrained, noting ironically that Mahler was trying to make more explicit 'the thoughts of the composer, who is supposed, for several reasons, not to have been able to express himself as clearly as he ought or might'. The *Sun* was more forthright, claiming that the performance 'must have left many questionings in the minds of Beethoven's worshippers, who love his music far more than they love conductors, no matter how distinguished'.

Most of the concert reviews were far from hostile but some were starting to have an ominous ring about them. The new tone was all the more striking since Mahler was continuing to reap acclaim for his work in the opera house. Indeed, his second season at the Met proved to be a still bigger triumph than his first, Toscanini's presence notwithstanding. Mahler's *Tristan* now drew praise even from the few who had had doubts before and his *Nozze di Figaro*, premièred on 13th January 1909, was widely judged incomparable. Again Mahler had a star-studded cast, with Scotti as Almaviva, Eames as the Countess, Sembrich as Susanna, Adamo Didur as Figaro and Geraldine Farrar as Cherubino. But what the critics loved most was the ensemble work and Mahler's way with the score. 'All the vivacious music foamed and sparkled and flashed like champagne,' enthused Krehbiel. So great was the triumph that plans were quickly made (but later dropped) to take *Figaro* on tour to Europe to show off the Met at its finest. Rather more unexpected was Mahler's success in February with Smetana's *Bartered Bride*. He had at his disposal the outstanding Prague-born soprano Emmy Destinn as Marenka and a team of dancers specially brought over from Bohemia, but the work had never been given in America before and there was some advance grumbling that New Yorkers shunned 'peasant opera'. In the event they loved it.

Mahler's second Met season was less taxing as well as more successful than his first. This time he conducted only three operas in nineteen performances, including a few on tour in Philadelphia. If at this stage he had returned to Europe for good his brief New York era would have been remembered as one of unsurpassed brilliance. But the lure of 'his' Philharmonic (plus a handsome salary) was far too strong to resist. With the start of the new season in November 1909, he took on a much heavier workload – forty-six concerts, some on tour, plus rehearsals, all packed into twenty-four weeks. He became less tolerant than he had been, to general surprise, at the Met and more easily depressed. Perhaps he expected too much too soon from his newly revamped orchestra. Whatever the cause his relations with the New York Philharmonic were tense, much as they had been with the Vienna Philharmonic a decade before.

That emerges clearly enough from memories of Mahler recorded in the 1960s by New York musicians who had worked under him. Not that the picture they give is wholly grim. Plenty of players respected Mahler's knowledge and commitment, his feeling for mood and his insistence on flexible phrasing which allowed the music to breathe. And when Mahler got what he was after he was overjoyed, on one occasion taking the whole orchestra off for a celebratory supper at the Liederkranz, a German club. But even his admirers admitted there were strains, especially during rehearsals. One recalls that Mahler had 'a pretty good stentorian voice. You wouldn't think it coming out of a little man like he was. And ... my – when he'd get into a rage, he'd scream; you could hear him three blocks away.' Others remember how he would pick on players he felt were not up to the mark and demean them in front of their colleagues. An elderly violinist, for instance, was told, 'You have no business to play in a symphony orchestra; you should be playing in the back room of a saloon.' As in Vienna, Mahler also encouraged a 'spy' from the orchestra to report to him on the backstage chat. Other players got wind of it and complained to the management. The man was later sacked.

Mahler made heavy demands on his audiences too, especially in his first Philharmonic season. Undiplomatically announcing that he aimed 'to educate the public', he put together four separate concert cycles (including a historical series) with some odd programmes. One consisted of Beethoven's relatively unfamiliar Second Symphony followed by the four overtures written for *Fidelio*. Another included an overture by Pfitzner, Bruckner's Fourth Symphony and preludes from Richard Strauss's *Guntram*. Interesting in their way, no doubt, but unlikely to bring queues at the box office. Nor did they. Mahler had some unexpected successes, including his arrangement for orchestra of Bach pieces which he directed from a piano converted to sound like a giant harpsichord. Concerts with the pianist/composers Ferruccio Busoni and Sergei Rachmaninoff, and with the violinist Fritz Kreisler, drew the crowds too. But often the halls were far from full and by the time the season closed the Philharmonic had run up a deficit of close to 90,000 dollars.

Among the season's flops was Mahler's First Symphony, given its American début on 16th December 1909 and repeated next day. At least, most of the critics panned it. By this time Mahler can hardly have been surprised. Ever since the stormy première (albeit of the raw, five-movement version) in Budapest twenty years before, the piece had been slow to win friends. Most New York reviewers were just as baffled as their European counterparts by the symphony's mix of perkiness, parody and pain. Even so Krehbiel's notice, calling Mahler among other things a 'prophet of the ugly', stood out for its venom. So much so that a few days later the *Musical Courier* took up the topic. It had been told, the *Courier* said, that Krehbiel's diatribe was 'the *Tribune* critic's petty manner of revenging himself for having been prohibited by Mr Mahler from airing "notes" on the subject of the symphony. This seems hardly credible, however.'

Credible or not, it was a fact. As well as being the *Tribune*'s critic (and part-time teacher at the Damrosch Institute), Krehbiel was the official annotator for the Philharmonic concerts. It was in the latter role that he had approached Mahler for background about the First Symphony. Specifically Krehbiel wanted to give details of the 'programme', i.e. the dramatic story which lay behind the music. Mahler refused. He had long since decided that offering 'programmes' did more harm than good. Worse, he told Krehbiel not to write any notes about the symphony at all because they would merely distract the audience. Krehbiel complied, fuming, but his pride was deeply hurt. Mahler was already facing a more strident critical chorus, but henceforth easily its shrillest voice would be Krehbiel's.

It wasn't all music. For a man supposed to be taking things easy, Mahler went out a great deal in New York. At least Alma did so, and writes that Mahler often accompanied her. Some of their trips were rather odd. On one occasion, doing some sightseeing with a music publisher, they ended up in an opium den in Chinatown where they were exhorted (unsuccessfully) to join in a smoke. On another night out they attended a seance with a group including the Met's banker-boss Otto Kahn, not usually a man to display other-worldly interests. As the session got under way and the room became bathed in phosphorescent light, a mandolin flew through the air and hit Mahler on the forehead, happily doing him no lasting damage. He seems to have been in more real danger when, travelling home alone on a winter's night, his hansom cab was blown over in a fierce blizzard. He crawled out of the wreck, retrieved his pince-nez from a snowdrift with the help of the tipsy driver and clawed his way through the deserted streets, finally reaching the hotel at 2 a.m.

Even straightforward-looking invitations brought surprises. Leon

Corning, an ultra-rich but miserly physician who had tended Alma after a fainting fit, served his guests an egg-cupful of champagne apiece and minute portions of food in a chamber feebly lit by tiny, sputtering candles. The frugal feast was preceded by a tour of the Corning home, a cross between palace and prison with a maze of steps and corridors, an iron-clad cell and a vast music room where the host paced up and down playing the flute. Similarly musical and no less eccentric was the interior designer Louis Tiffany, one of the Philharmonic's millionaire backers. On entering the Tiffany residence, the Mahlers found themselves in a chamber as big as a ballroom, with stained-glass windows, four fires burning in four different colours and an organ playing the prelude to *Parsifal* in the background. The host, who was painfully shy, muttered a few incomprehensible words and vanished. 'Silent footmen perambulated with costly glasses which although on trays never clinked,' Alma recalled. 'Palms and sofas, beautiful women in odd shimmering robes – or did we dream? It was the thousand and one nights – in New York.'

It was certainly more diverting than married life had been back home in the Auenbruggergasse. Vienna had its exotic side too but Mahler had always been frantically busy and for six years Alma had played housewife. Her domestic chores had hardly been heavy but in New York she was freed from them altogether. Even when Gucki joined her parents for the second and subsequent trips to America, she had her stern English nurse to look after her – as Alma ironically put it, to inculcate her with 'the stoicism of a Samurai'. Gucki responded to the tough discipline with a stubbornness only her father was able to get round. When she refused to eat, Mahler suggested she leave the room and return as a person of insatiable appetite called 'Gladys' (why 'Gladys' remains a mystery). The trick worked. When she lied to Alma about damage she had done with some scissors, Mahler knelt beside her and asked if perhaps the naughty scissors had taken on a will of their own. Gucki whimpered, then confessed. Like Putzi, she was her father's child.

Latterly, it is true, Alma turned against most of the matrons who ran the Philharmonic, and she ran foul of a vacuous society beauty who asked her with a smile of contempt how she had brought herself 'to marry such a hideous and old and altogether impossible man as Mahler'. No doubt the question was the more irritating because Alma, as her diary shows, had asked herself much the same from time to time. She had familiar bouts of ill health in New York too and, it seems, more than one miscarriage or abortion. At least it is hard to interpret in any other way a letter from Mahler to Carl Moll in March 1909 saying, 'Alma is very well. About her present state she has doubtless written to you herself. She has been relieved of her burden. But this time she actually regrets it.' Despite those troubles Alma, who turned thirty in 1909, generally had a splendid time. She was much invited, widely fêted and picked up a string of exotic acquaintances, from a woman who had camped out for years among the North American Indians to a Russian prince who strode about New York with a couple of wolves. 'All these people were friends of ours,' she wrote. 'We were more at home than in Vienna.'

Was that really how Mahler felt too? The evidence is mixed. He often wrote about America with enthusiasm, for instance telling Roller in early 1908, 'The people here are tremendously unspoilt – all the crudeness and ignorance are teething troubles. Spite and hypocrisy are to be found only among our dear immigrant compatriots.' On the other hand, just before returning to Europe three months later, he wrote to a Viennese countess, 'The homesickness that has tormented me all the time (I'm afraid I shall never be anything but a dyed-in-the-wool Viennese) is changing into that excited yearning which you too doubtless know.' No doubt Mahler was in part tailoring his message to his addressee. He would not have been the first to do so.

On balance, Mahler found much to admire in America even if his highest hopes there were not, in the end, fulfilled. But it is hard to believe that he embraced New York's social life with the ardour which Alma suggests. He may well have gone out much more than he did in Vienna. He certainly had more time to do so. The question is how much he enjoyed the experience. Olga Samaroff, a young pianist who later married the conductor Leopold Stokowski, has left one of the few independent accounts of how Mahler behaved at a New York dinner party. The details would have come as no surprise to Berta Zuckerkandl and other Viennese hostesses. According to Olga, Mahler sat next to her picking at his food and giving her neither glance nor greeting. Desperate to prise a word out of him and knowing of his fascination for Dostoyevsky, she finally asked provocatively if he did not consider *The Brothers Karamazov* much overrated. That did it. For the rest of the evening a furious Mahler lectured her on *Karamazov*, finally dragging her into the drawing-room to leaf through a copy and complete her conversion. That, indeed, is a familiar Mahler. 'I have often wondered what would have happened,' Olga commented, 'if he had known we were discussing one of my favourite books.'

A letter to Bruno Walter in early 1909 also gives an insight into what Mahler was really thinking and feeling as he sped with Alma from one function to another. 'How absurd it is to let oneself be submerged in the brutal whirlpool of life,' he wrote. 'To be untrue to oneself and to those higher things above oneself for even a single hour! But writing this down like this is one thing – on the next occasion, for instance, if I now leave this room of mine, I shall certainly again be as absurd as everyone else. . . . Strange! When I hear music – even while I am conducting – I hear quite specific answers to all my questions – and am completely clear and certain. Or rather, I feel quite distinctly that they are not questions at all.'

Being untrue to himself, for Mahler, meant above all to desert his composing. He had had to do so in the storm-ridden year of 1907 but already in 1908 he was back at work – not, of course, in New York or Vienna, nor Maiernigg with its painful memories, but in an isolated spot high in the Dolomites. It seemed the ideal retreat and for a time it served him well. But eventually the 'brutal whirlwind of life' was to catch up with him even there.

Chapter Nine

Das Lied von der Erde

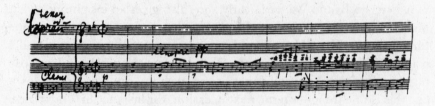

By a near miracle, Mahler's three composing huts have survived for around a century. The first one, by the Attersee, did interim service as a slaughterhouse and washroom but now, saved from imminent demolition in the 1980s, is a well-restored mini-museum. So is the second, after standing dank and empty for decades in the woods above the Wörther See. At least those two were stone-built and set in areas with a mildish climate.

Not so the third, a flimsy-looking wooden shack on a forest fringe about 4000 feet up in the northern Dolomites. Anyone coming on it unawares might mistake it at first for a storage shed unlikely to survive many mountain winters. Only scrutiny of several information plaques, one above the door and the rest in the cramped but refurbished interior, reveals that the place is hardier than it looks. It was here, in the summer breaks of 1908 to 1910 between European concerts and New York commitments, that Mahler composed *Das Lied von der Erde* and his Ninth and (unfinished) Tenth Symphonies.

A few minutes' walk away lies the hamlet of Alt-Schluderbach, where the Mahlers rented the whole upper floor of a massive farmhouse, and 2 miles further east the town of Toblach (Dobbiaco) sprawls below in the Puster valley. In Mahler's time the area was still part of the Habsburg

1910. Pragser Wildsee. Mahler dining with Alma, Maria Moll,
his daughter Anna (*centre*), the conductor Oskar Fried and
Anna Moll (Alma's mother).

(*Above left*) Arnold Schönberg
(1874–1951), revolutionary composer
and gifted painter, in characteristically
defiant mood. At first hostile to
Mahler's music, he later became a
passionate advocate.

(*Above right*) Willem Mengelberg
(1871–1951), Dutch conductor of the
Amsterdam Concertgebouw Orchestra
and (1921–29) of the New York
Philharmonic. Regarded by Mahler as
his finest interpreter.

(*Left*) Bruno Walter (1876–1962), Berlin-
born conductor who worked as assistant
to Mahler in Hamburg and Vienna and
propagated his music for more than half
a century.

Mahler (*right*) looks on as his friend and rival, Richard Strauss, strides confidently from the Graz Opera House on the occasion of the Austrian première of *Salome* in May 1906.

Anna von Mildenburg (1872–1947) as Kundry, the temptress in Wagner's *Parsifal*. One of the century's finest dramatic sopranos, she was Mahler's greatest love before Alma.

Natalie Bauer-Lechner (1858–1921), Austrian viola-player who adored Mahler and often spent summers with him and his sisters until his marriage in 1902.

Anna Bahr-Mildenburg
als „Kundry"
in „Parsifal".

Kunstverlag Emil Schwalb
Berlin-Charlottenburg 4

The Court Opera House in Vienna, opened in 1869
and directed by Mahler from 1897–1907.

The Philharmonic Society
of New York

1910...   SIXTY-NINTH SEASON   ...1911

Gustav Mahler ... Conductor

MANAGEMENT LOUDON CHARLTON

Carnegie Hall

TUESDAY NIGHT, JANUARY 17
AT EIGHT-FIFTEEN

FRIDAY AFTERNOON, JANUARY 20
AT TWO-THIRTY

Soloist
MME. BELLA ALTEN
(of the Metropolitan Opera House)

All-Modern Programme
1. OVERTURE "Das Kätchen von Hellbronn" . . . . Pfitzner
2. SYMPHONY No. 4, in G major . . . . Mahler
    I   Recht gemüthlich
    II   In gemächlicher Bewegung
    III Ruhevoll
    IV Sehr behaglich
           Solo Part: MME. ALTEN
3. "EIN HELDENLEBEN" Opus 40 . . . . Richard Strauss

The Steinway Piano is the Official Piano of the Philharmonic Society

Carnegie Hall, New York, 17 and 20 January 1911. The last occasions on which Mahler conducted a work of his own – the Fourth Symphony.

(*Below*) The Metropolitan Opera. Mahler made his triumphant New York debut at the Met with *Tristan und Isolde* on 1 January 1908, and conducted there regularly to great acclaim until he took over the New York Philharmonic in 1909. He briefly returned to the Met as a guest conductor in 1910 to give the first performances in America of Tchaikovsky's *Pique Dame*.

Mahler and his music inspired scores of caricatures.
(*Above*) conducting the first performance in Vienna of
his First Symphony on 18 November 1900 . . . and
(*below*) being told in 1910 that no audience is left
because everyone is needed onstage to give one of his
monstrous works.

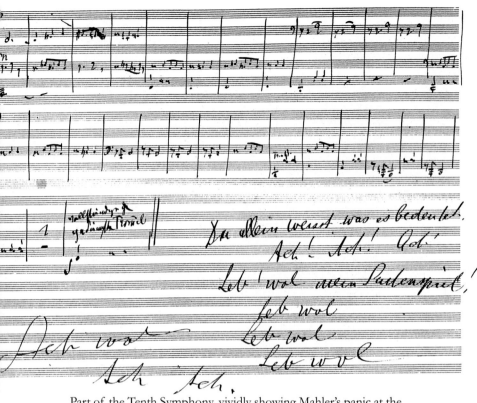

Part of the Tenth Symphony, vividly showing Mahler's panic at the thought of losing Alma. At the end he scrawled on the score 'for you to live! for you to die! Almschi'; here: 'Only you will know what this means. Farewell my lyre. Farewell.'

Silhouettes by Troianski. Like 'a cat with convulsions,' is how one wag described Mahler's dynamic conducting. In his last years, however, his style changed and he eschewed all expansive gestures on the podium.

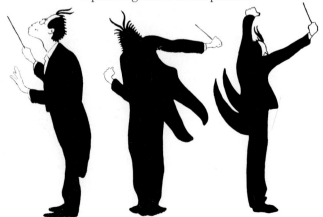

Mahler on his final crossing
from New York to Europe in
April 1911. He died a month
later in Vienna.

Death mask taken by Carl Moll.

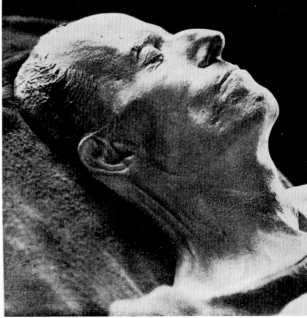

empire; after the First World War and the empire's collapse it and much else besides was ceded to Italy. Wars have come and gone, frontiers have shifted, skiers and hikers swarm by – but Mahler's last hut, protected by its unpretentiousness, remains essentially unchanged.

So does the view. Toblach itself has seen a great deal of tourism-induced new building but there is little to blot the panorama from Mahler's refuge; long rolling meadows, still snow-patched in late spring, and row upon row of mountain peaks beyond. Even distant details stand out sharply in the cool, clear air until close to sunset when shadows spread down the valley and rising mist briefly blurs the scene. Under moonlight, the landscape looks frozen into eerie immobility. Then, above all, it is hard not to ponder links between Mahler's works and the places where he composed them. Back in 1896 at the Attersee, Mahler joked that he had 'used up' the local mountains as raw material for his pantheistic Third Symphony. The Seventh Symphony, written nearly a decade later, has something of the stifling and scary atmosphere around his Wörther See home. The connection seems firmer still between Mahler's Dolomite environment and his last works, with their unsurpassed clarity of instrumentation and often curiously detached intensity. That goes above all for *Das Lied von der Erde*, full of delicate *chinoiserie* and moments of uncanny calm although scored for a large orchestra and two singers. It is even tempting to talk of Mahler's *Magic Mountain* period, drawing a parallel with the Thomas Mann novel in which isolation high in an Alpine sanatorium brings a sharpness of insight unmatched down below in 'the flat land'.

There is surely something in that theory but it doesn't do to push it far. There are too many exceptions. The sparse orchestration of *Kinder-totenlieder* and the cowbells in the Sixth and Seventh Symphonies suggest mountain composition, but all are Wörther See works. No doubt Mahler's lofty perch in the Dolomites had some influence on his last pieces, but that alone cannot account for their character.

What, then, does explain it? The usual answer is that after the blows of 1907 culminating in the diagnosis of a flawed heart, Mahler believed he faced certain premature death. All his subsequent work was shaped by that conviction. Knowing that Beethoven had died after writing nine symphonies (and, stretching a point, Schubert and Bruckner too), he resolved not to court fate and called his next composition, in effect his own 'Ninth', *Das Lied von der Erde*. Like its successors it is a work of regret and farewell. Mahler's superstitious juggling with numbers did not save him. Death came in 1911, less than four years after he learned the truth about his heart, with much of the Tenth Symphony still only in sketch.

That explanation is too neat by half. One reason to question it has been raised before. Mahler's works often do not reflect the circumstances of his life around the time he wrote them. A love affair, Mahler admitted, touched off composition of the First Symphony but did not determine its content. The tragic Sixth Symphony emerged during a seemingly happy period, the easeful Fourth during one of special stress. So how certain should we really be that the final works owe their character to the impact on Mahler of the grim events of 1907? If those events had happened the year before he wrote his Sixth Symphony, they would surely have been judged in retrospect as the reason for the work's nihilism. The connection would have seemed too obvious to deny. Since no such link is readily available, the 'explanation' that the Sixth prophesies Mahler's downfall comes in all the handier. It is a beguiling theory but that is no good reason to take it on trust.

The same goes for the rarely challenged tale, repeated by Alma among others, that Mahler was trying to cheat fate when he gave *Das Lied* a name, not the number nine. The origin of the story is obscure and there is no confirmation of it in Mahler's letters. If it is true, it seems odd that Mahler should have gone on to call his first work after *Das Lied* the 'Ninth' Symphony after all. He could just have dodged the issue again and called his new piece the 'Tenth', leaving *Das Lied* as the true but undeclared ninth. Apparently the bout of superstition which assailed him one year was gone by the next. However, other popular tales have it that although Mahler got as far as giving his Ninth a number, he balked at referring to it as such – nor could he bring himself to conduct his final works because of their doom-laden content.

Such stories are rarely pure invention. Facts are usually lurking in them somewhere. The problem is rather one of interpretation. Take the tale of the two birds which suddenly crashed through a window pane of Mahler's mountain hut while he was hard at work. According to Bruno Walter, Mahler jumped up in horror when the intruders, an eagle chasing a crow, burst in upon him and was deeply depressed by the incident long afterwards. 'His musical heaven had become a battlefield for one of the endless fights of "all against all",' Walter says. Is that his interpretation in retrospect (Walter was writing in the 1930s) or was it Mahler's? Walter does not quite call the incident a portent but he goes on at once to describe Mahler's final illness and death.

Walter's account is not the only one. Another comes from Marianna Trenker, an adopted daughter of the family which owned the farmhouse where the Mahlers stayed. According to her a vulture was chasing a raven, a sinister variation more fitting to Walter's tale, but she gives the story a humorous twist. Mahler, she says, went to 'old Trenker . . . and complained bitterly about the impudent intruder. Herr Trenker laughed in his face and Gustav Mahler had to laugh with him.' On another occasion, she says, Mahler asked what could be done to stop the cock crowing and waking him early in the morning. '"Ah well," said Herr Trenker, "you simply wring its neck." But Gustav Mahler did not want to hear of that.' Despite his oddities, Marianna Trenker says, Mahler was 'warm-hearted and unassumingly friendly'.

Alfred Roller too tells the story, this time involving a hawk and a jackdaw, but only to illustrate how deeply absorbed Mahler always was when composing. Although the hut was filled with screeching and fluttering, Roller says, 'Mahler had no idea all this was happening around him in the real world. It was only when the hawk flew out again and brushed his head with its wings that he came back to reality. The jackdaw cowering in a corner and the broken window enabled him to put together what had happened.' Roller gives the tale no macabre undertone, nor do his other remarks on Mahler's last years betray a sense of impending catastrophe. Rather the opposite. When Mahler returned briefly to Vienna after his first visit to America, Roller found him 'very much changed. I was taken aback when he stood there before me in the dim light of the station forecourt. The easier workload over there and the reduced amount of exercise had thickened him up. His clothes were smarter too.'

One incident, three versions – of which Walter's, not surprisingly, is the most often retold. It fits so well into the familiar picture of the dying composer. So do the claims about Mahler trying to cheat fate with a numbers game, but what evidence there is suggests the truth is less titillating. When Mahler began *Das Lied* he seems to have thought he was writing a song-series rather than a symphony, but gradually found he had a rare if not unique mixture of both. Quite recent research shows that he actually composed two versions of the work more or less simultaneously, one for voices and orchestra and another for voices and piano. Scrutiny of the manuscripts makes clear that the version with piano is no mere first draft of the one with orchestra but is meant to be performed in its own right (though it rarely is).

Those who know *Das Lied* only in its breathtaking orchestral garb may well find that hard to believe, but for Mahler the song-writer this procedure was nothing new. Nearly all his previous works in the genre, including the *Kindertotenlieder* and most of the *Rückert-Lieder* and *Knaben Wunderhorn* settings, were composed for performance with either orchestra or piano. That suggests *Das Lied* really belongs with the song cycles, yet it has symphonic elements. Mahler himself was uncertain how to describe his hybrid. In a letter to Bruno Walter in September 1908, as *Das Lied* neared completion, he wrote, 'I have been hard at work (from which you can tell that I am more or less "acclimatised"). I myself do not know what the whole thing could be called. A wonderful time was granted to me, and I think it is the most personal thing I have done so far.' Finally he hedged, naming the piece *Das Lied von der Erde* but giving it the subtitle 'Symphony for tenor and alto (or baritone) voice and orchestra'. He clearly had no doubts about the special place of the work in his symphonic output, and this was probably reason enough for him to set it apart, without a number. There is no need to claim that he acted from superstition.

It is true that Mahler never heard, let alone conducted, his last works but that does not prove he was afraid to do so. He often had a lengthy wait before his symphonies were first played. Sometimes the wait was even longer than it strictly need have been, as in the case of the Third, because Mahler insisted on near-ideal conditions for performance. At the end he simply ran out of time, dying eight months after conducting the première of the Eighth. Given another year or two of reasonable health he would very likely have got round to *Das Lied* and the Ninth as well – and to completing the Tenth. He may not often have referred to the Ninth specifically by number (though he did a few times in letters) but he mentioned the piece in general with evident affection, not apprehension. It was, he told Bruno Walter, 'a very satisfactory addition to my little family'.

There is no doubt that Mahler was initially in a black mood during his first summer near Toblach in 1908. In a letter dated 18th July to Walter he confessed that 'since that panic fear which overcame me that time, all I have tried has been to avert my eyes and close my ears. – If I am to find the way back to myself again, I must surrender to the horrors of loneliness.' Here, surely, is a man who has been told he is doomed and is belatedly facing up to the fact. Yet Mahler goes on, 'But fundamentally I am only speaking in riddles, for you do not know what has been and still is going on within me; but it is certainly not that hypochondriac fear of death, as you suppose. I had already realised that I should have to die.'

In a sense Mahler was just stating the obvious. Death was no stranger to him. It had taken many of his family and friends and he had barely escaped it himself at least twice, in Hamburg and Vienna. One way or another it haunts virtually all his work from the start, not just after 1907. Death was an obsession, but not necessarily more so for Mahler than for other great creative artists. Four years before he died, Mozart wrote to his father that he never went to bed at night without reflecting that he might not live to see another day. The thought did not frighten him. He even called death 'the best and truest friend of mankind' and 'the key which unlocks the door to our true happiness'. Mahler could rarely hold fast to that same conviction for long, but when he told Walter in 1908 that he did not have a 'hypochondriac fear of death' it is fair to assume that he meant what he said.

Mahler identifies the real problem later in the same letter. 'I cannot work at my desk,' he writes. 'My mental activity must be complemented by physical activity. The advice you pass on from doctors is of no use to me. An ordinary walk gives me such a rapid pulse and palpitations that I never achieve the purpose of walking – to forget one's body. I have recently been reading Goethe's letters – his secretary, to whom he was in the habit of dictating, fell ill, and this so put him off that he had to suspend work for a month. – Now imagine Beethoven having to have his legs amputated after an accident. If you know his mode of life, do you believe he could have drafted even one movement of a quartet? And that can hardly be compared with my situation. I confess that, superficial though it may seem, this is the greatest calamity that has ever befallen me.'

In other words Mahler's real fear was not that he was dying but that his life, stripped of exercise, would cease to be creative. All his doctors the previous year had warned him against over-exertion, even that Dr Hamperl who had assured him that otherwise he could lead 'a normal life'. The full implications of that advice probably only came home to Mahler when he began his summer break, hitherto a time for hiking and biking, swimming and – composing. When he wrote to Walter he was just getting down in earnest to *Das Lied*, his first major creative work since completing the 'Symphony of a Thousand' two years before. How much he must have dreaded that his efforts in the new, restricted, circumstances would come to nothing. This, incidentally, was also the moment when Mahler was sparring by letter with the Met about whether Toscanini should conduct *Tristan*. That can hardly have improved his morale.

Imagine Mahler's relief, therefore, when September came and *Das Lied* was all but complete. His letter to Walter about having been granted 'a wonderful time' is only one testimony to his change of mood. The following month he wrote to Alma from Munich, 'I feel now, after today's rehearsal with the incredibly willing orchestra, that it is really a pleasure to be the composer of a successful symphony.' Mahler here refers to his Seventh Symphony which he had premièred in September in Prague. The reaction to it had been respectful rather than enthusiastic but evidently that had not bothered Mahler for long. He even told Alma life in Munich was so cheap and the climate so superb that they should seriously consider settling there eventually. 'With our income we could live here like princes,' he enthused. 'In the middle of Europe – with first-rate communications in all directions.' Hardly the words of a man who thinks he is at death's door.

Mahler's mood was, if anything, even more buoyant during the next summer – 1909 – when he was composing the Ninth Symphony and putting the final touches to *Das Lied*. He was no longer ultra-careful about following his doctors' orders, revealing in letters to Alma – who was away on one of her periodic 'cures' – that he tramped down to Toblach and back every day in all weathers. That new-found vigour does not register strongly in Alma's edition of Mahler's letters to her because, for whatever reason, she cut out several references to it. But two photos taken that year help confirm the impression made by a reading of the full correspondence. They show Mahler on a mountain track, long stick in one hand and socks tucked into heavy walking boots. He is not out for a mere stroll.

All this seems to have an inconvenient corollary: that the leap Mahler made from the heady affirmation of the Eighth Symphony to the introspection of the last works is truly inexplicable. A closer look at the music and the philosophy behind it suggests it is not.

Many Mahler fans who particularly prize the Seventh Symphony find the Eighth rather an embarrassment. It is easy to see why. Unlike the Eighth, the Seventh is rich in daring harmony and bizarre orchestration with shocks at nearly every turn. Here it is tender and sophisticated, there jarring and elemental. The scherzo, a witches-round-the-cauldron dance marked '*Schattenhaft*' (shadowy) in the score, is about the spookiest movement Mahler ever wrote; the Andante amoroso which directly follows it is the most nearly erotic. In the Seventh Mahler outdoes himself. It is as though the hero downed in the Sixth has crawled to his feet again and is testing his weapons to their limits – and then a bit beyond. No wonder the radical young composers of the New Viennese School took to the piece right away. There certainly seem to be echoes of it in Schönberg's Serenade op. 24, Berg's Three Orchestral Pieces op. 6 and Webern's Six Pieces op. 10. But there is an even closer apparent affinity between the Seventh and Schönberg's Chamber Symphony op. 9, yet Schönberg had finished his piece well before he heard Mahler's. Pin-pointing influence is a dangerous business. At least it is safe to say that the avant-garde saw in their older mentor a fellow spirit, questing, idealistic and never more spectacularly bold than in the Seventh Symphony.

If the Seventh has a flaw it is the brassily jubilant rondo-finale, called empty and bombastic by its critics. Adorno, for one, accuses Mahler of being theatrical rather than sincere and repeats much the same charge he made about the Fifth Symphony, that the end of the work fails to counterbalance the start of it. Still, the movement has ingenious defenders. Some of them feel that with its strong hints of Wagner's self-important *Meistersinger* and of frothy Viennese operetta, the finale is one gigantic spoof. Mahler, they suggest, is poking fun at society's pomp and glitter, setting it against the 'real' worlds of love and nature he draws so vividly in previous movements. Others argue that Mahler is satirising not so much society as pretentious compositional technique. Ironically both claims resemble Adorno's theory about the Fourth Symphony, that its real meaning is the opposite of its apparent one. In the case of the Seventh Adorno has probably hit on the simple truth, that the finale is poor. As he puts it, 'only an apologist nervous to the point of obduracy could dispute that there are weak pieces by Mahler.'

Adorno calls the Eighth Symphony one of those weak pieces too. Indeed, he is even more scornful about it than about the finale of the Seventh, referring to 'the official *magnum opus*' (Mahler proudly dubbed the work 'a gift to the whole nation') and to a 'giant symbolic shell'. In similar vein, Hans Pfitzner responded to the opening chorus '*Veni, Creator Spiritus*' ('Come, Creator Spirit') with the sour reflection: 'But supposing He does not come.' Robert Simpson, a British composer who long championed neglected Mahler, gave the symphony's first part fair marks but called the second part 'an ocean of shameless kitsch'. The work's devotees claim its critics are so used to the tense, even neurotic Mahler that they cannot adjust when he composes something positive. That barb is aimed at Adorno in particular with his golden rule that 'Mahler is no yes-sayer.'

The rule is wrong but Adorno is on to something with his attack on the Eighth all the same. Mahler *is* a good yes-sayer; the question is only what he says yes in the teeth of. The apotheosis of the 'Resurrection' Symphony convinces because it is won only after fierce struggle. Much the same goes for the Fifth. The main trouble with the Eighth is that relatively little struggle occurs. Mahler seemed to have a brilliantly original concept; to marry two texts written in different languages a thousand years apart – '*Veni, Creator Spiritus*' and the end of Goethe's *Faust* – into a single drama of redemption. In fact he laid a trap for himself and fell into it.

Arguably, Mahler was unwise to choose a work of Goethe's at all. Hitherto he had very largely avoided setting indisputably great poetry to music, claiming that to do so would be profane. By turning to Goethe, the poet and dramatist he revered most, Mahler was breaking his own rule and taking a chance. The best he could hope for was to live up to the words. That might even have worked had he found the right Goethe text for his symphonic purpose, but he did not. The first part of *Faust* plunges from heaven to the world and hell; the second part, more intellectual and mystical but less dramatic, rises from earth to heaven and Faust's salvation. By the time the last scene is reached, the one Mahler set, the battle for Faust's soul is over. Mephistopheles has already admitted defeat and no longer appears. The stage is taken by a bewildering array of heavenly apparitions including 'angels', 'younger angels', 'more perfect angels' and 'blessed boys'. In context, the scene convinces; presented alone it falls flat.

Mahler might have saved the situation in two ways. He could have made the symphony's first part – '*Veni, Creator Spiritus*' – more tortured, so that the second part emerged as a victory hard won. Or he could have built more drama into that final scene by rewriting it or combining it with some of the earlier *Faust* material. No doubt in deference to Goethe, Mahler changed the text very little. He does take full advantage of what scope for tension Goethe offers; mainly in the opening section set in a craggy, wooded wilderness, and in the impassioned plea of Pater Profundus ending, 'O God, have mercy on my thoughts, Give light to my impoverished heart.' But much elsewhere is bland. Instrumentation used to pungent effect in other works (like the celesta in the Sixth Symphony) here goes for little, key themes return relatively undeveloped. Rhythms do not vary much either, but then Mahler is sticking closely to the purposeful tread of Goethe's heaven-bound verse.

Mahler is only one of many composers tempted by *Faust*, some fatally. Liszt shrewdly remarked that 'anything having to do with Goethe is dangerous for me to handle' but he went on to write a *Faust-Symphonie* all the same. It turned out to be one of his stronger works, thanks to its sharply contrasted three movements with their vivid character portraits of Faust, Gretchen and Mephistopheles. Even so the devilry seems too easily dispatched to make way for the triumphant choral finale, like Mahler's a setting of Goethe's concluding poem '*Alles vergängliche, Ist nur ein Gleichnis*' (All that is past of us Was but reflected). Berlioz came closer to avoiding bathos in his *Damnation de Faust*, a mix of opera and cantata he called a 'dramatic legend'. In his finale, Marguerite wins heavenly redemption while Faust, getting his just deserts, tumbles into the abyss.

That solution would not have done for Mahler any more than it did for Goethe. The two of them shared the same view about the meaning of *Faust*. Shortly before he died, Goethe quoted the lines '*Wer immer strebend sich bemüht Den können wir erlösen*' (Whoever strives unceasingly Him we can redeem), adding that they contained 'the key to Faust's salvation'.

Faust is not damned although he succumbs to temptation; he is saved because, driven by discontent with all the world offers, he develops through his mistakes and finally rises above them. He needs God's grace too but he has to earn it first by effort and suffering. How close that divine deal is to Mahler's conviction, or at least to his ever-recurring hope. He ends his 'Resurrection' Symphony with the words '*Was du geschlagen Zu Gott wird es dich tragen*' (What thou hast fought for Shall lead thee to God). He compares himself to the Old Testament's Jacob, extorting a blessing from God through 'my terrible struggles to bring my own works into being'. No wonder that he felt drawn to *Faust* and its author; that he talked so strikingly of Goethe to Erica Conrat that summer in Maiernigg as he finished his Sixth Symphony, an apparent 'last work' if ever there was one, and pushed on right away to the next.

At the end of *Faust* the hero's soul is left (presumably) enjoying the fruits of salvation, but that is not really how Goethe saw the after-life himself. Ever restless, he admitted he would not know what to do with eternal beatitude unless it gave him new tasks and problems to overcome. 'To me the eternal existence of my soul necessarily arises from my idea of activity,' he told Eckermann, his amanuensis. 'If I work on incessantly till my death, nature is bound to give me another form of existence when the present one can no longer sustain my spirit.' Here too he is close to Mahler. So close in fact that it might seem Mahler simply took over the idea from Goethe, but there were plenty of other influences too like Nietzsche, Fechner and Lipiner. Not least there was Wagner, fascinated by the doctrine of reincarnation and again pondering his old scheme for an opera about the Buddha when death claimed him.

'We will all return,' Mahler told Richard Specht, and stories abound showing he believed exactly that – not always, certainly, but fairly consistently. On one occasion he muttered, 'You too are immortal,' as he reluctantly crushed an injured fly; on another he carefully pushed to safety a moth which had landed on the score from which he was conducting. Such creatures, after all, had souls too; even plants and stones did so, according to Fechner. All were part of that indestructible chain of creation 'from the lowest to the highest things' Mahler extolled in the Third Symphony. Not, it should be said, that this insight stopped him from raging over the distracting bird-song in Steinbach or the early cockcrow in Alt-Schluderbach!

In *Das Lied von der Erde* Mahler grapples with the issue of immortality yet again. That he adopts a different approach after the 'Symphony of a Thousand' should be no surprise. Whatever its artistic merit, the Eighth was an act of gigantism not to be repeated. Where could Mahler go from there? He had faced a similar problem after completing the marathon Third Symphony and had solved it with the deceptively simple-seeming Fourth. *Das Lied* is very far from simple but much of it has the intimacy of chamber music. It confides where the Eighth proclaims; it is daring in many ways and yet it is not wholly new. The often astringent instrumentation harks back to the *Kindertotenlieder* and *Rückert-Lieder*; so in part does the pentatonic (five-note) technique used in *Das Lied* to help evoke oriental atmosphere. Even the work's complex heterophony (the simultaneous variation of a single melody, often associated with non-Western music) has popped up here and there in Mahler before. Now, though, all these elements are combined in one large-scale piece, and with such unobtrusive skill that the whole thing sounds improvised. By 1908, at the height of his powers and with the Eighth behind him, Mahler was ready for *Das Lied*. Perhaps he would have got down to it a year earlier but for that dreadful summer – and assuming that by then he had already come across the anthology of poems called *Die chinesische Flöte (The Chinese Flute)*.

Alma claims that Mahler did, in fact, make a start on *Das Lied* in 1907 but again her account looks suspect. She says that in the late summer, after Putzi's death and the verdict on his heart, Mahler recalled the melancholy contents of *Die chinesische Flöte* which a friend had given him some time before. He now selected verses from it, she says, and began to sketch the piece which a year later took final shape as *Das Lied von der Erde*. That seems unlikely because the anthology was first published (in Leipzig) only in October 1907, though conceivably Mahler might have got an advance copy. Alma is certainly wrong when she calls the book 'a recent translation from the Chinese by Hans Bethge', an error often repeated since. Bethge, a young German lyric poet fascinated by Arabic and oriental culture, had no Chinese. In *Die chinesische Flöte* he simply paraphrased versions of (mainly ancient) Chinese poems already produced by various other European literati. He made a sensitive job of it but some of the material he selected had itself been wrongly attributed and poorly translated.

Mahler was thus far from the original sources but there is no sign that that bothered him, if indeed he was aware of it at all. The haunting reflections on youth and loneliness, on love and farewell, and on earth's endless beauty, stirred his creativity – and not only his. Composers including Schönberg, Webern and Richard Strauss also drew inspiration from *Die chinesische Flöte*, which Bethge followed up with a series of similarly exotic and popular collections. Orientalism, loosely defined, was 'in the air'. The wealthy used Asian motifs in home decoration; Puccini scored a hit (in Vienna too) with *Madam Butterfly*; Debussy, Ravel and Stravinsky exploited pentatonism; Guido Adler wrote a learned tract underlining the heterophony in Siamese, Javanese and Japanese music; a banker friend gave Mahler recorded cylinders of Chinese music which he had found on sale in Vienna. Wholly distinctive though it is, *Das Lied* was part of a trend.

Much to the work's advantage, Mahler treated Bethge's verse with far less respect than he did Goethe's in the Eighth. He retitled, rearranged, cut and added to the texts with such vigour that it is fair to call him co-author as well as composer of *Das Lied*. From Bethge's eighty-three poems Mahler chose seven and fashioned them into six strongly varied movements – a weighty one at the start and another at the end, sandwiching a quasi-adagio, a quasi-scherzo and two brief intermezzi. That structure is, of course, close to that of the Third Symphony, itself a kind of *Song of the Earth*, although the order of the inner parts differs. Both six-movement works (the only ones Mahler wrote) might have split under the pressure of their ultra-diverse material; both are held together above all by thematic cross-reference and the cunning transformation of a mood. There are major differences too, of course. *Das Lied* is much shorter (usually lasting just over an hour to the Third's hundred minutes or so) and it is far subtler. No Mahler score, perhaps no score at all, better repays prolonged scrutiny.

With '*Das Trinklied vom Jammer der Erde*' ('The drinking song of earth's misery'), after the eighth-century poet Li-Tai-Po, *Das Lied* does not so much start as leap out of nowhere for the jugular. The key is A minor, like that of the tragic Sixth Symphony, the tone by turns violent, defiant, despairing. Condemned by Mahler to sing this horror-tale of man's mortality in an unnaturally high register, most tenors sound strained, hysterical even – which here is as it should be. Rising and falling themes hurled out simultaneously threaten to split the orchestral texture. Flutter-tongued woodwind interjections add to the terror, culminating in the ghastly vision of an ape howling on graves in the moonlight. Three times the implacable refrain returns: 'Dark is life and dark is death'. After the third, the movement is felled by a single sharp knockout blow.

Still, tucked away at the heart of the piece is another vision. 'The firmament is blue eternally,' sings the tenor/poet, 'and the earth/Will long stand fast and blossom in spring.' Just those few words, gone too soon to be a real cause for hope, and sure enough the next lines are contemptuous. 'But thou, O man, how long then livest thou?/Not a hundred years canst thou delight In all the rotten trash of this earth.' That seems to settle that. And yet the little episode ending with 'spring' lingers in the memory, thanks to the tender scoring with high strings, harp and woodwind and (with luck) the tenor's *piano ma appassionato* delivery. Mahler here drops a clue; the solution emerges only five movements later. Meanwhile, what he does not do is almost as interesting as what he does. Bethge's version of the poem includes the lines: 'There is but one possession you can be sure of:/That is the grave, the grinning one, at the end.' Mahler scraps them.

The second song, *'Der Einsame im Herbst'* ('The lonely one in autumn'), brings contrast but no relief. The nightmare scenes of the *'Trinklied'* give way to a landscape of frost and blue mist; universal calamity becomes personal pain too intense for full expression. It is the world of the *Kindertotenlieder* and, sure enough, Mahler uses similarly sparse orchestration. Trumpets, trombones and percussion have no place here. Just once passion bursts out, with the final lines: 'Sun of love, will you never shine again,/And dry up, tenderly, my bitter tears?' But although the phrase begins *'Mit grossem Aufschwung'* (with great impetus) it ends quietly *'ohne Ausdruck'* (without expression). The question catches in the singer's throat because the answer seems all too clear. On the whole Mahler sticks closely to Bethge's text but he makes a tiny change to the title. Bethge's *'Die'* (feminine) *'Einsame im Herbst'* becomes *'Der'* (masculine) *'Einsame im Herbst'*. This song, like numbers four and six, is usually performed by an alto but Mahler suggests a baritone as an alternative. He does so in a bracket as though offering a second-best option, but the title change here suggests he has a male victim/protagonist in mind all the same. Himself?

Relief comes at last, but never really reliably, in the following three songs – '*Von der Jugend*' ('Of youth'), '*Von der Schönheit*' ('Of beauty') and '*Der Trunkene im Frühling*' ('The drunkard in spring'). It is not clear who wrote the first poem, wrongly attributed by Bethge and hence by Mahler to Li-Tai-Po. But whoever it was devised a charming scene; elegant friends drinking and chatting in a porcelain pavilion, a little arched bridge of jade, the whole reflected in a peaceful pool. Mahler gives it some of his daintiest music with tinkling triangle and swishing cymbals. Weighty issues do not belong here. Death, if perceived at all, seems no more daunting than distant thunder. Everything pleasingly lacks substance, like the images in the water.

The world of '*Von der Schönheit*' seems just as fragile at the start, but not for long. Under the longing gaze of maidens picking flowers on a river-bank, young men on horseback come galloping by. Adding detail and drama to Bethge's version, Mahler briefly lets his very full orchestra off the leash. Piccolo, triple woodwind, four horns, two trumpets, three trombones, tuba, tambourine, mandolin, bass drum, cymbals, harps and strings – all get an outing. Even the timpani join in, for the first and last time in *Das Lied*. The hoofs stamp, the hearts beat faster – but the horse-men pass and the piece dies away in tremolos of unfulfilled yearning. Perhaps there will be other young men; or perhaps, as Joseph Conrad puts it at the end of one of his tales, what is hoped for from life is already gone 'in a sigh, in a flash – together with the youth, with the strength, with the romance of illusions.'

In the rollicking little fifth song, the drunkard wastes no valuable boozing time on fruitless matters like hope and love. 'If life is but a dream,' he cries, 'why then toil and fret?' Even when he wakes to hear a bird singing that spring has come (piccolo, solo violin and distant echoes of the Seventh Symphony's Andante amoroso), he shrugs and reaches again for the bottle. 'For what does spring matter to me? Let me be drunk.' For the second time in *Das Lied*, spring comes and goes in a trice.

What lasts? The obvious answer comes tolling in at the start of '*Der Abschied*' ('The farewell'), the sixth song, which is nearly as long as the other five put together. With their hushed tam-tam strokes and *pizzicato* lower strings, the opening bars have chilling inevitability as if plucked from the ether (though, amazingly, Mahler added the tam-tam here only as an afterthought). The soloist is directed to sing '*In erzählendem Ton, ohne Ausdruck*' (like a narration, without expression). What need is there for more? Death is imminent, inescapable. It alone endures. Having established that at the outset, Mahler sets out to show it is wrong.

For one thing he radically alters the text. In '*Der Abschied*' Mahler runs together two of Bethge's poems, '*In Erwartung des Freundes*' ('Awaiting a friend') after Mong-Kao-Jen, and '*Der Abschied des Freundes*' ('The friend's departure') after Wang-Wei. In Bethge's versions the tone is largely resigned and the regular stanza form adds to the sense of inevitability. Mainly by insertions, Mahler shakes up the stanzas and produces a positive denouement which would have surprised Bethge, and presumably the ancient Chinese too. Where Bethge's wanderer simply goes to the mountains to seek rest for his lonely heart, Mahler adds the line: 'I am journeying to the homeland, to my resting place.' Bethge rounds off the piece with the dispassionate 'The earth is everywhere the same,/And eternal, eternal the white clouds . . .' Mahler transforms this to 'The dear earth everywhere/Blossoms in spring and grows green again!/ Everywhere and for ever the distance shines bright and blue!/For ever . . . for ever . . .'. Spring comes again to *Das Lied* and this time rounds it off.

Has Mahler, desperate for a happy ending, simply produced some brighter words and composed music to fit them? A look at the draft scores shows that here and there he did just the opposite. He first wrote the music and then, dissatisfied with the text, rewrote Bethge. That is not all. As often before, but never with greater mastery, he matched musical technique and structure to a philosophical message. Or was it, rather, that the message flowed inevitably out of the music? No doubt Mahler would have been hard pressed to decide which. In writing the Third Symphony he felt he had rediscovered 'profound and eternal laws' applying not just to composition but to all creation. In the Fourth, he unravelled a complex start into the 'peace which passeth understanding' of the childlike finale. How much was accident, how much design?

Against first appearances, '*Der Abschied*' is a single, titanic struggle. On one side is that so-familiar Mahler device, the march. Sometimes it is unmistakable, as in the bleak orchestral interlude before the longed-for friend finally appears; sometimes it is quite unobtrusive, but it is rarely absent for long. Set against it are passages so free in their rhythm and polyphony that they seem close to anarchy; for instance, when 'The brook sings, full of melody, through the darkness', or when 'The birds huddle silent on the branches./The world falls asleep!' These near-chaotic moments check the steady tramp of the march much as Mahler's insertions in the text break up Bethge's over-tidy stanzas. Years before in a talk with Natalie Bauer-Lechner, Mahler had linked his idea of polyphony to the sounds he heard as a child, flooding to him from all sides and in all rhythms in the woods near Iglau. There are plenty of passages in the symphonies which suggest exactly that, but none more daring or complex than here. Mahler realised that very well. 'Have you any notion how this should be conducted?' he asked Bruno Walter on showing him the score of 'Der Abschied'. 'I haven't!' Walter had to solve the problem himself. He gave Das Lied its première in Munich in November 1911, six months after Mahler's death.

The struggle is resolved, or rather dissolved, close to the movement's end after the words 'Still ist mein Herz und harret seiner Stunde!' (My heart is still and awaits its hour!). The music falters, appears to die; then an ever more intense crescendo builds on the high strings and from it soars the soloist's 'Die liebe Erde. . .' It is a moment of ecstatic release. There is no more pulse, no more weight. Terms like strictness and freedom no longer apply. Once more the music surges, then fades bit by bit as 'Ewig' is repeated and repeated. After setting out in C minor, the key of Todtenfeier, 'Der Abschied' takes its leave in C major.

Adorno decided that Das Lied was pessimistic. The universe may be eternal, the earth may go on renewing itself (though not quite indefinitely), but man's days are few. He mistook the message of the first song for that of the whole work. Not so Benjamin Britten. Writing to a friend in 1937, when Mahler's music was ill known in Britain, he commented, 'The same harmonic progressions that Wagner used to colour his essentially morbid love-scenes (his "liebes" is naturally followed by "Tod") are used here to paint a serenity literally supernatural. I cannot understand it – it passes over me like a tidal wave – and that matters not a jot either, because it goes on for ever, even if it is never performed again – that final chord is printed on the atmosphere. Perhaps if I could understand some of the Indian philosophies I might approach it a little.'

Britten's last point is specially acute. 'What we leave behind us is only the husk, the shell,' Mahler said in a letter to Alma in 1909. 'The Meistersinger, the Ninth [Beethoven's], Faust – all of them are only the discarded husk! No more, properly speaking, than our bodies are! I don't of course mean that artistic creation is superfluous. It is a necessity of a man for growth and joy, which again is a question of health and creative energy. – But what actual need is there of notes?' A dangerous question for a composer. Musically, philosophically, Mahler had come a long, long way.

And yet he went on. In principle that should be no surprise by now. As assiduous as Goethe, Mahler had constantly produced startling follow-ups to works which seemed to have said everything. But what on earth (or beyond it) could he find to say after *Das Lied*, and with what means? He had hovered on the border of tonality, arguably creating a greater sense of tension than by crossing it altogether. And like Webern later, he had refined music to the point where every silence seemed to count as much as every sound. 'What actual need is there of notes?'

Yet he found a sequel and it was Schönberg who put his finger best on its special character. In the Ninth Symphony, he said in a speech a year after Mahler's death, 'the author hardly speaks as an individual any longer. It almost seems as though this work must have a concealed author who uses Mahler merely as his spokesman, as his mouthpiece. This symphony is no longer couched in the personal tone. It consists, so to speak, of objective, almost passionless statements of a beauty which becomes perceptible only to one who can dispense with animal warmth and feel at home in spiritual coolness.' That is well said. There are plenty of eruptions in the Ninth, but they seem more witnessed than experienced – like the scene at dusk at the start of '*Der Abschied*'. The piece burns with a cold flame.

While Mahler was composing the first parts of the Ninth at Alt-Schluderbach in June–July 1909, Alma was 60 miles further south taking a cure in Levico. Did she really need treatment, or could she just not face a whole summer in the country with a touchy husband who spent much of his time in a hut? 'I was in a state of profound melancholy,' Alma writes in her *Memories*. 'I sat night after night on my balcony, weeping and looking out at the crowd of gay and happy people, whose laughter grated on my ears. I longed to plunge myself into love or life or anything that could release me from my icy constraint.' She and Mahler were in constant contact, or rather they wrote to one another. 'We exchanged letters daily on abstract topics,' Alma says.

If Mahler realised his marriage was close to crisis, his letters give no sign of it. Several of his friends and ex-friends were more perceptive. One of them, Guido Adler, actually got as far as writing to Mahler about his fears. His letter has not survived but the sharp reply has. 'I have to say something about my wife, to whom your views and remarks did a great injustice,' Mahler writes. 'You should know her well enough by now. When have you ever found her guilty of extravagance or selfishness . . . my wife is not only a courageous, faithful companion who shares all my spiritual interests, but also (a rare combination) a sensible, level-headed manager of our domestic affairs.' Alma, Mahler reassured his worried friend, 'has *nothing* but my welfare in mind.'

The letter was written in New York on New Year's Day 1910.

Chapter Ten

Inferno

AT THE START of June 1910, Alma went for another rest-cure, this time to the fashionable spa of Tobelbad near Graz in Styria. From the account in her *Memories and Letters*, the stay was not much happier than the one a year earlier in Levico. She was so solitary and melancholy, she writes, that the head of the sanatorium introduced her to young people who would keep her company on walks. 'There was an architect, X, whom I found particularly sympathetic, and I soon had little doubt that he was in love with me and hoping I might return his love. So I left.'

From the moment it appeared (1940), this version seemed suspect; all the more so since the mysterious Mr X was not hard to identify as Walter Gropius, one of the century's most influential architects and from 1915 to 1920 Alma's second husband. Did she really resist him, as she claimed, when they first met? Gropius was then twenty-seven (nearly four years younger than Alma) and was just starting to make his way with a practice of his own in Berlin, his home town. He was still years away from his breakthrough to fame as director of the revolutionary Bauhaus school of applied art and architecture (broken up by the Nazis in 1933). But special talent, even in embryo, always drew Alma. Besides, Gropius was athletic, full of humour and single; no wonder she found him 'sympathetic'. Just how much so did not emerge until the 1980s when hitherto private correspondence between the couple was revealed in Gropius's authorised biography.

The truth is that Alma met Gropius on 4th June, soon after her arrival in Tobelbad, and was at least as drawn to him as he to her. The same evening they went for a long moonlit walk together and at some stage they became lovers. Alma recalls hours together broken only by a nightingale's song and the dawn light. 'By my side lay a handsome young man. And that night two souls had found each other, their two bodies forgotten.' The Tobelbad idyll ended in the second half of July when Alma returned to Mahler at Alt-Schluderbach, but neither she nor Gropius dreamed of saying goobye for good. For the time being, they agreed to stay in touch via the poste restante in Toblach.

Did Mahler suspect nothing? He was, as usual, very busy. Soon after his arrival in Europe in April he had given the French première of his Second Symphony in Paris, the last time he conducted the work anywhere. Debussy, for one, walked out during the performance. A disastrous visit to Rome followed. Mahler gave two concerts there but, furious with the wretched orchestra, cancelled a third and stormed off to Vienna. For much of May and June he was flitting between Vienna, Leipzig and Munich rehearsing some of the huge forces needed for the première of his Eighth Symphony, planned for September.

It was while he was in Munich that he began to feel something might be really wrong with Alma. She was sending him sad little notes, sometimes none at all. 'Are you hiding something from me?' he wrote on 21st June. 'For I feel there is something to be read between the lines.' A week or so later he went briefly to Tobelbad to check on things, then left for Alt-Schluderbach mightily reassured. 'Just a word to let you know I found Almschi much fresher and fitter,' he told Anna Moll on his departure, 'and am firmly convinced her cure here is doing her a great deal of good.'

Alma had only been back with Mahler for a week or two when the blow fell. Gropius wrote her a letter begging her to join him but addressed it instead to Mahler. 'Whether the young man made a mistake in the stress of emotion or whether it was his unconscious wish that it should come into Mahler's hands, remains a mystery,' Alma writes in her *Memories*. What, of course, she did not care to reveal was the scheme she and Gropius had devised for communicating behind Mahler's back. It seems hardly likely that Gropius would have written 'Herr Direktor Mahler, Alt-Schluderbach' on the envelope when he really intended it for Alma 'Postlagernd, Toblach'. Probably Gropius aimed to force the issue. At any rate he did.

Mahler returned from his hut, opened the letter and chokingly asked Alma, 'What is this?' Apparently he made no accusations – quite the contrary. It was Alma who went on the attack. She told him how she had 'longed for his love year after year and that he, in his fanatical concentration on his own life, had simply overlooked me. As I spoke, he felt for the first time that something is owed to the person with whom one's life has once been linked. He suddenly felt a sense of guilt.' Both weeping, they summoned Anna Moll, just as they had done when Putzi had died three years earlier. If Alma still bore her mother a grudge for marrying Moll, she none the less looked to her for help. As for Mahler, he trusted Anna completely – wrongly as it proved.

Gropius came to Toblach, without warning according to Alma. She says she happened to catch sight of him hiding under a bridge when she and Mahler were out driving. Apparently he had tried to approach the Alt-Schluderbach farmhouse but a dog chased him away. Mahler did not. When Alma admitted whom she had seen, he went off by night to find Gropius and, lantern in hand, led him back home. He left the two of them together and retired to read the Bible by candlelight, saying Alma should make her decision. 'But I had no choice,' she writes. The next day she saw Gropius off at Toblach railway station. Half-way home she met Mahler who had hurried after her, in dread that she had left for good after all. And that, as far as Alma's *Memories* are concerned, was the end of her link with the young Mr X.

In fact it was only the start. Alma and Gropius henceforth made one hurried tryst after another and, even when Mahler was dying, continued to exchange love letters. Alma's became increasingly ardent. She signed herself 'Your Wife', yearned for a child from him and for the moment when 'you lie naked against my body and nothing but sleep can separate us'. Less emotionally, she observed that 'for the heart and all other organs, nothing is worse than enforced asceticism'. Alma was probably now achieving sexual fulfilment for the first time – despite all her early flirtations and some post-marriage ones, for instance with Pfitzner and Ossip Gabrilovich, a handsome young Russian-born musician torn between passion for Alma and reverence for her husband's work. None of this dallying seems to have gone beyond a few fleeting embraces.

As for Mahler himself, Alma constantly dropped heavy hints that he was a poor lover, sometimes impotent. 'I knew that my marriage was no marriage and that my own life was utterly unfulfilled,' she writes in *Memories*. Not that this view of Mahler's sexual prowess seems to have curbed her fears that he was carrying on with other women, notably Anna von Mildenburg. The probable truth is that Alma simply did not find Mahler physically attractive. In a diary entry in 1905, she records telling Mahler that when they first met she found his smell 'unsympathetic'; to which he replied, 'That is the key to a lot – you have acted against your nature.' If anything their physical relationship got worse. According to a much later diary entry, Alma kept her bedroom door firmly shut in the last years of her marriage so that Mahler would not come to her while she was asleep.

An all-too-busy husband of middle age, a seductive younger wife with too much time on her hands and a vigorous interloper in his twenties – on the face of it a banal tale. Gropius's allegedly misaddressed letter and his attempted concealment under a bridge even add elements of farce. Perhaps Mahler had feared something of the kind all along: he had written warningly to Alma before their marriage about 'Sachs and Evchen', a reference to the philosopher-cobbler in *Die Meistersinger* and the girl he wisely sees is too young for him. Though any presentiment Mahler may have had can scarcely have softened the blow when it came. Arguably, he never suffered a worse one – not even in 1907.

Mahler was often impatient and schoolmasterly with Alma, he apparently failed to satisfy her sexually (few ever did for long) but he adored her all the same. 'I live only for you and Gucki,' he wrote to her in Tobelbad. 'Everything else is so insipid – a bad woodcut next to a Titian.' Eager to surprise her on her thirty-first birthday at the end of August, he ordered a diadem to be made to a design he had selected. Between rehearsals that same summer he went on trips near Vienna looking for a house, a castle even, where he and the family could settle – not at once of course but . . . sometime soon. He finally decided to build, not buy, and acquired a plot of land high up at Breitenstein am Semmering, where he and Alma had spent happy breaks in the Vienna Opera days. Rumours spread, perhaps nourished by this home-hunting, that Mahler might even

be induced to return to his old opera job. Weingartner was already planning to step down after less than three years as director and the hunt was
on for a successor. An informal approach was, indeed, made to Mahler in
the autumn but there is no evidence he seriously considered it. In the
event the post went in 1911 to Hans Gregor, no musician but (evidently
more important) a canny businessman.

Back in Alt-Schluderbach (and with Alma still away), Mahler was
deluged with letters and telegrams to mark his fiftieth birthday on 7th
July. He claims he 'cursed and swore' at the thought of having to answer
them all, but two at least greatly pleased him. One was from Siegfried
Lipiner, again on friendly terms with Mahler after years of estrangement,
the other from Schönberg who begged Mahler to 'come back soon to our
hated, beloved Vienna and stay here'. A book in his honour had been
compiled too with contributions from, among others, Richard Strauss,
Max Reger, Paul Dukas, Alfredo Casella, Romain Rolland, Gerhard
Hauptmann, Stefan Zweig, Hugo von Hofmannsthal and Arthur
Schnitzler. Whether he cared or not, Mahler was a famous man.

A few weeks after that birthday came the crash. Mahler lost his bearings. Alma says he would lie on the floor of his hut weeping for fear of
losing her. One night she found him unconscious on the landing, a
lighted candle beside him. He left notes for her, agonised, pathetic. 'My
darling, my lyre, Come and exorcise the spirits of darkness, they claw
hold of me, they throw me to the ground,' he wrote in one. In another,
'Breath of my life!/I have kissed your little slippers a thousand times and
stood yearning at your door . . . but the demons have punished me
because again I thought of myself and not of you, my dear one.' Desperate for ways to please her, Mahler even unearthed some of Alma's early
songs and pronounced them 'excellent. I insist on your working on them
and we'll have them published.' It was not quite nine years since he had
ruled there could not be two composers in the family. Alma claims she
felt no triumph. True or not, she was certainly alarmed. Mahler's 'idolatrous love and reverence,' she wrote, 'can hardly be called normal any
more.'

Mahler must have felt the same himself. At least he decided to go and
see Freud. It is often said he did so because he had become impotent, a
claim seemingly backed by Freud's comment that Mahler sought him out
because of 'his wife's resentment of the withdrawal of his libido from

her'. Since Alma was keeping her bedroom door shut on Mahler, it is fair to ask who had withdrawn from whom. At any rate Mahler was desperate for help to save his crumbling marriage. He must have been, to seek out Freud at all (with a distant relative of Alma's acting as go-between). Mahler thought little of Freud's work and the two men had never previously been in touch, although they had lived within a short walk of one another in Vienna for years. Now, at his wits' end, he made and cancelled an appointment three times. Finally the two agreed to their now famous meeting on 26th August at the Dutch town of Leiden, close to where Freud was holidaying. Mahler left Toblach on the 25th, sending telegrams and a poem fluttering back to Alma from each stage of the long trip.

Naturally enough, much has been made of the Mahler-Freud talk. The mere thought of an exchange between the father of psychoanalysis and one of the most complex of composers is mightily intriguing. Something revealing, surely, could not fail to come out of it. Perhaps it did and the evidence is too thin to show it, or perhaps the pair needed considerably more time than a four-hour stroll round town. In any case the content of the 'analysis', as reported, seems suspiciously superficial. That certainly goes for the claim, described in chapter one, that thanks to Freud Mahler suddenly saw a link between an unhappy childhood incident and his music's failure to achieve 'the highest rank'. The tale of the 'name game' between the two men rings hollow too. Freud is said to have expressed wonder that Mahler had married a woman named Alma although his mother, who 'evidently played a dominating part' in his life, was called Marie. Mahler, reportedly 'greatly impressed' by Freud's perception, replied that his wife's second name was Maria but that he called her Marie. If he did so there is no record of it. In his letters he calls Alma all sorts of things – from 'Lux' to 'Almschilitzilitzilitzili' – but not Marie. Mahler may well have been encouraged by Freud's insight that Alma, conditioned by her deep love for her father, was attracted to older men. There was surely something in that view, at least there had been a decade or so before. But did Freud know about Gropius?

While both men seem to have found the talk worthwhile neither made great claims for it. Freud did say later that 'If I may believe reports, I achieved much with him' but he added that 'No light fell at the time on the symptomatic façade of his obsessional neurosis. It was as if you would dig a single shaft through a mysterious building.' Mahler was briefer. In a telegram to Alma on the trip home he reported, 'I am happy. Interview interesting. Mountains made out of molehills.' Perhaps the most interesting thing about the talk is what, apparently, was not discussed at all – Mahler's physical health. It seems that Freud did not ask about it and Mahler did not raise it. If Mahler had felt he was close to death from a heart ailment presumably he would have thought it worth a mention – even to a psychoanalyst.

Can't this anguished tale be heard loud and clear in the work Mahler was composing that summer, his Tenth Symphony? So much of the piece is desolate although, like most of its predecessors, it struggles to a kind of victory in the end. Mahler wrote nothing more terrifying than the nine-note *fortissimo* for full orchestra, dissonance piled on dissonance and pierced by a high trumpet A, which erupts in the first movement. The shock of Gropius's letter? Alma's accusations? Hardly less appalling is the muffled drum stroke which ends the fourth movement and is repeated in the fifth. Alma links it to the sound they once heard together from a funeral cortège which passed far below their hotel window during their first winter in New York. Perhaps that is where Mahler got his raw material, but doesn't he use it here to relate to a deeper and more recent blow? Then there is the title *Purgatorio* Mahler gave the biting little third movement with its echoes of '*Das irdische Leben*', the *Wunderhorn* song about a child left to starve to death. Isn't Mahler now (or again) the abandoned one?

Above all there are the tortured words Mahler scrawled on the manuscript; among them '*Erbarmen!! O Gott! O Gott! Warum hast du mich verlassen?*' (Mercy!! Oh God! Oh God! Why hast thou forsaken me?) and '*Der Teufel tanzt as mit mir/Wahnsinn, fass mich an, Verfluchten!/Vernichte mich/Dass ich vergesse, dass ich bin!*' (The devil dances it with me/Madness seize me, accursed one/Destroy me/That I forget, that I am!). How like several of the notes Mahler left for Alma in the farmhouse. He may have written something even more shocking on the bottom half of the *Purgatorio's* title page but the section has been sliced off, presumably by Alma.

This is reason enough, one might think, to give the symphony a subtitle like 'The summer of 1910' or simply 'Inferno'. Some even directly link the work's unfinished state to Mahler's talk with Freud. Emanuel Garcia, an American psychoanalyst, puts this case eloquently in a paper made public in 1994. He argues that Mahler had always suffered from an Oedipal conflict which, at huge cost to his personal life, he had sublimated in artistic creation. When Freud showed him the extent of his unconscious love for his mother and its effect on his marriage, Mahler faced a stark choice: to pursue his old ways and risk losing his wife or to choose Alma and forsake artistic creativity. He picked the latter, doing no more work on the Tenth, but he could not live without creating. Paradoxically he thus wrote his own death sentence.

Faced with so much conjecture and apparent evidence it is worth looking more closely at Mahler's work schedule that summer. What exists of the Tenth Symphony was almost certainly written between 3rd July, when Mahler arrived in Alt-Schluderbach from Tobelbad, and 3rd September when he left for Munich. It is impossible to be precise but Mahler may have lost, all in all, around a fortnight's composing because of birthday and business letter-writing, proof-reading, his marriage crisis and the trip to see Freud. That would have left him some seven weeks during which he produced a five-movement symphony of more than 1900 bars: quick going, although only the first two movements and part of the third exist in full-score draft, i.e. with much of the orchestration already in place. Mahler would have revised even this had he got round to the final stage of a definitive full score. The rest of the work is thin, sometimes skeletal, in texture but reasonably clear in outline. When Gropius's letter arrived in late July or early August Mahler had probably been at work for around three weeks. Exactly how far he got in that time is a matter of intense and probably endless debate. But the key point is that the Tenth Symphony must have been well under way when the crisis broke.

How did Mahler react to the shock, not as a husband but as a composer? He neither stopped work altogether, at least not for long, nor did he drop the piece he was writing and start another. He went on with the same symphony, and it is hardly likely that he abruptly gave it a different character because of the crisis, revamping what he had already done and composing the rest to match. It is true that he made changes as he went along and that, until a late stage, he was in doubt about the order of the movements. But for Mahler that was nothing new. It is certainly not proof that the events of his life at the time were affecting the content of his work.

Perhaps the most striking aspect of the Tenth is the musical sense it makes although unfinished. It was well on the way to being one of the best structured of Mahler's symphonies – long, slowish movements at the start and finish enclosing two scherzos and, as fulcrum, the painful (cleansing?) *Purgatorio*. No wonder several Mahler enthusiasts have since produced their own 'complete' versions of the Tenth, or at least have filled out the original enough to permit orchestral performance of all five movements. By comparison the Ninth Symphony, for all its virtues, seems lop-sided with a weighty first movement never quite counter-balanced by the succeeding three. Mahler may often have lain weeping in his hut during that dreadful summer of 1910, as Alma says, but his mastery of symphonic form did not desert him. Indeed, it was never more telling.

It does no justice to the Tenth to see it as the immediate product of a domestic crisis, however terrible, or even as a delayed reaction to the blows of 1907. That approach is common but too narrow. So is the tendency to tidy the work away along with the Ninth Symphony and *Das Lied von der Erde* as an example of Mahler's 'late style'. Since much of the tonal daring and pungent orchestration in all three pieces was foreshadowed in works years before, the 'late style' is something of a misnomer. Indeed all efforts to slot Mahler's output into neat categories, from the so-called *Wunderhorn* period on, tend to mislead. There is too much overlap.

If the Tenth Symphony can be docketed sensibly at all, then it is as the last, unfinished, stage of a lifelong quest. Over decades, in work after work, Mahler developed his musical language and perfected his technique but the questions he posed stayed essentially the same – 'What did you live for? Why did you suffer? Is it only a vast terrifying joke?' He extracted many different answers, from the brassy triumph of the First Symphony to the mystical release of *Das Lied*, but he went on asking. He was still doing so when he began what turned out to be his last piece. Gropius's and Alma's accusations were no reason for Mahler to change course in his work. On the contrary, they added a bitter emphasis to all-too-familiar questions.

Whatever the stimulus for the music itself, it seems obvious (almost always a danger sign with Mahler) that the tortured words on the manuscript must be directly related to the marital crisis. No doubt some are – but not only to that. For instance, the phrase *'Der Teufel tanzt es mit mir'* may well have been written before the fateful letter had even arrived. *Purgatorio* could, of course, be a reference to Dante's *La Divina Commedia* but it is also the title of a group of poems by Lipiner, whose work Mahler was rereading that summer. And Lipiner, as Mahler well knew, had recently been undergoing painful radium treatment for cancer. Other jottings on the score seem to betray Lipiner's influence too, and surely Mahler might well have scribbled them in anyway, marital crisis or not, believing (correctly) that his rediscovered poet-friend was a doomed man. Or perhaps, consciously or not, he identified Lipiner's agony with his own. We shall never know for sure.

At least there is no room for doubt about the words Mahler wrote close to the sigh of consolation on the strings with which the work ends: *'Für dich leben! Für dich sterben! Almschi'* (To live for you! To die for you! Almschi). In later years Alma kept the score with its final tribute on display in her living-room – 'like a hunting trophy' as one visitor put it.

There is no sign that Mahler ever worked on the Tenth Symphony again after his visit to Freud, but then time was short. He returned to Alt-Schluderbach from Leiden on 28th August and left six days later for final rehearsals of the Eighth Symphony in Munich. Perhaps only then did Mahler really believe the première, set for 12th September, would come off after all. Preparations had been fraught – no wonder, with the small army of performers to bring by train from widely separated cities – and several times over Mahler lost heart. In a letter to Bruno Walter in April he had compared the planned performance to a 'catastrophic Barnum-and-Bailey' show and, still later, he had fired off a furious complaint to the impresario Emil Gutmann about efforts to cut rehearsal time. 'I am simply dumbfounded,' Mahler wrote. 'Either every item in our agreement is kept to – i.e. the full three days are at my disposal, without any restriction (incidentally, that is the minimum necessary) – or you may take this as my final withdrawal.'

Mahler got virtually all he wanted. Even the bells of passing trams were muffled to ensure that the concert, in the 3200-seat Neue

Musikfesthalle (New Music Festival Hall) of Munich's Exhibition Park, would be undisturbed. The event could have been a disaster all the same, not least for Gutmann who no doubt cursed 'pig-headed' Mahler much as Richard Strauss had done years earlier before the first performance of the Third Symphony. Instead it was a triumph – so much of one, in fact, that the long list of notables present has since been extended by myth. Despite claims to the contrary little royalty was there, nor was Georges Clemenceau (it was his brother Paul), nor Otto Klemperer (who was only at rehearsals), nor Edward Elgar, nor Rachmaninoff. The report, repeated ever since, that 'more than a thousand' performers took part is suspect too. It was the publicity-conscious Gutmann who (to Mahler's dismay) coined the nickname 'Symphony of a Thousand' and, indeed, about 1030 instrumentalists and singers were scheduled to appear. Not all did so, however. Records show that the special train bringing one of the choirs, supposedly 250-strong, from Vienna was shortened by one carriage because of last-minute cancellations.

It was easily Mahler's biggest lifetime success and one of the last great premières before the old Europe began to disintegrate, four years later, in the First World War. Among those who really did attend were the composers Richard Strauss, Siegfried Wagner and Anton Webern; the conductors Bruno Walter, Willem Mengelberg and the young Leopold Stokowski (who was to give the American première in Philadelphia six years later), the singers Erik Schmedes and Anna von Mildenburg (Mahler's Vienna Tristan and Isolde); men of the stage like Alfred Roller and Max Reinhardt, of science like Arnold Berliner, of painting and design like Koloman Moser, of literature like Thomas Mann. 'When Mahler finally appeared on the podium,' wrote Maurice Baumfeld, a friend from New York, 'the entire audience, as if responding to a secret signal, rose to its feet, initially in silence. The way a king is greeted. Only when Mahler, visibly surprised, gestured his gratitude did a cheering erupt of a kind that is seldom heard at such an event. All this, before the performance began.' At the end the jubilation lasted nearly half an hour. The same evening Mann visited Mahler at his hotel but, still over-whelmed, was uncharacteristically lost for words. Later he sent round a copy of his new novel *Königliche Hoheit (Royal Highness)*, calling it a modest gift for 'a man who seems to me to embody the most serious and sacred artistic purpose of our time'.

How far from the devastated figure weeping in his mountain hut only weeks before! That Mahler still (or again) had the highest hopes of his marriage is clear from his letter to Alma from Munich on 5th September. His yearning, he told her, was more intense than ever. 'But what a torment, what an agony, that you can no longer return it. But as truly as love must reawaken love, and faith will find faith again, as long as Eros remains the ruler of men and gods, so truly I shall reconquer everything again, the heart which once was mine . . .' In passing Mahler said he had had a sore throat again but that, wreathed in blankets, he had more or less sweated the ailment away. It was, he rashly insisted, nothing serious. His friends, though, were more worried and the soprano Lilli Lehmann found his appearance 'positively alarming'. When Alma finally arrived in Munich she found her hotel room smothered in roses and a copy of the Eighth Symphony, dedicated to her, lying on her table. Mahler, she noted, 'was ready to take offence at the slightest sign that I was not paid enough honour or not received with enough warmth.'

Gropius was there too, at another hotel naturally. He and Alma snatched time together while Mahler was at rehearsals, and tried to come to terms with their looming, longer-term separation. Mahler was due to return to New York the following month and Alma seems to have had no real doubt that she would go too. She told Gropius that Mahler would die if she left him, and perhaps she really believed that. But she must have relished the thought of having both: a famous husband, doting on her as never before, and a potent lover. It was dangerous, of course, but thrilling – and Alma had long felt starved of thrills. Now she was making up for lost time. On 12th October she proposed a last secret assignation, this one on the train for Paris, before she and Mahler took the boat for America. 'Rendezvous would be Munich,' she wrote from Vienna to Gropius in Berlin. 'I leave here on Friday the 14th October at 11.55 a.m. on the Orient Express. My compartment bed no. 13 is in the 2nd sleeping car . . . I would advise you (if you are coming) to have your ticket issued in the name of Walter Grote from Berlin – as G. is travelling 2 days later and might ask to see the list.' The plan worked.

In her *Memories* Alma claims that Mahler boarded the liner for New York in Bremen, north Germany, and that she joined it later in France. If true, that would imply that Alma and Gropius had even more time together undisturbed in Paris before parting. In fact what is known of

Mahler's schedule suggests he could not have got to Bremen in time to catch the boat. In all likelihood, therefore, the Mahlers embarked together in Cherbourg after all. During the voyage Mahler took part in a benefit concert for sailors' widows and orphans, accompanying the tenor John McCormack on the piano. Otherwise, Alma says, they used the time 'to have a complete rest'.

Chapter Eleven

Finale

HINDSIGHT CAN MISLEAD. We now know that when Mahler arrived in New York for the fourth and last time on 25th October 1910, he had less than seven months to live. He had been through a shocking and exhausting summer, his throat was giving him trouble and he was in dispute with the Philharmonic over his pay and workload for the coming season. How natural to assume that as he walked down the gangplank he felt an almost beaten man, perhaps already at death's door. Natural but wrong.

Mahler was a fighter and despite all the blows, he was far from giving up, particularly not on Alma. There is no evidence that he realised she had not broken with Gropius, but it is hard to believe he did not suspect something. Perhaps he now inwardly acknowledged that she might sometimes take lovers and did not regard that prospect, however painful, as the end of his marriage. At any rate he battled for her favour like a newly smitten suitor, showering her with adoring notes, plying her with more gifts and (no doubt most persuasive) encouraging her composing. He also pressed on with his scheme to build a family villa south of Vienna, and warned Gutmann not to book him for concerts the following summer as he wanted the time for 'creative work'. During his last New York stay Mahler was still looking to the future. His plans firmly included Alma and, as she surely realised, she had more than ever to lose by backing out of them.

Professionally, Mahler had plenty of options. The première of the Eighth Symphony had brought him an acclaim even Richard Strauss had rarely enjoyed. Opera houses in Berlin and Vienna were keen to sign him up, a Vienna conservatory job allowing time for some conducting and a lot of composing was almost certainly his for the asking. For the moment he elected to stay with the New York Philharmonic, despite the upheavals of his first season. Although Anglo-Saxons lacked artistic temperament, he told the Austrian writer Ernst Decsey, 'the 96 musicians that he had to conduct followed him better than any previous orchestra because he had them to himself'. Besides, he was well paid, albeit in his view not well enough. During the summer, without consulting him, the Philharmonic had proposed raising the number of concerts for the 1910–11 season by around twenty to more than sixty. When told of the plan Mahler demanded an extra 5000 dollars for the 'vast increase in workload'. He finally got 3000, though the dispute dragged on until January 1911.

That was not the only sign of friction. According to Alma, Mahler was summoned by the orchestra's ruling guarantors' committee to the house of Mrs Sheldon, the chairwoman, and taken to task for alleged misconduct. After he had defended himself, a curtain was drawn aside to reveal a lawyer who had been taking down every word. 'A document was then drawn up in legal form, strictly defining Mahler's powers,' Alma writes. 'He was so taken aback and so furious that he came back to me trembling in every limb.' She may exaggerate and the date she gives for the meeting (mid-February) is suspect. But the Sheldon group did set up a sub-committee to 'supervise' the choice of programmes, which had hitherto been Mahler's sole prerogative, and it is clear that around the turn of the year the search was already on for a new conductor for the 1911–12 season. It might seem that Mahler was being pushed out by the very people who had signed him up with glee just two years earlier.

In fact he was not, despite the seemingly damning evidence. He still had powerful allies on the committee; especially Mrs Sheldon, who called him 'the greatest conductor either in Europe or America', and Mrs Minnie Untermeyer, an influential lawyer's wife described with rare warmth by Alma as Mahler's 'guardian angel'. But the Philharmonic was in a fix. A few highlights apart, the public response during the 1909–10 season had proved disappointing and the final deficit heavy. More money was raised, a business manager appointed and – hardly a sign of fear for the

Philharmonic's future – the number of concerts increased. But part of the season's poor result was blamed on Mahler's ambitious and sometimes arcane programming. This was not, in fact, an unreasonable conclusion. Mahler's concert plans for 1910–11 show that he too felt a different mix was needed, though naturally he was riled by his employers' move to 'supervise' his choice. Whether the changes which emerged were, in fact, to the good seems doubtful. A new cycle of 'National Programmes with Great Soloists' (Italian, French, Norse et cetera) looked attractive in theory but in practice its offerings were ill balanced. The 'English-American' concert, for example, combined (mainly shortish) works by George Chadwick, Charles Villiers Stanford, Edward Elgar, Charles Loeffler, Edward MacDowell and Henry Hadley. Even the most patriotic of Anglo-Saxon music-lovers must have wondered if attendance was a 'must'.

The tug-of-war over programming brought strains on both sides, but that was not why the hunt began for another conductor. By the end of 1910 Mahler had still not made clear whether he aimed to stay on for the next season, and the committee's time was running out. A successor with anything like comparable prestige would be hard to find, especially at short notice, and without one the 'new Philharmonic' experiment might be doomed. Ironically, one person considered was Weingartner, who had taken over from Mahler at the Vienna Opera and whom Mahler, in turn, was now being urged fruitlessly by the Viennese to replace. Another possibility was Henry Wood, founder of the popular Promenade Concerts in London.

Perhaps Mahler was genuinely in doubt about whether to stay on, perhaps (far from impossible) he was playing hard to get to help win a better deal. At any rate, in January he finally stated his terms: a higher salary of 30,000 dollars for a 1911–12 season of between ninety and a hundred concerts. The committee balked at the salary demand and flirted with Weingartner, but a compromise with Mahler would probably have been reached eventually. The truly amazing thing is that Mahler was ready to take on so many concerts, a good thirty more than he was committed to in the already taxing 1910–11 season. It is hard to believe but the details are carried in the committee's minutes – further proof, if any were needed, that Mahler no longer took his doctors' warnings from 1907 seriously.

Despite the behind-the-scenes sparring Mahler was often winning plaudits with the orchestra, though his biggest triumphs were out of town. After a hectic start (eleven November concerts in Manhattan and

Brooklyn), he took the Philharmonic on a pre-Christmas tour to Pittsburgh (Pennsylvania), Cleveland (Ohio) and four towns in New York state, Buffalo, Rochester, Syracuse and Utica. The performances were well attended and the critics enthusiastic, sometimes embarrassingly so. 'Little Mahler with the big brain,' bubbled the *Cleveland Plain Dealer* after a concert of Bach, Beethoven and Wagner in the city's 5000-seat Gray's Armory hall. 'Little Mahler with the mighty force. Little Mahler with the great musical imagination. Little Mahler, whose gigantic power makes the other conductors seem like pygmies.' The *Buffalo Express* was a little more restrained, but called Mahler's reading of Beethoven's 'Pastoral' Symphony 'remarkable . . . A more tremendously realistic portrayal of the thunderstorm has certainly never been given, and the conductor himself seemed like the very genius of the storm, driving his forces on to fiercer and yet fiercer outbursts.'

Later the legend was born (and persists) that Mahler did not get the chance to conduct the 'Pastoral' until he went to America. In fact he had given the work five times (in Vienna and Hamburg) before arriving in New York, but that Buffalo performance must have been outstanding. Earlier that day Mahler and Alma had lingered in wonder on the observation platform at nearby Niagara Falls, almost deafened as the water roared by. But after the 'Pastoral' in the evening, Mahler stepped beaming from the podium and proclaimed, '*Endlich ein fortissimo*' (A *fortissimo* at last). 'I have realised today,' he told Alma, 'that articulate art is greater than inarticulate nature.' He went on to finish the tour in high spirits while Alma returned alone to New York, reading *The Brothers Karamazov* at Mahler's behest on the trip. 'Splendid journey with Alyosha' (the youngest of the brothers), she cabled to him on arrival. 'Journey with Almyosha much more splendid,' he wired back.

The New York critics were more reserved than their provincial colleagues (and the *Tribune*'s now-embittered Krehbiel, of course, liked next to nothing). The orchestra was generally felt to be playing better than a year earlier but was still not the equal of Boston's. Mahler was both praised for moments of 'exquisite poetic insight' and blamed for 'almost incessant and sometimes far-reaching modifications of tempo, of accent and rhythm'. The response was mixed, too, when Mahler gave his (newly revised) Fourth Symphony in Carnegie Hall on 17th and 20th January, the last occasions on which he conducted a work of his own. Like most of their European counterparts, the New York critics were unsure whether to take the piece seriously. But the *Times* admitted that the audience applauded with gusto and, in his last known letter a month later, Mahler said that 'the work had a great success' – one of several signs that he had long since stopped bothering with reviews. Perhaps if he had returned for a third Philharmonic season, he would finally have won over the critics and public as fully in the concert hall as he had done in the opera house. But that was a feat he had never really achieved in Vienna (let alone Hamburg), and in 1910–11 he was still some way from doing so in New York.

Six weeks after those hearings of her husband's Fourth Symphony, Alma made her New York début as a composer. It was a brief one – a performance on 3rd March of one of her shortest songs by the soprano Frances Alda, then wife of the Met director Gatti-Casazza. But Mahler got as excited, and touchy, about the event in advance as if it were one of his own massive premières. Five of Alma's songs had just been published, and when Madame Alda said she could fit only one into her recital Mahler angrily tried to insist she perform the lot. He even claimed in a letter to Anna Moll that the works were 'causing a furore here' and would soon be given by two different singers. If they were, there is no record of it. Madame Alda stuck to her guns and included only Alma's '*Laue Sommernacht*' ('Mild summer night') in her concert. Mahler, ill in bed, was unable to attend but on hearing the piece had been encored he repeatedly muttered, 'Thank God.' After nearly a decade ignoring Alma's talent, he now overrated it. None of those five early songs is truly memorable, though all are accomplished and sometimes tonally daring. Didn't she write better ones after Mahler's death, Alma was asked in a New York interview decades later? '*Ja*. Hah. Certainly,' she replied in her still halting English. 'I could, because I was free.'

Meanwhile Alma and Gropius had stayed in contact via the poste restante in New York and had found a ready confidante in, of all people, Anna Moll – 'little Mama' as Mahler fondly called her. She and Mahler had always been close, so close in fact that Alma once drily noted, 'If Mahler had gone to my mother and said: "I've had to put Alma to death," she would simply have replied: "I'm sure you were right, Gustav."' But when Frau Moll learned of Alma's affair with Gropius, apparently soon after it began, she gave it her backing while wringing her hands. 'The sad thing is that for the present one is so helpless,' she wrote to Gropius in November 1910. 'One must leave everything to time, and I am quite sure that the love you two have for one another will survive all difficulties. I have complete confidence in you and am sure that you love my child so much that you will do everything to avoid making her even more unhappy.'

Frau Moll's confidence notwithstanding, Gropius's feelings seemed to Alma worryingly changeable. In January he went to a performance of Mahler's Seventh Symphony in Berlin and came out deeply shaken 'as though by a strange, distant Titan'. On that evening, he reported to Alma, 'something important became clear to me about Gustav and you – and me. More of that face to face.' Alma's anguish on reading that cryptic message is easy to imagine. Was Mahler's music stealing her lover away? 'I want you!!!,' she wrote back in late March after a long silence. 'But you?? – You – me also?'

By that time Mahler was dying. His sore throat had returned just before Christmas but he seemed to get over it, sticking to his work, going snowballing with Gucki in Central Park and preparing surprises for Alma. Among them were two promissory notes: one 'to the value of 40 dollars/for a fine spree/along the Fifth Av./For Herr Gustav Mahler on a country ramble with his Almschili'; the other 'for the purchase of a/Solitaire/worth over 1000 dollars'. On Christmas Day their hotel room was full of pink roses and presents piled round the tree.

Two months later Mahler's throat again became inflamed and his temperature jumped to 104 degrees Fahrenheit. Insisting that he had often conducted himself back to health, he went off to give a concert at Carnegie Hall on 21st February. It was his forty-eighth that season and it turned out to be the last of his life. The programme was hardly what he would have chosen for his farewell appearance, although it included the première of the touching *Berceuse Élégiaque* (subtitled 'A man's cradlesong at the grave of his mother') by his friend Busoni. The other pieces were an overture by Leone Sinigaglia, Giuseppe Martucci's Piano Concerto, an intermezzo by Marco Bossi and – the sole masterpiece – Mendelssohn's 'Italian' Symphony. Toscanini was present, presumbly because it was an 'all-Italian' evening, not because Mahler was conducting.

Once more Mahler seemed briefly to recover but when the fever returned his (Viennese-born) doctor, Dr Joseph Fraenkel, called specialists to the hotel. Since Mahler's death, like Mozart's, has proved the stuff of legend, it is worth making clear what the experts on the spot found out. One of them, Dr George Baehr, later recalled, 'On arrival I withdrew 20 cc of blood from an arm vein with syringe and needle, and squirted part of it into several bouillon flasks and mixed the remainder with melted agar media which I then poured into sterile Petri dishes. After 4 or 5 days of incubation in the hospital laboratory, the Petri plates revealed numerous bacterial colonies and all the bouillon flasks were found to show a pure culture of the same organism which was subsequently identified as streptococcus viridans.'

Diagnosis: subacute bacterial endocarditis – a serious ailment afflicting hearts which, like Mahler's, have suffered valvular damage. In those days before antibiotics almost no one survived it. That does not imply that Mahler had, after all, been given a death sentence in 1907 when told the valves of his heart had defects, albeit 'compensated' ones. He had lived with that heart problem a long time, perhaps since birth, and might have gone on doing so indefinitely without getting bacterial endocarditis. But he was unlucky. Somewhere he picked up the deadly bug, possibly in the summer of 1910 in Vienna where it had long been endemic, and failed to shake it off. His bout of fever in Munich in September, taken so lightly at the time, could have been a sign he already had more than just another sore throat. But this is far from sure. The only certainty is that once his heart became seriously infected he stood virtually no chance. Penicillin, discovered less than two decades later, would probably have cured him.

Alma, for one, claimed there was more to it than bad luck. 'You cannot imagine what Mr Mahler has suffered,' she told a correspondent of the *New York American* on return to Europe. 'In Vienna my husband was all-powerful. Even the Emperor did not dictate to him, but in New York, to his amazement, he had ten ladies ordering him about like a puppet. He hoped, however, by hard work and success to rid himself of his tormentors. Meanwile he lost health and strength.' The interview was carried widely in the European press, along with further 'evidence' of humiliating treatment in America which had pushed Mahler towards an early grave. One newspaper claimed he had been forced to take an exam before an American jury in piano playing and music theory. Later, a vicious obituary by Krehbiel calling Mahler's influence in New York 'prejudicial to good taste' was seized on in Europe as yet another sign of American barbarity. Other, favourable, New York obituaries were largely ignored.

Alma may not have been wrong when she linked Mahler's illness to physical and mental stress, but she identified the wrong culprits. Stress can indeed harm the immune system and Mahler suffered plenty of it, thus perhaps becoming more vulnerable to the infection which killed him. Still, his irritation with the 'ten ladies' was surely modest compared with his torment over Alma's infidelity. Besides, Mahler was himself responsible for much of the pressure he was under – and which he no doubt found productive even while cursing it. Once the shock of the 1907 diagnosis had worn off, he ignored his doctors' counsel to take things easier and gradually became a workaholic again. 'I see by now that I am incorrigible,' he admitted in a letter to Bruno Walter in December 1909. 'People of our kind cannot help doing thoroughly whatever they do at all. And that, as I have come to realise, means overworking. There it is, I am and remain the eternal beginner. And the little bit of routine I have acquired serves at best to increase the demands I make on myself.' He was right. Mahler was his own greatest taskmaster.

According to Dr Baehr, when the results of the blood tests were known Mahler 'insisted on being told the truth and then expressed a wish to die in Vienna. Accordingly, he and his wife left shortly thereafter for Paris, where the diagnosis and prognosis were reconfirmed, and then proceeded to Vienna.' In fact events were more painfully drawn out than that account suggests. Alma says that since neither she nor Mahler had previously heard of streptococci, they were not at first alarmed by the findings. New York doctors came and went, injections of this and that were tried, Fraenkel spoke of hope (which he surely did not feel) that nature would give the patient enough strength to pull round. Through it all Mahler hung on to his sense of (black) humour. As his temperature soared and plunged, he talked of his little bugs which were always either dancing or sleeping. 'You will be in great demand when I am gone, with your youth and looks,' he often joked to Alma. 'Now who shall it be?' He ran over a list of possibles but always ended with 'It'll be better after all, if I stay with you.' Did he mention Gropius, one wonders, or even Fraenkel, who was already drawn to Alma and later abortively begged her to marry him?

Every time Mahler felt stronger he talked of returning to the

Philharmonic; he even arranged a rehearsal which promptly had to be called off again. Instead Theodore Spiering, the orchestra's leader, took over the baton for the season's last concerts while New York buzzed with rumours that Mahler might be feigning sickness out of pique with his employer. Later, after failing to get Weingartner, the Philharmonic in some desperation signed up Josef Stransky, a Czech conductor close to Mahler in only one respect – the two had been born within 5 miles of one another. Stransky had little flair but much diplomacy; qualification enough, it turned out, to keep him in the New York job for more than a decade. He then became an art dealer.

Gradually Mahler got weaker but he still had enough willpower to throw out nurses he found fault with. One's shoes squeaked, another snored. So Alma did most of the caring herself, sleeping in her clothes in Mahler's room and feeding him like a child. 'When I'm well again we'll go on like this,' he enthused. 'You'll feed me – it's so nice.' With Alma wilting, her mother rushed from Vienna to help but accidentally set the hotel apartment on fire while cooking. 'Poor Mamma', Mahler sympathised once the blaze had been doused and everyone, by a fluke, had escaped injury. For him Anna Moll could do no wrong.

By now, according to Alma, doctors were urging that Mahler be taken to Paris to consult bacteriologists there, though it is not clear whether that was the main reason for returning to Europe or whether Mahler, aware he had little time left, really wanted to see 'hated, beloved Vienna' one last time. The New York physicians must have known that even their highly reputed French colleagues would be equally helpless. Whatever the truth, on 8th April Mahler, Alma, Gucki, Anna Moll and Miss Turner (the English nurse), along with more than forty pieces of luggage, boarded the SS *Amerika* bound for Cherbourg. Mahler shivered and sweated in his cabin, only rarely making it up to the deck. He looked, Alma writes, 'disturbingly beautiful. I always said to him "Today you are Alexander the Great again." Black, radiant eyes, his white face, the black locks, a blood-red mouth. Frighteningly beautiful.' Busoni was also aboard and tried to amuse Mahler with crazy bits of counterpoint. So was the young Stefan Zweig, later a libretto writer for Richard Strauss. He caught a brief glimpse of Mahler silhouetted 'against the grey infinity of sky and sea. There was boundless sorrow in this sight, but also something transfigured by greatness, something resounding into the sublime, like music.'

Ten days later they reached Paris. Exactly a year earlier, Mahler had conducted his 'Resurrection' Symphony there. Now, miraculously, he seemed to throw off his sickness straight away. After a night's sleep at the Élysée Palace hotel Alma found him up, shaved and dressed and proposing a drive to the Bois de Boulogne. He had done nothing for himself for weeks. He got into the car laughing and making plans – a trip to Egypt, a new opera production . . . An hour later he was back, deathly pale and close to collapse. In bed he wept, telling Anna Moll he wanted to be buried with no pomp next to Putzi in Grinzing cemetery. He could not, he said, bear to talk of it to Alma – but she overheard.

Mahler was moved to a clinic in suburban Neuilly where Professor André Chantemesse, a fellow of the Pasteur Institute, took great professional interest in his case. 'Come and look,' he urged Alma excitedly after taking a culture from Mahler's blood. 'Even I – myself – have never seen streptococci in such a marvellous state of development.' A serum treatment was tried but Mahler grew so weak he could no longer lift a book. He managed to read Eduard von Hartmann's *Das Problem des Lebens (The Problem of Life)* all the same, tearing out the pages one by one. His thoughts often turned to the impoverished Schönberg whom he had helped with cash (in part anonymously) the year before. 'If I go, he will have nobody left,' he kept repeating. Alma promised she would help Schönberg out whatever happened, and she did.

By this time at the latest Alma must have known she would soon be a widow. What did she feel? Intense longing for Gropius, certainly. In letters to him from Paris she yearned for his 'warm, soft, dear hands' and signed herself 'Your Lover'. But during those final months her tenderness for Mahler had never been greater and at some stage she began to make love to him again. She admitted as much to Gropius soon after Mahler's death, expecting him to be understanding. He was not. Alma's behaviour, he claimed, showed her passion for him was an 'aberration'. It was their first serious row. There were many to come. Years later, her marriage to Gropius breaking down and her other affairs palling, Alma described the men in her life as 'microbes' compared to Mahler. 'I suddenly know with terrible clarity that I love Gustav and only Gustav,' she wrote in her diary, 'and that since his death I have always been seeking and have never found – and never will.'

In Paris another professor was summoned, this time Franz Chvostek from Vienna who at least knew how to raise his patient's spirits. 'Now then, Mahler, what's all this about?' he boomed cheerily on entering the sick-room. 'Working too hard, that's what it is. You'll have to knock off for six months or a year.' When Mahler, dumbfounded, asked if he would really be able to work again, Chvostek replied, 'Of course. Why not? Keep your heart up, that's all. This evening we'll be off to Vienna together.' In private he told Alma to be quick because Mahler might have a relapse and then it would be too late to move him. They packed madly and caught the night sleeper, Mahler on a stretcher but thanks to Chvostek looking blissful. The journey was, Alma said, like that of a dying king. Journalists came to the door at every station in Germany and Austria asking for the latest bulletin. On arrival in Vienna next morning, 12th May, they went straight to the Löw sanatorium in Mariannengasse. Mahler knew it well. He had been operated on there a decade before. Close by was the Zuckerkandls' house where he had fallen for Alma, beyond it the road where he had proposed to her in the snow.

Vienna went into mourning, much of it false according to Mahler's friends and fans. In a furious letter later to her sister in Paris, Berta Zuckerkandl claimed that all the people who had fought Mahler in his opera days shed crocodile tears when he returned on a stretcher. 'Under sensational headlines,' she wrote, 'the press issued daily bulletins from his bedside. Sentimental anecdotes were peddled everywhere. In the salons and coffee houses, memories were sparked off like cheap fireworks – of the great age of opera that had existed under Mahler. His sparkling *Don Giovanni* . . . His magnificent *Fidelio* . . . His *Figaro*. . . . His like would never be seen again.'

Mahler would have shaken his head in resignation at the spectacle, Berta said, but probably he was unaware of it. She was right. Crowds gathered outside the sanatorium, bouquet after bouquet was delivered but Mahler, now often delirious, noticed little. When Justi came to visit he asked dazedly who she was. His leg swelled and radium was applied. Twice he muttered 'Mozartl' (little Mozart), one finger conducting on the quilt. It has often since been claimed that these were his last words but, as in many such cases, the evidence is flimsy. During the final agonising hours, Alma says she was sent into the next room. A thunderstorm was raging. Mahler died just after 11 p.m. on 18th May. As usual his music sketch book was by him – at the ready, as it were.

Epilogue

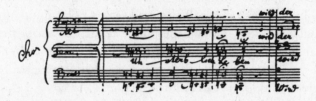

'MY TIME WILL COME,' Mahler is said to have prophesied. That is not quite what he wrote (in a 1902 letter to Alma saying his time would be when Strauss's had gone) but it is near enough. Today Mahler is widely thought to have been rescued from almost total neglect only in the 1960s, by a generation sadder and more knowing than his own. Mahler's audiences, claimed Leonard Bernstein, could not or would not face up to the brutal truth that his music reflected Western society in decay. It was only after half a century or more of horrors (Bernstein gives a list ranging from Auschwitz to the arms race) that 'we can finally listen to Mahler's music and understand that it foretold all'.

When Bernstein wrote that in 1967 he had just completed the first cycle of Mahler's symphonies on records. Thirty years on there are more than a dozen recordings of the full cycle and over 1000 of individual works (including the songs). Crowds flock to Mahler concerts from Berlin to Boulder, London to Ljubljana, Tokyo to Tanglewood. There are Mahler symposia, Mahler T-shirts, Mahler Internet sites. The word 'Mahlerian', vague though it be, has passed into many languages. Undeniably there has been a 'Mahler boom', but that does not mean Mahler was an outcast until 'the age of anxiety' was ready for him. His time came, or at least was well on the way, while he was still alive.

In 1913, two years after Mahler's death, Guido Adler tried to work out how often his old friend's music had been performed. Adler did not include the songs in his list nor, for some unfathomable reason, the Seventh Symphony but his findings are striking all the same. They show that since the Budapest première of the First Symphony in 1889, works by Mahler had been played more than 260 times, mainly in Europe but also in Russia and America. The Fourth Symphony had been given most often (61 times) but even the lavish Second (44 times) and Eighth (22 times) had been far from ignored. Mahler had been his own busiest advocate, conducting his symphonies (up to and including the Eighth) about 70 times. But most performances, around 200, had been led by others – Strauss, Nikisch, Mengelberg, Walter and Oskar Fried among them. The works usually shocked, though the public tended to adopt them more readily than most critics did; but they were increasingly often heard and some, like the Third and Eighth Symphonies, had instant success. How many modern composers can claim as much?

After his death Mahler thus had well-placed disciples to carry on his cause, at least in Europe. Progress was slower at first in America, though Stokowski's première of the Eighth Symphony in Philadelphia in 1916 proved such a hit that the work was repeated six times and then taken to New York. That success rather obscured Stokowski's other notable American 'first' – *Das Lied von der Erde* – in the same year. Slowly the message spread. In the 1920s New York had a steady diet of Mahler thanks largely to Mengelberg, who spent half of each year there and the other half with his Concertgebouw Orchestra in Amsterdam. Frederick Stock premièred the Seventh Symphony in 1921 with the Chicago Symphony, Serge Koussevitsky the Ninth Symphony a decade later in Boston. Others giving Mahler concerts in America included Walter (both before and after his flight into exile there in 1939), Klemperer, Artur Bodanzky, Artur Rodzinski, Fritz Reiner, Dimitri Mitropoulos and Eugene Ormandy. They were joined after the Second World War by conductors like George Szell (Cleveland), Maurice Abravanel (Utah) and William Steinberg (Pittsburgh). This is not to say that Mahler was already staple fare in American concert halls by the middle of the century. But when Bernstein took over the New York Philharmonic in 1958 and began his (first) complete Mahler cycle, the ground had been well prepared.

In Europe, the Dutch proved the greatest Mahler fans. The reason is plain – Mengelberg. Between 1911 and 1920 alone he included Mahler's works in more than 200 of the Concertgebouw's concerts, an example followed (albeit less intensively) by the two other Dutch orchestras in The Hague and Utrecht. In no other country did the public get the chance to hear Mahler played so often so soon; certainly not in Britain, despite early advocacy by Henry Wood and far-sighted commentary by the critic Ernest Newman, let alone in France, Italy or Spain. Amsterdam was the world's Mahler capital and proved it in 1920 with a festival at which all the symphonies were played to packed houses. Near-complete cycles followed elsewhere soon afterwards, in Vienna under Fried and in Berlin under Klaus Pringsheim (who went on to première five of the symphonies in Japan in the 1930s). Zemlinsky, Webern, Clemens Krauss, Jascha Horenstein, Hermann Scherchen, Carl Schuricht (as well as the indefatigable Walter and Klemperer) – all these and others kept Mahler alive in the concert halls of (mainly) Germany and Austria.

The Nazis put a stop to that. Mahler was banned along with rest of so-called 'degenerate art' and only began to reappear after 1945. All things considered, his recovery was remarkably quick, at least it was in Holland (under Eduard van Beinum, Eduard Flipse, Willem van Otterloo and later Bernard Haitink) and in Vienna under too many conductors to mention. It is simply not true that the Vienna Philharmonic only began to learn Mahler in the late 1960s thanks to Bernstein, a myth fostered in part by the conductor but also (more surprisingly) by some in the orchestra. The Philharmonic learned part of its Mahler, admittedly not always with delight, from the composer himself. It went on to give about 70 performances of the symphonies alone between 1911 and Austria's *Anschluss* with Germany in 1938, and over 30 more between 1945 and Bernstein's Vienna début. That is not to belittle Bernstein, one of the century's finest all-round musicians, but merely to put his Mahler contribution in context.

Although the claim that Mahler was ready for adoption only after Western society had been through the hell he 'foretold' sounds plausible, it sells Mahler short. The demons he called up in his music are those of every age, not just his and ours (though naturally we are inclined to consider those we face to be the most diabolical ever). A soldier's terror ('*Revelge*') was surely no less during the Thirty Years War than in Vietnam; a starving child ('*Das irdische Leben*') no less anguished in Babylon than in Bosnia; the concept of the 'blows which fell the hero' (in the Sixth Symphony) easily recognisable to the ancient Greeks. The real reasons holding Mahler back from the widest acceptance early on are so obvious they tend to be overlooked. His music is very long (especially if you take the symphonies, like Wagner's *Ring*, as a single vast work of interlocking parts) and it is very complicated.

This book began by asking whether Mahler was devilish or saintly, cunning or naïve, extrovert or withdrawn. The answer, of course, is that he was all those things and much besides; brandishing his contradictions in music of stinging intensity and battling through to a synthesis time after time. In principle that is the source of his universal appeal. Contradictory is what most people are and harmony, on earth or at least beyond it, is what they long for. But on first impressin Mahler's music, as Adler put it, 'produces attraction at one place, repulsion at another and must be courted lovingly'. Courting demands time and opportunity. When people were given the chance to hear Mahler frequently they took to him, as in Holland. Even there, though, the later non-vocal works had more of an uphill struggle than the songs and early symphonies.

It was the long-playing record, rather than the *Zeitgeist*, which made a comprehensive breakthrough possible. Mahler's work became accessible and repeatable in the home. It is intriguing to think that he might almost have lived to see it (Strauss, after all, died only in 1949); still more so to speculate on what he might have composed by then. A few years later the coming of stereo benefited no composer more than Mahler, with his huge choral and instrumental forces and precisely conceived spatial effects. By his centenary year in 1960 almost all his work existed on record, often in several different versions. Not everywhere, admittedly. 'No recording available in this country,' a British centenary discography noted against the Third, Seventh and Tenth Symphonies as well as *Das klagende Lied*. That soon changed though. Britain came late to the Mahler feast but once present it indulged with zest. There, as elsewhere, the problem is no longer famine but glut, and with it the tendency to take for granted the least complacent of all composers.

Recommendations

Keeping abreast of Mahler literature and recordings is no job for the faint-hearted (or the impecunious). More than 2500 books and essays are listed in Simon Namenwirth's critical bibliography *Gustav Mahler* (three volumes (in English), Verlag Otto Harrassowitz, Wiesbaden). Less comprehensive but more manageable is Susan Filler's *Gustav and Alma Mahler: A Guide to Research* (Garland Publishing Inc., New York). Both books are vital navigational aids but they were issued in the late 1980s and even more on Mahler has been published since.

Much the same goes for Peter Fülöp's *Mahler Discography*, issued by The Kaplan Foundation, New York, in 1995. Easily the best of its kind, it not only lists all known Mahler recordings at that time – 1168 of them – but often goes behind pseudonyms on CD labels to identify the true performers. How many people, for instance, realise that the recording of Mahler's Fifth Symphony attributed to Joseph Kreutzer with the Royal Danish Symphony Orchestra is really by the London Symphony Orchestra under Rudolf Schwarz? Few, surely, and still fewer care. But Schwarz, who was born in Vienna in 1905 and imbibed his Mahler there as a young man, is one of the rare conductors to take the Fifth's Adagietto at close to Mahler's own probable (relatively swift) tempo. Here it is not only fair but historically important to give credit where it is due.

Given the flood of material, it would be even more absurd than usual to claim particular books and recordings as 'definitive'. What follows is a personal choice, liable to brings squawks of outrage here and there both for what it includes and for what it leaves out. I make a few standard recommendations but also point to less widely known work I have found specially rewarding. Some things will be hard to find, but persistence pays.

Two authors bestride the Mahler world like colossi, Henry-Louis de La Grange and Donald Mitchell. If that sounds daunting it is meant to. De La Grange has spent nearly half a century working on his life of Mahler, easily the most comprehensive biography and indispensable to anyone with a serious interest in the topic. But it is hard to pin down. French-readers can go for the only complete edition so far (three volumes totalling 3782 pages) issued by Fayard in Paris in the 1980s. English-readers long had to make do with a single volume on the early years, published a decade earlier. Now the whole work (updated) is coming out gradually from Oxford University Press, but it is tantalisingly slow going.

While de La Grange's volumes broadly concentrate on the life, Mitchell delves deeper into the music. Very deep and sometimes obscurely, it must be said, but rewardingly. His main books (all published by Faber in London) are *Gustav Mahler: the Early Years*, *The Wunderhorn Years*, and – best of all – *Songs and Symphonies of Life and Death*. More than either Mitchell or de La Grange, Constantin Floros in Germany probes Mahler's religious, philosophical and literary background in the first of his three volumes on *Gustav Mahler* (Breitkopf and Härtel, Wiesbaden). Alas, only the third volume, on the symphonies, so far exists in English translation (Amadeus Press, Portland, Oregon) but for German-readers nothing by Floros should be overlooked, controversial though his conclusions often are.

Still, if one were forced to rescue a single Mahler book from a burning house it would have to be his *Selected Letters*, originally chosen by Alma and first published in German in 1924. Mahler's personality leaps off the page, the peaks and troughs of his career as he records them leave one breathless. An English translation edited by Knud Martner was issued by Faber in 1979 but needs revision. German-readers should go for the 1996 edition *Gustav Mahler: Briefe* (Paul Zsolnay Verlag, Vienna) edited by Herta Blaukopf. Two other collections edited by Herta Blaukopf have, happily, been translated into English and are well worth digging out. They are *Mahler's Unknown Letters* (Victor Gollancz, London) and *Gustav Mahler, Richard Strauss, Correspondence 1888–1911* (Faber, London). Fascinating though they are, these volumes do not include any of Mahler's letters to Alma. A collection of those in English can be found in Alma's *Mahler: Memories and Letters* (John Murray, London, repeatedly revised), edited by

Mitchell and Martner. The fullest edition (reinserting Alma's deliberate omissions) is so far available only in German: *Ein Glück ohne Ruh'* (Siedler Verlag, Berlin), but an English version is planned by Oxford University Press.

Alma's *Memories* and her *And the Bridge is Love* (Harcourt Brace, New York) demand to be read but need to be treated warily. To a lesser extent the same goes for Natalie Bauer-Lechner's *Recollections of Gustav Mahler* (Faber, London) and Bruno Walter's *Gustav Mahler* (Hamish Hamilton, London). Guido Adler's little *Gustav Mahler* (Cambridge University Press) is easy to miss in the crowd. A pity because it more than makes up in balance and insight what it lacks in length. Much the same is true of Kurt Blaukopf's *Gustav Mahler* (Allen Lane, London), a compact work with unsurpassed 'feel' for the Habsburg and especially the Vienna background. Reading Theodor Adorno's *Mahler: a Musical Physiognomy* (University of Chicago Press) is a battle even for fanatical Mahlerians, but it is one well worth fighting. Less of a struggle is his Mahler centenary address (1960) published in *Quasi una Fantasia* (Verso, London).

Finally, a few indispensable compendia: *Mahler Remembered*, put together by Norman Lebrecht (Faber, London); *Mahler: his Life, Work and World* by Kurt and Herta Blaukopf (Thames and Hudson, London); *Gustav Mahler: the World Listens* published by the Concertgebouw, Amsterdam, to mark the Mahler festival there in 1995; and *Gustav Mahler's American Years* by Zoltan Roman (Pendragon Press, New York). Add to those the comprehensive collection of photos in *The Mahler Album* (Thames and Hudson, London, with The Kaplan Foundation, New York) and you have Mahler seen through many eyes from every angle. Those wanting to keep abreast of every fascinating twist and turn in Mahler research should join the Internationale Gustav Mahler Gesellschaft, Wiedner Gürtel 6, A-1040, Vienna.

RECORDINGS

First, a short cut. Buy the complete sets of the symphonies conducted by Georg Solti with the Chicago Symphony Orchestra (Decca) and by Rafael Kubelik with the Bavarian Radio Symphony Orchestra (DG). True, there are plenty of other sets, some in marginally more up-to-date sound. But no one does all the works equally well and these collections offer nicely contrasting approaches by two masters at less than full price. The best of Leonard Bernstein's often riveting performances, incidentally, are not be found on CD but on video – nearly all with the Vienna Philharmonic. Again the sound is not the most modern but the artistry is stunning and the price relatively cheap.

Then, two collections, about as far apart technologically as could be. The first on BMG Conifer includes Gilbert Kaplan's performances with the London Symphony Orchestra of Mahler's 'Resurrection' Symphony and the Adagietto from the Fifth, all Mahler's own piano roll recordings in the best transfers they have had, and many pictures from *The Mahler Album* on CD-ROM. Kaplan's realisation of the symphony is fanatically, arguably uniquely, close to the score and the sound is among the best the piece has had. Also thrown in are interviews with New York musicians who played under Mahler, part of a brilliant eight-hour *Mahlerthon* broadcast originally compiled by the late William Malloch of Los Angeles. The whole thing should be made available by some enterprising company.

The second collection (on two Pearl CDs) goes back to the 1920s. It includes the first Mahler recording ever made (barring Mahler's piano rolls) – the 'Resurrection' Symphony conducted by Mahler's protégé Oskar Fried with the Berlin State Opera Orchestra, and the *Kindertotenlieder* sung by Heinrich Rehkemper and conducted by Jascha Horenstein. Compare Fried's often wildly passionate performance of the symphony with those of Walter and Klemperer, two other disciples, and you will never talk of a 'true Mahler tradition'. All are so different. Rehkemper's *Kindertotenlieder* is the more moving for its dignified restraint and Horenstein's accompaniment is as one would expect from arguably the finest of Mahler conductors. A bold claim, of course, but whatever else you buy be sure not to miss Horenstein's recordings of the First and Third Symphonies (on Unicorn-Kanchana) and of the Ninth Symphony and *Das Lied von der Erde* (on Music and Arts). His versions of the Fourth, Sixth, Seventh and Eighth Symphonies are only marginally less recommendable. Almost uniquely, Horenstein revealed the strength of Mahler's symphonic structures without underplaying any of the quirky detail. It is amazing that no major company signed him up for a complete cycle.

And so to recordings of individual works, beyond but not necessarily above those already mentioned. For the First Symphony try the Amsterdam Philharmonic (no, it is not the Concertgebouw) under the

Hungarian conductor Árpád Joó, on various labels including Aurophon and Arts. It is strikingly fresh and accurate and can often be found for a knock-down price, perhaps because the performers are not 'big names'. For the 'Resurrection' Hermann Scherchen (with the Vienna State Opera Orchestra on various labels including Palladio) will enlighten and infuriate but never leave you cold. For No. 3 (an eccentric recommendation, this) seek the original LPs of Charles Adler's recording with a Vienna orchestra (on Society of Participating Artists, with notes by Alma Mahler, no less). You will be rewarded with one of the most gripping of all Thirds, in sound which lost so much in later transfer to other labels and CD that the performance itself has been widely underrated. For the Fourth, go for the Philharmonia under Paul Kletzki (EMI) in a performance so expert but natural that the score seems simply to play itself.

The sound is rather dim and there are a few instrumental mishaps, but no one has realised the Fifth Symphony more convincingly than Bruno Walter in his 1947 recording with the New York Philharmonic (on Sony Classical). This was another work Horenstein performed wonderfully well, and perhaps a recording will one day emerge from someone's archives. For No. 6 I unhelpfully have to admit that I know of no recording I can recommend without serious reservation. Bernstein's (DG) comes closest to the ideal, but for an over-fast first movement march. For No. 7 Claudio Abbado is exemplary, achieving an intensity with the Chicago Symphony (on DG) he rarely seems to manage in Mahler with his own Berlin Philharmonic. Klaus Tennstedt is one conductor (John Barbirolli was another) who very rarely achieved in the studio what he could in the concert hall. His 'Symphony of a Thousand' (EMI) with the London Philharmonic is a fine exception to that rule. For an unexpectedly magnificent alternative, turn to Robert Olson's account with the combined forces of the Colorado MahlerFest (traceable via the MahlerFest at P.O. Box 1314, Boulder, CO 80306-1314, USA). For No. 9, try Karel Ančerl with the Czech Philharmonic (Supraphon) for a startlingly different, at times almost jaunty, approach. A jaunty Ninth; surely that can't be right – or can it? Mahler once wrote that his Ninth could, perhaps, best be ranked with his (relatively sunny) Fourth. Ančerl's Bohemian performance without neurosis makes most sense of that odd claim. For a more mainstream approach, no one has bettered Bernard Haitink's recording with the Concertgebouw (Philips).

That leaves two complex cases. One is *Das Lied von der Erde*. Of the orchestral versions with tenor and alto, the best sung in stereo is Klemperer's (with Fritz Wunderlich and Christa Ludwig on EMI), in mono Walter's (with Julius Patzak and Kathleen Ferrier). The famous studio version of the latter is on Decca but a concert version, even more intense in parts, is available on CD from Willem Smith Productions, De Akkeren 45, 3762 An Soest, Holland. Of the orchestral version with tenor and baritone, Simon Rattle's with Peter Seiffert and Thomas Hampson (EMI) heads a small but strong field. Nor should you miss Mahler's version with piano (try the one with Cyprien Katsaris on Teldec) and the chamber orchestra version partly by Schönberg (on Harmonia Mundi conducted by Philippe Herreweghe).

The other problem case is the Tenth Symphony. Argument still rages about whether it is right for others to make 'completions' or 'performing versions' of Mahler's sketches. Irrespective of your view, it is too late to put the genie back in the bottle. It popped out when Deryck Cooke produced his (first) 'performing version' and finally won Alma's consent to its public performance. For fine realisations of Cooke's revised score, go to Simon Rattle (EMI) and Jean Martinon with the Chicago Symphony (in a package of recordings issued by the orchestra). But Cooke's version has its rivals. One is Remo Mazzetti's (recorded under Leonard Slatkin on RCA); a second is Clinton Carpenter's (by Harold Farberman for Golden Strings); a third Joe Wheeler's. The latter has not yet been recorded but a few cognoscenti claim it is the best of the lot. Many conductors still insist on performing only the first movement Adagio, which Mahler largely completed. One is Haitink and he does it very well (rather better first time round with the Concertgebouw than later with the Berlin Philharmonic – both on Philips).

A final lap of vocal recordings: for *Das klagende Lied*, Riccardo Chailly (Decca), and for *Lieder eines fahrenden Gesellen*, Fischer-Dieskau with Wilhelm Fürtwängler (EMI). I have not forgotten Janet Baker, one of the finest of all Mahler singers. Hear her in *Des Knaben Wunderhorn* with Geraint Evans (under Wyn Morris on IMP); in the *Rückert* songs (under Barbirolli with the New Philharmonia on EMI) and in the *Lieder und Gesänge aus der Jugendzeit* (*Songs of Youth*) with Geoffrey Parsons (piano) on Hyperion.

Chronology

1860   7 July
Gustav Mahler born in Kalischt (Kalištĕ), Bohemia. Son of Bernard Mahler (1827–89) and Marie, née Hermann (1837–89). Second of fourteen children.

October
Family moves to Iglau (Jihlava) in Moravia.

1870   October
First public appearance as pianist (in Iglau theatre).

1875   September
Enters Vienna conservatory (diploma 1878).

1877–79   Enrolled at Vienna university.

1880   May–August
First job as conductor (in Bad Hall).

By November
Completes first version of *Das klagende Lied*.

1881   September
Conductor in Laibach (to April 1882).

1883   January–March
Conductor in Olmütz (Olomouc).

August
Second conductor in Kassel (to July 1885).

1884–85   Composes *Lieder eines fahrenden Gesellen*.

1885	July Conductor at German Theatre in Prague (until July 1886).
1886	July Second conductor (to Nikisch) at Leipzig Municipal Theatre (to May 1888).
1888	20 January Première of Weber's *Die drei Pintos* (completed by Mahler). March Completes First Symphony. September Completes *Todtenfeier*. October Director of Royal Hungarian Opera, Budapest (to March 1891).
1889	20 November Première in Budapest of First Symphony (called Symphonic Poem).
1891	March First conductor at Hamburg Municipal Theatre (to April 1897).
1892	May–July Guest conductor in London (Covent Garden and Drury Lane Theatre).
1893	Summer Works on Second Symphony (in Steinbach am Attersee).
1894	Completes Second Symphony.
1895	Summer Works on Third Symphony. 13 December Conducts première in Berlin of Second Symphony.
1896	Completes Third Symphony.

1897   11 May
        Début as a conductor at Vienna Court Opera with *Lohengrin*.

        15 October
        Becomes director of Vienna Court Opera (to December
        1907).

1898   6 November
        First concert with Vienna Philharmonic.

1899   Summer
        Works on Fourth Symphony. First meets Alma Schindler
        (1879–1964), his future wife. Buys land at Maiernigg am
        Wörthersee to build villa and composing hut.

1900   June
        Concerts with Vienna Philharmonic in Paris.

        Summer
        Completes Fourth Symphony in Maiernigg.

1901   17 February
        Conducts première of *Das klagende Lied* in Vienna.

        April
        Resigns from Vienna Philharmonic concerts.

        Summer
        Work on Fifth Symphony and songs.

        7 November
        Again meets Alma and this time falls for her.

        25 November
        Conducts première of Fourth Symphony in Munich.

1902   March
        Marries Alma in Vienna (9 March). Honeymoon in St
        Petersburg.

        9 June
        Conducts première of Third Symphony in Krefeld.

Summer
Completes Fifth Symphony in Maiernigg.

3 November
Daughter Maria Anna (Putzi) born (1902–7).

1903   Summer
Works on Sixth Symphony in Maiernigg.

October
Visits Amsterdam for first time to conduct Concertgebouw
Orchestra.

1904   15 June
Daughter Anna Justine (Gucki) born (1904–88).

Summer
Completes Sixth Symphony and *Kindertotenlieder* in Maiernigg.
Works on Seventh Symphony.

18 October
Conducts première of Fifth Symphony in Cologne.

1905   29 January
Conducts premières of works including the *Kindertotenlieder*
and four of the *Rückert-Lieder*, in Vienna.

Summer
Completes Seventh Symphony in Maiernigg.

9 November
Records four piano rolls for Welte-Mignon.

1906   27 May
Conducts première of Sixth Symphony in Essen.

Summer
Composes Eighth Symphony in Maiernigg.

1907   May
Requests release from contract as director of Vienna Opera.

June
Signs contract with Heinrich Conried of Metropolitan Opera,
New York.

July
Putzi dies in Maiernigg (12 July). Mahler's heart condition
diagnosed.

15 October
Conducts at Vienna Opera for last time *(Fidelio)*.

24 November
Conducts his Second Symphony at farewell concert in
Vienna.

9 December
Leaves Vienna *en route* for New York.

1908   1 January
New York Metropolitan Opera début with *Tristan und Isolde*.

Summer
Composes *Das Lied von der Erde* in Toblach.

19 September
Conducts première of Seventh Symphony in Prague.

8 December
Conducts US première of Second Symphony in New York.

1909   31 March
First concert with New York Philharmonic.

Summer
Composes Ninth Symphony in Toblach.

16 December
Conducts US première of First Symphony in New York.

1910   26 January
Conducts US première of *Kindertotenlieder*.

Summer
Sketches Tenth Symphony.

12 September
Conducts première of Eighth Symphony in Munich.

1911   21 February
Conducts last concert (New York).

8 April
Leaves New York for Europe.

18 May
Dies at Löw sanatorium in Vienna.

22 May
Buried at Grinzing cemetery.

Works

1880

Three lieder for tenor and piano (words by Mahler)
a) '*Im Lenz*'
b) '*Winterlied*'
c) '*Maitanz im Grünen*'

*c.*1878–80

Das klagende Lied (words by Mahler) for soprano, contralto, tenor, baritone, bass solos, chorus and orchestra. Original version in three movements completed 1880, later heavily revised.
a) '*Waldmärchen*'
b) '*Der Spielmann*'
c) '*Hochzeitsstück*'

1880–83

Five lieder for voice and piano
a) '*Frühlingsmorgen*' (words by Richard Leander)
b) '*Erinnerung*' (Leander)
c) '*Hans und Grete*' (words by Mahler)
d) '*Serenade aus Don Juan*' (words by Tirso de Molina)
e) '*Phantasie aus Don Juan*' (Tirso de Molina)

1884–85

[Four] *Lieder eines fahrenden Gesellen* (words mainly by Mahler)
a) '*Wenn mein Schatz Hochzeit macht*'
b) '*Ging heut' morgen übers Feld*'

c) *'Ich hab' ein glühend' Messer'*
d) *'Die zwei blauen Augen'*

1884–88
Symphony No. 1, D major, completed 1888, later heavily revised

1887–90
Nine *Wunderhorn-Lieder* for voice and piano (words from *Des Knaben Wunderhorn* collection of Achim von Arnim and Clemens Brentano)
a) *'Um schlimme Kinder artig zu machen'*
b) *'Ich ging mit Lust'*
c) *'Aus! Aus!'*
d) *'Starke Einbildungskraft'*
e) *'Zu Strassburg auf der Schanz'*
f) *'Ablösung im Sommer'*
g) *'Scheiden und Meiden'*
h) *'Nicht Wiedersehen!'*
i) *'Selbstgefühl'*

1888–94
Symphony No. 2, C minor, for soprano, contralto, mixed chorus and orchestra (later revised)

1895–96
Symphony No. 3, D minor, for contralto, women's chorus, boys' chorus and orchestra (later revised)

*c.*1888–98
[Twelve] *Wunderhorn-Lieder* for voice and piano or orchestra (words from the von Arnim/Brentano collection partly adapted by Mahler)
a) *'Der Schildwache Nachtlied'*
b) *'Verlor'ne Müh'*
c) *'Trost im Unglück'*
d) *'Wer hat dies Liedlein erdacht'*
e) *'Das irdische Leben'*
f) *'Des Antonius von Padua Fischpredigt'*
g) *'Rheinlegendchen'*
h) *'Lied des Verfolgten im Turm'*
i) *'Wo die schönen Trompeten blasen'*
j) *'Lob des hohen Verstandes'*

k) *'Es sungen drei Engel'*
l) *'Urlicht'*

1899–1900
Symphony No. 4, G major, for soprano and orchestra (later revised)

1899–1902
Seven lieder called, after Mahler's death, *Aus lezter Zeit* made up of:

[Two] *Wunderhorn-Lieder* for voice and orchestra (words from the von Arnim/Brentano collection)
a) *'Revelge'*
b) *'Der Tamboursg'sell'*

[Four] *Rückert-Lieder* for voice and orchestra (words by Friedrich Rückert)
a) *'Blicke mir nicht in die Lieder!'*
b) *'Ich atmet' einen Linden duft'*
c) *'Ich bin der Welt abhanden gekommen'*
d) *'Um Mitternacht'*

[One] *Rückert-Lied* for voice and piano (orchestrated by Max Puttmann)
'Liebst du um Schönheit'

1901–2
Symphony No. 5, C sharp minor* (later revised)

1901–4
[Five] *Kindertotenlieder* (words by Rückert)
a) *'Nun will die Sonn' so hell aufgeh'n'*
b) *'Nun seh' ich wohl, warum so dunkle Flammen'*
c) *'Wenn dein Mütterlein'*
d) *'Oft denk' ich, sie sind nur ausgegangen'*
e) *'In diesem Wetter'*

1903–5
Symphony No. 6, A minor (later revised)

1904–5
Symphony No. 7, B minor* (later revised)

*Key in which works begin

1906

Symphony No. 8, E flat major*, for eight soloists (three sopranos, two contraltos, tenor, baritone, bass), mixed chorus, boys' chorus and orchestra (nicknamed 'Symphony of a Thousand')

1908

Das Lied von der Erde, subtitled 'Symphony for tenor and alto (or baritone) voice and orchestra' (also for voices and piano), words adapted by Mahler from Hans Bethge's collection *Die chinesische Flöte*

1909

Symphony No. 9, D major*

1910

Symphony No. 10, F sharp*
(unfinished by Mahler, several 'completed' versions by others)

EARLY WORKS, FRAGMENTS

1875
Herzog Ernst von Schwaben
Opera, libretto by Josef Steiner (lost)

c.1875–76
Sonata for Violin and Piano (lost)
Quintet for Piano and Strings (lost)

c.1876–78
First movement of Piano Quartet, A minor
Fragment of scherzo for Piano Quartet, G minor

c.1878–80
Die Argonauten
Opera, libretto by Mahler and possibly Josef Steiner (lost)

c.1879–83
Rübezahl
Opera (music lost, Mahler's libretto survives)

*Key in which works begin

*c.*1882–83
Symphony, A minor (lost)

1884
Der Trompeter von Säkkingen
Incidental music (lost) to Viktor von Scheffel's play

ARRANGEMENTS AND EDITIONS

Including:
J.S. Bach
Suite aus seinen Orchester-Werken

Beethoven
Quartet No. 11, F minor, op.95 (string orchestra version)

Bruckner
Symphony No. 3 (piano arrangement for four hands, possibly with R. Krzyzanowski)

Schubert
Quartet No. 14, D minor, *Der Tod und das Mädchen* (string orchestra version)

Weber
Completion of opera *Die drei Pintos* (Mahler also revised libretto with Carl von Weber)

Also much rescoring of orchestral works (e.g. Beethoven and Schumann symphonies) and libretto changes (e.g. Weber's *Euryanthe* and *Oberon*)

Index

Berg, Alban 3, 118, 155
  Lulu 118
  Three Orchestral Pieces op. 6 185
  Violin Concerto 118
Berlin 3, 35, 57, 77, 83, 112, 145, 197,
  215, 223
  Berlin Opera 46, 113, 114, 211, 228
  Berlin Philharmonic 36, 159, 229,
  230
Berliner, Arnold 27, 207
Berlioz, Hector 85, 133, 141
  Damnation of Faust 187
  Symphonie Fantastique 39, 60, 94
Bernstein, Leonard 6, 221, 222, 223,
  228, 229
Bethge, Hans, ed.: *Die chinesische Flöte*
  189–90, 191–4
Bezecny, Count Josef von 81, 82, 86, 95
Bismarck, Otto von 6–7
Bizet, Georges: *Carmen* 33
Blaukopf, Herta 226, 227
Blaukopf, Kurt 227
Blech, Leo 84
  Das war ich 141
Blumenthal, Dr Carl 152–3
Bodanzky, Artur 222
Bonci, Alessandro 160, 161
Bossi, Marco 215
Boston Symphony Orchestra 49, 150,
  159, 165, 167, 213, 222
Brahms, Johannes 19, 23, 36, 42, 55–6,
  57, 74–5, 80, 82, 88, 115, 117–18
  Second Symphony 118
  Violin Concerto 118
Breslau 68, 142, 145
Britten, Benjamin 194
Brno 139, 141
Bruckner, Anton 19, 21–3, 28, 92, 133,
  179
  First Symphony 23
  Second Symphony 23
  Third Symphony 22–3
  Fourth Symphony 60, 88, 173
  Fifth Symphony 98
  Ninth Symphony 22

Budapest 25, 30, 36, 63, 83
  Royal Hungarian Court Opera 3, 6,
  29–30, 50, 51–7, 74, 80, 82, 94,
  137, 173, 221
Buffalo 213
Buffalo Express 213
Bülow, Hans von 36–7, 42, 48, 57–8,
  60, 65–6, 88, 93, 112
Busoni, Ferruccio 60, 173, 218
  Berceuse Élégiaque 215
Burckhard, Max 99, 101, 104, 106, 110,
  151

Calvé, Emma 160
Canetti, Elias 105
Carnegie Hall, New York 169, 215
Carpenter, Clinton 230
Caruso, Enrico 150, 160, 161
Casella, Alfredo 201
Cervantes, S.M. de: *Don Quixote* 14
Chadwick, George 212
Chailly, Riccardo 230
Chaliapin, Feodor 161
Chantemesse, Prof. André 219
Charpentier, Gustave: *Louise* 145
Chicago Symphony Orchestra 159,
  222, 227, 229, 230
Chotzinoff, Samuel 161
Chvostek, Prof. Franz 219–20
Cincinatti 159
Clemenceau, Georges 99, 100, 207
Clemenceau, Paul 99, 100, 207
Clemenceau, Sophie 99, 100, 101
Cleveland, Ohio 158, 213, 222
Cleveland Plain Dealer 213
Colorado MahlerFest 229
Conrad, Joseph 192
Conrat, Erica 136, 188
Conried, Heinrich 150–1, 152, 157, 158,
  162, 164, 166, 167
Cooke, Deryck 72, 230
Corfu 103
Corning, Dr Leon 175
Covent Garden Opera 59
Craig, Gordon 140

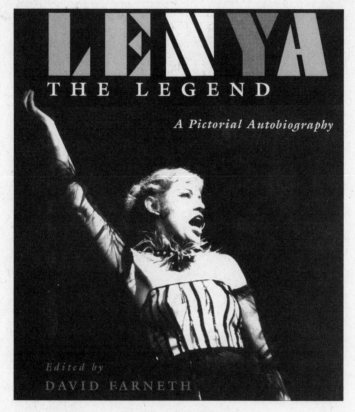

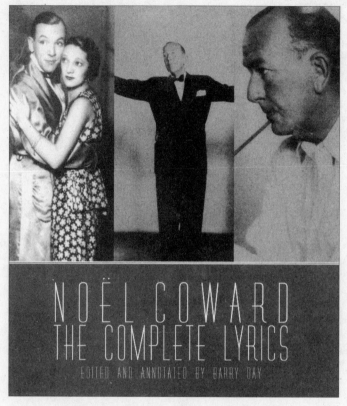